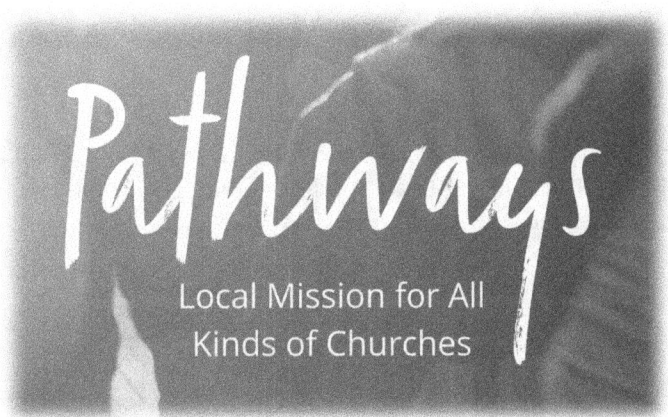

First published 2017

Copyright © K. L. Morgan 2016

ISBN: 978-0-6481050-0-8

Published By K.L. Morgan
3 Watersedge Cl
Knoxfield Vic
Australia 3180

E-mail – info@pathways4mission.com

Web – www.pathways4mission.com

Unless otherwise noted, Bible quotations are taken from THE HOLY BIBLE, NEW INTERNATIONAL VERSION®, NIV® Copyright © 1973, 1978, 1984, 2011 by Biblica, Inc.™ Used by permission. All rights reserved worldwide.

Some quotations are paraphrased.

All rights reserved. No part of this publication may be reproduced, stored in a retrieval system, or transmitted in any form or by any means—electronic, mechanical, photocopy, recording, or any other—except for brief quotations for printed reviews, without prior permission of the publisher.

Cover Design – Leanne Beattie

Cover Photo – Sami Sert

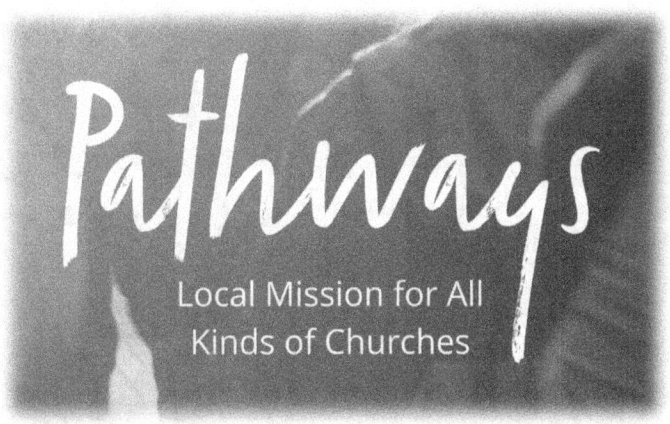

KEN MORGAN

K. L. Morgan
Melbourne

Since 1998 Ken Morgan has worked as a consultant, trainer and coach to church planters, church ministers and denominational leaders in a wide variety of traditions across Australia and beyond. He's currently the Head of Parish Mission Resourcing for the Anglican Diocese of Melbourne. A graduate of Tabor College and Victoria University, he makes his home in Melbourne.

Contents

Introduction	1
Part 1—Purpose and Principles	3
Chapter 1 On a Mission from God	5
Chapter 2 Principles of Disciple-making	23
Part 2—Seven Stages Explained	47
Chapter 3 Clarify Your Mission Focus	49
Chapter 4 Potential Contact	51
Chapter 5 In Touch	59
Chapter 6 Belonging	67
Chapter 7 Embracing the Gospel	75
Chapter 8 Following Jesus	95
Chapter 9 Serving in Ministry	121
Chapter 10 Leading Ministry	145
Part 3—Implementation	169
Chapter 11 Leading the Learning	171
Chapter 12 Analysing Your Own Church	179
Chapter 13 Starting Work	203
Chapter 14 Managing and Evaluating	227
Chapter 15 Expand the Possibilities	235
Appendix 1: Identifying a Mission Focus Group	245
Appendix 2: Rites of Profession	253
Appendix 3: Faith and Obedience	257
Appendix 4: Leadership Problems of Position, Authority and Power	261
Appendix 5: If You're Planting	267
Appendix 6: The Fundraising Trap	275

Introduction

Does it have to be this hard?
The idea of the local church as an agency of God's mission has lately gained a lot of attention. Sermon series have been preached with conviction and passion. Churches have restructured, reimagined and re-engineered in order to become more 'missional'. Christians have quit conventional churches and struck out on their own, trying to find ways to engage the people around them and share the good news of Jesus. Some of these endeavours have been successful; some have not lived up to expectations.

The most common description of the missional journey seems to be this: it's *hard*.

I'm not suggesting mission is necessarily easy. Of the churches I've served as a trainer and coach that have been effective in mission, all of them have worked hard both in planning and execution. They've been purposeful, thoughtful and at times willing to make some tough decisions.

However, I'm wondering if we're making mission too hard by expecting too much of the individual. Paul's writing in 1 Corinthians 12 and Ephesians 4 argues for a corporate, interdependent approach to ministry. The mission of Christ is the occupation of the *whole* body of Christ. If each of us can find our place and pull our weight, we might just accomplish the great undertaking with which Jesus has commissioned us.

To be more specific, much of the popular training and methodology for mission charges individuals to go out, engage their surrounding culture, bind up wounds, form relationships, share their faith, proclaim the gospel, form converts in Christian spirituality and then bring them along to church. There are some problems with this approach.

Few people are gifted to do all of this, and almost no one can do it all at once. Even more importantly, it's uncommon for such an approach to produce the desired results. For all the attention and emphasis it has received lately, the 'each-person-being-a-solo-missionary-in-their-sphere' approach is not delivering a whole lot of new disciples.

In the following pages I want to think about things a little differently. Instead of upending almost everything we currently do, what if we could think about the small things each of us can do to play our part on the mission of Jesus? And what if we had a way of joining these small things together in a logical sequence, so that we could easily understand the most important thing to do in the various contexts in which we find ourselves? In short, what if mission could be a collection of simple things, thoughtfully assembled so that mission actually becomes the occupation of the whole body of Christ (or at least the local expression you belong to)? If those questions sound interesting, this book is for you.

Part 1 is all about foundations - what I mean by 'mission' and 'making disciples'. There's a range of different definitions for these terms, so it's important that we get clear from the outset. I also clarify what I am talking about, and what I'm not.

Part 2 is about the Pathways theory, and the various theories that support it. If like me you love a theory that works, this is your sweet spot. It's grounded in field experience, so it's not too abstract.

Part 3 is just for you if you really love the practicalities. It's the nuts and bolts of making Pathways work in real time. There are plenty of examples to keep you engaged.

Part 4 is not in this book – It's the emerging conversation at www.pathways4mission.com where you can find helpful resources and a community of fellow travellers. You're welcome to join in.

And just to reassure you, when churches *do* adopt the kind thinking I'm describing, more often than not they see steady growth through new faith commitments—usually after about eighteen months.

Part 1
Purpose and Principles

Chapter 1
On a Mission from God

If you're a fan of the 1980 cult film *The Blues Brothers*, you'll get my now rather dated pop culture reference. For the uninitiated, the whole plot of *The Blues Brothers* revolves around two orphan brothers engaging in increasingly unbelievable antics to overcome the resistance of former bandmates, a murderous ex-fiancée, the Nazi Party and the entire Chicago police force in order to save an orphanage from closure (all to a classic, walking-bass-and-blaring-horns soundtrack).

Because they sincerely believe they're on a God-ordained mission, they equally believe nothing will stop them from fulfilling their mission, not even the immutable laws of physics and a blanket approval of the use of unnecessary violence in their apprehension.

Jesus told his disciples that he was sending them as the Father sent him (John 20:21). Like Jesus, and as successors to his first disciples, we're on a mission from God.

What is 'mission' anyway?

Since you've got past the front cover, and endured a diversion into a thirty-six-year-old film, I'm going to assume a couple of things. First, you're interested in the whole idea of mission. Hopefully, you'll stay with me when I say that 'mission', for the follower of Jesus, means continuing his work in the world. Second, you have some sense that the local church, as a community of followers of Jesus, is charged with taking up his mission. So far so good?

A lot has been written on the local church and mission. If you've been around a while you'll have come across books and courses and facilitation kits designed to step you through clarifying the unique mission God has instilled into your church. Much of it is useful stuff written by people with more expertise and experience than me. This book is not about that.

There's also been a lot written about the nature of mission, from some very big picture thinking that develops the idea of mission bringing the entire creation back into its intended order, through to some very specific thinking about how to most efficiently help people make their first act of repentance and faith. These are valid and important themes, but they're not my primary focus either.

All the gospels recount Jesus undertaking a vast array of compassionate acts. From the spectacular (healing and feeding of thousands) to the intimate (esteeming a grateful prostitute over the cold indifference of the 'righteous' religious men), Jesus felt the pain of others and acted to alleviate it. With such a vivid example to follow, continuing the mission of Jesus must also embrace acting with similar compassion.

According to Matthew's gospel, Jesus' parting directive to his closest followers was to make disciples, baptising them and teaching them to obey Jesus' commandments. I'm going to assume that, being a parting directive, this is important—perhaps even central—to the mission of the local church.

For the purposes of this book, I'm going to work with these two ideas (acting with compassion and making obedient disciples) as a rough description of mission. And hopefully demonstrate how they're profoundly interdependent.

Structure-driven mission?
A few years back I had a coaching conversation with a church leader. It was one of those first-time *pro bono* coaching appointments where he and I were checking to see if we wanted to work together. He described to me his intention to implement a new structure in his church, since the current one was ineffective. He had just returned from a conference overseas, where a particular approach was being advocated as the key to efficient organisation of the church. Over the previous five years this leader had restructured the church three times, and yet he still felt that poor structure was the primary barrier standing between the church and mission effectiveness. The question I asked is probably the question you're asking as you read: *'Since the last three restructures failed, what gives you confidence that this one will succeed?'*

I confess it was not a particularly empowering question, and the conversation ran out of gas soon after (and, unsurprisingly, he didn't take me on as his coach). However, the story illustrates the preoccupation we have with structure. This book is not about rewriting your organisational chart. I'm not advocating any kind of ideal way of setting out your management and governance systems.

Instead of changing how you assign responsibility and authority, my focus is on organising your activities so that they work together. It's about how apparently unrelated activities such as a community garden and Alpha could become quite closely linked.

A lot has been written since the mid-1990s consigning the 'inherited' model of church to the historical dustbin. My friends in the emergent church movement claim 'it's easier to have kids than to raise the dead', implying there is no hope and no future in attempting to revitalise existing churches. Yet my experience in the field has been much less polarised. Early in my career I watched and wondered as a nearby 'hip' church plant folded, even though its leaders seemed to have all the right answers to all the right questions. Meanwhile, a more conventional church not far away saw consistent growth through first-time faith commitments year in and year out. What I observed didn't square with the books I was reading.

Some church plants have flourished, others have failed. Some conventional-type churches have declined and even closed, others have grown into large regional centres with multiple congregations. Despite much of the rhetoric, and despite gloomy predictions, the vast majority of mission as I've roughly described it is currently being undertaken by reasonably conventional churches (in the Western world at least). These churches will generally be characterised by fairly standard public worship services consisting of congregational singing, a sermon, prayer, an offering and the Lord's Supper at varying frequencies. They will likely have paid staff, a board or council and regular programs through the week, and will usually occupy a complex of buildings. These features are not essential to mission, and they're not necessarily hindrances either.

Whether you're working in a mission-shaped church plant or a cathedral, Pathways is not so much about wiping out your existing activity and starting from scratch as it is about being thoughtful and strategic regarding the things you're already doing, and evaluating them based on their potential to contribute to the overall mission of the church.

Dissing the emergent church?

Is all this to say that the recent emphasis on the emergent or missional church can be waved away as a reactive flash in the postmodern pan? Not at all. A significant proportion of my time over the past decade has been spent working with church planters: some planting more conventional-style churches, others pioneering forms less recognisable as church in the traditional sense. (I struggle with language in this sphere. There has been so much bandying about of terms like 'emergent', 'missional', 'organic' and 'fresh expression' that the terms seem to have lost function to communicate common ideas.)

The groundwork that underpins this book has been conducted on both sides of the traditional/emergent divide. In the process it has become apparent that regardless of forms and traditions, local churches that act with compassion *and* make disciples are effective for largely the same reasons. While the observable activity of the churches may vary immensely, the less-visible processes of disciple-making that occur in the context of those activities are remarkably similar. My interest is the effective commonalities of disciple-making across a spectrum of forms and traditions.

Seven-steps-to-guaranteed-success?

Have you ever wondered why a program like Alpha is highly effective for making new disciples in one church and yet is apparently ineffective in another? Or why a church on one side of town finds a sporting club to be a missional harvest-field and yet a similar church on the other side sees no fruit from an almost identical club?

Others have written helpful books on the merits or otherwise of the various approaches and activities undertaken by local churches. I'm not writing to instruct you about which activities you should do. You're the expert on your context (at least you should be), and you're in the best position to know and understand what will engage and serve your local population. This book attempts to understand the common dynamics *inside* various activities, and how they work together to facilitate mission (and, yes, I will explain why Alpha 'works' sometimes and not others).

Since the 1980s there has been a range of off-the-shelf church growth programs produced. These programs carry a tacit (and sometimes explicit) promise to reproduce in your church the stellar results accomplished in the church where they were first developed. Some are single-program add-ons to the existing activity of the church; others attempt the religious equivalent of business process re-engineering.

My first exposure to organisational consulting was in the early 1990s, when the Total Quality Management (TQM) movement was sweeping through the manufacturing industry in Australia. I learned some very helpful principles, picked up some very useful tools and developed skills I still use today. And I also learned that it's not as easy as Tom Peters seemed to suggest in the video case-studies.

Back then, Toyota Motor Corp was the pin-up company for quality and efficiency achieved through worker empowerment. Toyota would welcome visits by management teams from rival manufacturers. They would demonstrate their systems of cards and cords and teams to anyone who was interested, confident that rivals would never be able to emulate Toyota's success. Why? Toyota's systems were supported by a culture that had been established over decades.

Trying to carbon-copy the structures and programs of 'successful' churches is no more likely to succeed in your context than copying the observable features of Toyota would work to make rival manufacturers more effective. Without the culture, the structural and programmatic stuff is just stuff.

Likewise, churches that grow by acts of compassion and making disciples have generally developed a disciple-making culture. Effective and sustainable mission requires careful, thoughtful and disciplined leadership. I make no promises of quick success through implementing the ideas in this book. The church plants and existing churches that have grown through the application of Pathways principles have made steady progress over years. Some have experienced 'growth spurts' where a large number of people have come to faith in a short period, but these events are generally not readily reproducible. Pathways is a way of thinking. It takes time for that way of thinking to permeate the various levels of the church organisation.

More 'keys' to mission effectiveness?

I've read books teaching that mission is a matter of prayer. I've attended workshops teaching that the key to mission is relationships. You can implement growth programs built around teaching people techniques to share their faith. There's a whole shelf of books in my local Christian bookshop espousing the centrality of a clear vision. I've worked with churches that over years have pushed hard into one thing and then the next and still not seen much result for their efforts.

What if they're all (or most of them) at least partially right? I think Christian Schwarz is on to something in describing a church as a kind of ecosystem where you need a range of characteristics all working interdependently to produce health, which leads to growth.[1]

Pathways is a way of focusing and aligning various activities so they work together. Fervent prayer *and* clear vision *and* serving the disenfranchised *and* careful implementation (and a bunch of other dynamics) work together for sustained mission effectiveness. The genius and elegance of Jesus' life was his ability to be masterful in all of these without behaving like a stressed-out CEO.

Another restructure, revitalise, revolutionise?

Just about every church with which I've worked has made some kind of attempt at 'strategic planning' where creating core ideas (like a vision and values statement) provides a basis on which to develop plans for the various activities of the church, redesign organisational structures, set budgets, establish KPIs and set up plans for review. While I frequently help churches with those kinds of rational-comprehensive planning processes, I'm not writing about that here. There are dozens of books and resources around. There are more than enough competent consultants—some of them are my friends. Use them as you need to.

What I have learned is this: encouraging the church to think Pathways *before* embarking on a whole-of-church planning and organising adventure has proven helpful in keeping the planning and design process focused and simple.

---

[1] Schwarz, Christian A. Natural Church Development: A Guide to Eight Essential Qualities of Healthy Churches (Church-Smart Resources, Chicago 1998.) If you're using Schwarz's Natural Church Development process, please don't use Pathways as a rationale to quit your cycle of surveys. Pathways thinking will work right alongside it. If your Need-oriented Evangelism or Functional Structures scores are low, Pathways thinking will be especially helpful to you.

My heart's desire for this book
I'm committed to the idea that people who don't currently go to church or profess faith can—and do—become followers of Jesus and co-labourers in his church. I'm convinced that churches can become increasingly effective in helping people make the transition we once called 'conversion'.

I've seen otherwise unremarkable churches serve and disciple people with no church background through activities intentionally designed and coordinated as a series of simple, obvious and attractive steps. This book is about what I've learned from churches with effective pathways made up of these steps, and what I've learned in helping churches become increasingly effective in mission by organising their activities into pathways.

Making disciples in the post-Christian Western world isn't easy. Yet it's not necessarily complex. In the hurly-burly of church life it can be hard to see the mission forest for the crisis trees.

This book is to help pastors and lay leaders (and in time everyone else in your church) to see clearly how the activities of your church work to fulfil the mission of Jesus—or not. Once you have an unambiguous picture of your current mission effectiveness—no matter how sketchy—this book will help you figure out the next step (and the next, and the one after that) to helping your church become better-organised and more effective for mission.

If you're planting a church, you have the advantage of creating a mission-oriented culture from the outset, and aligning your activities as you begin them. If you're applying Pathways thinking in an established church, you'll be able to make some positive changes almost immediately, but a change in culture and consistent, sustained results may take several years.

Pathways is as much about how you think about church as it is about how you do church. It's as much about the 'Why?' of your various activities as it is about the 'What?' and 'How?'

The theoretical framework for Pathways was developed through study of historical and contemporary examples of effective churches and mission movements—from the early church to the Celtic monastic movement, to Wesley and Booth, through to 20th century and contemporary churches. This book is based on over a decade of field testing the Pathways model in dozens of local church settings in Australia, New Zealand and the UK. The

Pathways approach has proven helpful in a wide variety of traditions and cultures, from welfare-class church planting contexts through to traditional, conservative churches in leafy suburbs; and from the outback to the inner city.

Stories of conversion
Before we get into technicalities, I'd like to share with you four stories. They're all true, although the names and some incidental details have been changed to protect me from my relatives!

Let me take you on a journey back in time (if this were movie, I'd make the image on screen go blurry and wobbly while playing weird and dreamy music). The year is 1964 and the place is Adelaide, South Australia. Andrew and Jackie are a couple of young adults barely out of high school.

Andrew and Jackie had been dating for about four years when they decided to marry. Although the young couple had no church affiliation, they made an appointment with the minister at their local Anglican church (that's what everyone did in those days). The minister was delighted to officiate and met with them several times in the lead-up to the happy occasion.

Not long after the big day, the minister dropped in on the couple to see how they were settling in to married life. On a second visit the minister invited them to join several other newlywed couples to chat over marriage and how to make the most of it.

In joining the group, Andrew and Jackie made new friends and found encouragement as they navigated the adjustment to married life. As the minister and some of the others in the group shared about the importance and value of their faith, Andrew and Jackie took interest.

The minister invited them to study the Bible, and a little later took them through confirmation class. Andrew and Jackie became regular attenders at services, and began helping with other activities in the life of the church. In time Andrew joined the church council and became involved in the governance of the denomination at a state level.

Let's jump to the early 1970s and about 500 miles east to Melbourne, where Frank and Therese are living the great Australian dream. Frank has a secure and well-paid job as a trade teacher, while Therese cares for their two little boys and keeps their triple-fronted brick suburban home spotless and sparkling. A six-cylinder Holden in the driveway completes the picture of domestic bliss.

When the boys begin school, Therese meets Dora, who has two boys the same age as Therese's. Dora and her husband, Les, have much in common with Frank and Therese: they also live in a triple-fronted brick home nearby, with the prerequisite Holden in the drive. Les works in a government department while Dora keeps the home. The boys become friends, the two women become friends and in time Frank finds himself serving with Les on the school council.

What is different about Dora and Les was their faith in Christ, and their participation in a Baptist church in the next suburb. Dora invites Therese to afternoon tea with a group of her friends from church. Therese is enfolded into the group of women and begins attending a Bible study—not because she has any particular spiritual interest, but simply to enjoy the social interaction.

When the Baptist church decides to begin a Boys' Brigade company, the boys go along. Frank hangs around to watch and help.

Frank is a born organiser and soon becomes more than just a helper. At the same time, he is befriended by several other men in the church. Meanwhile, the Christian message shared at Boys' Brigade begins to nag at him. Frank wrestles with the Christian faith, and speaks at length with the minister of the church. In time, Frank's faith takes root and he is baptised along with Therese.

Being from the ever-faithful 'builder' generation, Frank and Therese quickly cement themselves as permanent fixtures in the Sunday service. The minister is a gifted teacher, which not only impresses Frank (who relentlessly sought to improve his own teaching skills) but also gives him a solid grounding in the basics of discipleship.

Frank becomes a section leader and then captain of the Boys' Brigade company. Under his leadership the company grows to become the largest in the state, serving 150 boys and reaching about 120 families.

The screen in front of you is going blurry and wobbly again as we move into the 1990s and to the beachside suburbs of Melbourne. Now you're looking at Mike: about thirty years old, tall, fit and working as a physiotherapist. A new client recently showed up at his clinic with a knee injury. In conversation Mike learns that his client hurt his knee playing basketball.

After several treatment sessions, Mike's client invites him to come and meet the team, do a little training and see if he wants to get involved. Mike figures he could use some extra exercise and a wider social circle (and maybe a few new clients!), so he agrees.

The atmosphere in the basketball team is upbeat, humorous and fiercely competitive. In no time Mike feels like he belongs and is valued, despite being only an average player. About half the guys on the team are a part of a large Baptist church that meets in the local high school. They talk about their faith in a matter-of-fact kind of way, but never put any pressure on Mike to attend church.

A couple of months later one of the guys on the team invites Mike to a theatre production that he and some others from his church are putting on. By this time Mike has become curious about these Christians, so with just a little apprehension, he agrees to go.

Mike is blown away by the quality of the show—he wasn't expecting a full-scale professional production from a bunch of churchgoers. He is also moved by the plot, which depicts a young man who had wasted his father's money and destroyed his reputation, yet is greeted with hugs, tears and gifts when he finally returns home.

At the end of the show, the minister of the church takes the stage. He explains that the story in the play was originally told by Jesus and that the welcoming, gracious father is a representation of God. Then the minister says this story pretty much encapsulates the message Jesus came to bring. He invites anyone who is interested to know more to sign up to a program called Alpha where people can 'kick Jesus' tyres'.

At this point, Mike's friend elbows him to get his attention, then looks him in the eye and says, 'I did Alpha last year—it changed my life. I'm gunna do it again this year. Wanna come?'

There is an Alpha promo booth at the back of the theatre, and Mike signs up on his way out. During the program, Mike listens, asks questions and thinks deeply. During a weekend retreat, Mike accepts the invitation to pray a prayer of repentance and faith.

The following week, Mike accepts an invitation to church, and at the end of Alpha he joins a life transformation group with two other blokes from church. A year later, Mike recruits a work colleague to join a mixed basketball team with him, with the hope of inviting her to the next theatre production.

I hope I've done a good-enough job with the stories that you're seeing a pattern emerging. Indulge me with one more. No wobbly screens this time—it began only recently.

Julie migrated from mainland China with her husband, Nelson, a couple of years ago. Nelson completed his tertiary education in Australia, during which time he developed his English language skills. He works as an electronics engineer with a subsidiary of a multinational telecommunications company. Julie studied enough English at high school to get by with the basics of life in Australia, but not enough to develop real friendship with native English-speakers.

Julie and Nelson rent a townhouse in a leafy inner suburb of Melbourne. While Nelson works long hours to build his career, Julie feels isolated. She has developed a habit of taking long walks to get herself out of the house and to help her acclimatise to Australian culture.

Walking past a local church, her attention is caught by a huge real estate-style sign. (In the US and UK real estate signs are small and elegant, swinging from arched posts. In Australia they're huge—five feet high and six feet wide is not unusual.) Half the sign is taken up by a photo of three young adults, each obviously from a different corner of the world. They smile out at Julie while the text of the sign encourages her to join a conversational English group. Julie makes a mental note of the time and day the group met. She turns up at the next session.

Julie is welcomed at the door with a warm smile and some friendly small talk in simple English. She is offered a place at a table shared with six others, about half of whom are Chinese like her. Each takes turns talking about an aspect of their lives prompted by the group facilitator.

After the formal session the minister of the church wanders over to the small group where Julie is enjoying coffee with other participants. He introduces himself and asks Julie a little about herself. Learning of her country of birth, the minister tries out some of his newly acquired Mandarin. Julie smiles and responds in kind, speaking slowly enough for the minister to pick the tonal variations. The minister grins and promises to have some new phrases to try out with her the following week.

Over the following weeks Julie builds some solid friendships, and is invited with Nelson to meals at the homes of her new friends. Her confidence with English improves quickly (as does the minister's confidence with Mandarin). Julie also notes that a number of the people in her group, when it is their turn to share about some aspect of their lives, speak about the importance and value of their Christian faith. Julie is intrigued, as all religious involvement is discouraged in her homeland.

Over coffee with one of her new friends, Julie cautiously inquires about faith. Her friend explains how she had become a believer a few years before, and invites Julie to read Mark's gospel with her.

They meet weekly after the conversational English class, reading Mark both in English and Chinese. Julie asks questions and her new friend answers those she could with patience and sincerity. Something is stirring inside Julie's heart.

After several months punctuated by a number of long conversations with her new Christian friends, Julie kneels by her bed one night and prays a simple prayer of commitment to Christ. A couple of months later she asks to be baptised.

Nowadays you'll find Julie (and sometimes Nelson) in the weekly Sunday service. Recently Julie began attending a home fellowship where the group studies the Bible and prays both for its members and for those yet to meet Jesus.

The associate minister invited Julie to complete a giftedness-discovery course, which helped her to think about where she might best use her unique blend of gifts, interests and skills to serve Jesus. If you visit Julie's church on a Thursday morning, you'll find her serving as part of the team that runs a music-based playgroup for mothers and pre-schoolers.

Pathways in the stories
Stories like these are unremarkable in themselves—until you begin to pile them up together. Growing churches like the four that produced these

examples seem to create a steady trickle, and perhaps even a consistent stream, of people coming to faith and joining the church. They seem to have a process for making disciples, whether it's intentional and explicit or just instinctive and implied. Churches that are plateaued, declining or just growing by transfer may run similar programs, but they are far less likely to have people making the journey toward Christ and his church. The activities of those churches generally don't link to form a pathway.

What do I mean by a mission pathway? Let's look first at the beginning of each story. Each of the churches had some kind of program or activity that served the needs of a particular group within their local community. These were, in order of appearance: a support group for newlyweds, a Boys' Brigade company, a basketball team and a conversational English class.

Each story began with people within the reasonable span of influence of the local church for whom these activities were meaningful, enriching or—in marketing speak—a 'value add'. In Pathways parlance, we say such people have *'potential for contact'*. They're only an introduction away from connecting with someone from the church. That introduction could come by finding a phone number in a directory, meeting in the course of daily life, seeing a sign or visiting a website.

Once that contact is made, that person is '*in touch*' with the church (even if they may not yet know it). It may be that they've had a meeting with the minister, or they've begun a friendship with a church member, or a church member has entered their professional circle, or they've been greeted warmly at the door of a church-run program. Whichever way, there's someone at church who knows their name and is interested enough to nurture the relationship.

A person 'in touch' with a local church is only an invitation away from beginning to feel like they *'belong'* with the church community. This means that they fairly regularly participate in a group that includes a number of Christians. This is often where their felt needs are met—be it the marriage support group where Jackie and Andrew started to feel at home with church people, or the Boys' Brigade company where Frank found his niche. It might be the basketball team where Mike picked up his fitness (and no doubt the new clients he was hoping for), or the conversational English class where Julie's isolation turned into friendships and fluency.

People who feel some sense of belonging are only an invitation away from beginning to consider the claims of Jesus Christ. We call this stage '*embracing the gospel*'. Here people come to understand the good news that God loves them, that sin has alienated them from God, that God has made the way of reconciliation through Jesus, and that they can be restored to their intended relationship with God through repentance and faith. This could happen through traditional means such as the confirmation class where Jackie and Andrew embraced the good news, a series of conversations as was the case with Frank, a process-evangelism course like Alpha where Mike came to faith or a study group like the one Julie attended.

In days gone by, 'embracing the gospel' activities tended to take the form of large-group public preaching, whether it was Whitfield, Wesley or Billy Graham. Nowadays the trend seems to be toward conversation. If you read the book of Acts, you'll note that Paul used both. An 'embracing the gospel' activity has served its purpose when a person makes a profession of faith, marked by a rite such as confirmation or baptism.

People who have embraced the gospel can naturally be invited to environments that help them shape their lives and values to the teaching and example of Jesus. We call this stage '*following Jesus*'. While no one truly graduates from this stage, immediately after conversion is the ideal time to help a person embed habits that will lead to a lifestyle of discipleship. (I use the term 'conversion' advisedly, and you'll find out why a little further in.)

'Following Jesus' activities might be a Sunday service, as we saw in the first two stories (although many Sunday worship services do not serve this purpose), or it may be a triplet-sized group as we saw in Mike's example. It may be a home Bible study such as the one Julie joined. The key similarity is that people are taught, challenged and resourced to become more like Jesus.

The next stage, '*serving in ministry*', sometimes begins as a way of belonging, as we saw with Frank's involvement with Boys' Brigade, or it may begin soon after conversion, as we saw with Andrew and Jackie helping with the various tasks around their Anglican church. Mike took a little longer, and his way of serving was primarily to bring others along the same pathway he had followed. Julie found her way of serving in ministry at the music playgroup.

'Serving in ministry' activities simply help and support people to contribute to the ministry of Jesus and his church. They include processes like the course Julie took, the good old roster system that quickly got Andrew and Jackie involved, or meetings of ministry teams like Boys' Brigade leaders.

The final stage in the pathway is '*leading ministry*'. Andrew found himself in a leadership role representing his parish at a denominational level. Frank's management skill inevitably took him into the leadership of the Boys' Brigade company. Mike and Julie aren't there yet—and they may never move to this stage since leadership is not everyone's cup of tea.

Pathways for Mission: Seven steps illustrated

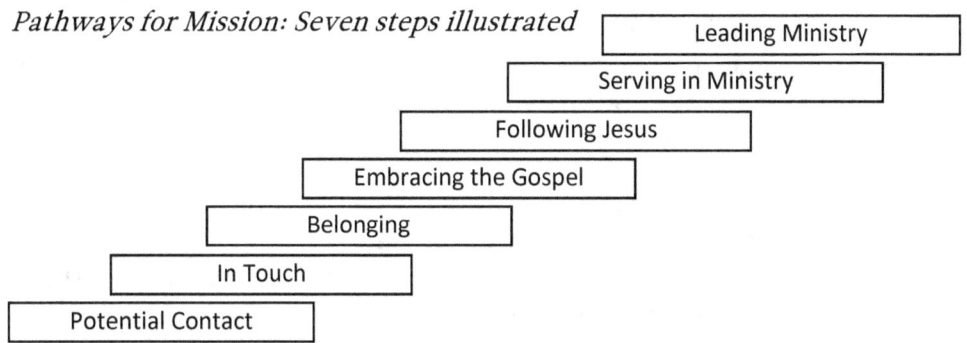

Explaining the process

Jesus repeatedly used stories about the cycle of sowing, growing and reaping to explain the kingdom of God. In Mark 4:26-29 he asks rhetorically, 'What is the kingdom of God like?' He goes on to explain it's like 'a man [who] scatters seed on the ground. Night and day, whether he sleeps or gets up, the seed sprouts and grows, though he does not know how. All by itself the soil produces grain—first the stalk, then the head, then the full kernel in the head. As soon as the grain is ripe, he puts the sickle to it, because the harvest has come.'

Exegesis of parables hinges on getting the main point and not getting lost in the details. The point here is that the soil produces grain without our work, observation or understanding—that is, we can't manufacture grain, it grows as God designed it. So too we can't manufacture the kingdom of God: it grows as God designs.

But this parable is not Jesus instructing us to simply 'let go and let God' or absolving us from the responsibility of mission.

If we're going to do a decent job of exegesis, we need to appreciate the original context and audience of the text. Jesus told this story in early first-century Galilee, which at the time was the backblocks of post-exilic Jewish culture. He was speaking in a town or just near to one—but not in the major city of the region (which was the more Gentile-dominated Tiberias). His audience would have been closely linked to primary production—they knew a thing or two about farming. Jesus, who would have spent hours of his adolescence making and repairing wooden ploughs, would have had a fair working knowledge of grain growing too.

The idea that farmers have to work to produce a harvest would have been common knowledge of the day. Jesus cites sowing and harvesting, but you can be sure his agrarian audience would have appreciated that there was a bit more to it. Producing a grain harvest is a cooperative partnership between human effort and God's design.

The idea of cooperative partnership with God can be traced back to Genesis. Genesis 2:5 tells us that 'no shrub had yet appeared on the earth and no plant had yet sprung up, for the Lord God had not sent rain on the earth and there was no one to work the ground'. Later in v. 15 we read that God 'took the man and put him in the Garden of Eden to work it and take care of it'. God created the process, but human beings must steward the process to gain the ideal outcome.

Likewise we have to work to produce growth in the kingdom. We have to put the 'seed' in an environment where it can germinate, grow and mature. God's Spirit must cause the gospel seed to germinate and flourish in order to produce maturity and multiplication. We can't force it, but we can do much to create optimal growing conditions.

Farming is the metaphor that informs the Pathways process. A 'pathways church' is not a factory where we seek to control everything, nor is it a jungle where we let everything grow wild and hope for the best. A 'pathways church' is a farm, or a garden, where we cooperate with the Spirit of God to produce a spiritual harvest of well-formed disciples.

Between my foray into pastoral ministry and my career as a church growth consultant, I was for a time a human resources manager, working firstly in manufacturing and then for a vertically integrated agribusiness. In other words, I worked in a factory and then on a farm (actually bunch of farms, growing mostly apples). Making the transition to primary production meant I had to learn some new things, and to unlearn some others.

I learned that, in Australia, apples grow in the southern half of the continent. They grow where there's good rainfall, cool nights (but not too cold) and plenty of sunshine without too much heat. Apples need reasonable quality soil that's well-drained. They are labour intensive, so they are grown not too far from population centres.

I learned that growing apples profitably requires a huge chain of judgment calls beginning with selection of land and including design and layout of farm blocks and dams, choice of varieties and rootstocks, choice of irrigation and trellising systems, planting densities, tractors, spray equipment, staging and storage areas—all before a single tree gets planted.

Once the orchard is planted, there are more decisions to make—pruning techniques, pest management, soil moisture, crop load, harvesting times. And that's before an apple gets picked.

My point is this. Good farmers understand intimately what they grow and how their particular crop interacts with its environment. They have a thorough grasp of the complex interactions between the effects of various decisions. And those decisions will vary from location to location, variety to variety, season to season. In short, the better farmers understand their context and their crop, the more profitably they can farm.

Likewise, if we're cooperating with God to grow disciples, we'll be more effective if we can understand how disciples grow, both generally and in the context of our own parish and people group. If we understand what kind of environment disciples need at their various stages of development, we'll be better able to use our resources wisely to support a healthy 'crop'.

Let's return to Mark 4. The farmer scatters seed (by implication, having chosen the grain to sow and the appropriate season to sow it, and having prepared the ground to receive the seed). The farmer's work completed for the time being, it's up to God's design to kick in for the seed to germinate and grow. The farmer may not understand the biology of it, but no matter: the ground produces the crop. However, when the farmer judges that the grain is mature for harvest, the sickle is swung and the crop is gathered. The moral of the story is this: how the kingdom grows is to some extent a mystery, but humanity has an active part in its coming.

And my thesis runs along the same lines. The better we understand the environments required for each stage in the growth process for disciples, the better we can partner with God's unseen work to produce a 'crop' of Jesus-followers.

Chapter 2
Principles of Disciple-making

Church is a community of disciple-making disciples—an integrated growth environment
As a model of church, Jesus led his band of disciples into different contexts with people at different stages of spiritual maturity. Jesus offered healings and parables to huge multitudes, gave more detailed teaching to the more interested, explained everything to the twelve and revealed more intimate truths to an inner core of three. Jesus ministered to match the discipleship needs of his audience.[2]

Based on the Acts narrative, it seems that the early church used a similar model. Peter healed a crippled man begging at the temple gate in Acts 3, which created a stir in the temple. His subsequent explanation and challenge were matched to the audience. He was in the temple, so we can assume that the audience was Jewish. He addressed them as brothers, identified the ultimate source of the miracle as the God of the patriarchs, and implied that the miracle in the name of Jesus was clear evidence that Jesus was in fact the Holy and Righteous One, the author of life. He challenged them about their involvement in the recent execution of Jesus, and reminded them of the prophet foretelling that the Christ would suffer. Finally he called them to repent and to embrace the promise given long ago to their ancestor Abraham.

Peter's audience already knew and identified with the heritage of Abraham, the redemptive history of Israel and the predictions of the prophets. They knew of Jesus of Nazareth and the miracles he had recently performed prior to his crucifixion. They would have heard about this new community of his followers. They were ripe for the gospel message that Peter brought.

---

[2] For the academic types, here's an advance warning. I'm not attempting to set out a comprehensive theology. Instead, I'll outline the principles with which we're working. If you're attuned to systematic theology, you'll inevitably feel yourself protesting that I've failed to answer all the questions, and that I've missed some things—and you're probably right.

Contrast this with Paul's address to the Athenians in the Areopagus (Acts 17:16-34). He leveraged their religious interest and idol worship to introduce the idea of the supreme Creator-God who gave them life and who was close by. He explained that this God does not dwell in temples and is not like artworks of metal and stone. He urged repentance and predicted a coming judgment by one who was raised from the dead, but he didn't mention Jesus by name.

Paul's audience were pagan philosophers. They had no identification with Abraham or Israel and no knowledge of Jesus. The net effect of his sermon was to divide the group into sceptics and inquirers. We can assume that further conversation in a different environment led to Dionysius and Damaris becoming believers.

Much of Paul's activity recorded in Acts was geared toward those outside the church. Paul preached, discussed and debated in all kinds of contexts with the goal of helping people come to a saving knowledge of Christ. At the same time, much of the teaching preserved in his letters to the churches is specifically geared toward helping believers sort out their issues and become mature disciples. In his pastoral letters he specifically addresses leaders labouring to make disciples in the contexts of Ephesus and Crete. Taken together, it's obvious that Paul had different approaches for people at different stages of the discipleship journey.

By the end of the first century, Christians at times had to work differently in some contexts to avoid being discovered and arrested by the hostile Roman state. Their primary means of outreach became works of charity, from rescuing exposed infants to supporting widows who had no family to care for them. Depending on the political wind of the time (persecution and reprieves ebbed and flowed with the politics of region and empire), the kind of public announcements that Peter and Paul made in the passages above would have landed Christians in a dungeon, awaiting an unpleasant demise.

Suspected of cultish behaviour and subterfuge, the Christians adapted their approach. Inquirers drawn toward believers by their acts of charity or private conversations were put through several stages of rigorous discipleship before their baptism and acceptance into the community. Even in the face of persecution, the early church had a clearly identified pathway by which an unbeliever could become a believer, a member of the Christian community and, in time, a mature disciple.

The gospel accounts, Acts and the early church consistently paint a picture of concurrent ministry to people across the spectrum of the discipleship journey, from those with no knowledge of the gospel (and perhaps no interest in it) right through to committed believers who were striving to run the disciples' race toward Christlikeness.

In every age and in every context, the purpose of the church is to produce mature, Christlike disciples, beginning with those who are unconnected and unaware of Christ and his gospel. Therefore our concept of 'church', wherever we are, must encompass ministry across the spectrum of spiritual maturity in an integrated way—not unlike the way a farm works across the growth cycle from bare soil right through to mature and fruitful plants.

Examples from history

If we leave the early church and move toward the medieval period, much of the mission of the church was accomplished through monasteries. When we think of monks and monasteries nowadays, we tend to think of those living a cloistered lifestyle, contemplating and chanting, wearing rough habits and bad haircuts, walled in from the 'real' world and real temptations: people committed to their own spirituality rather than more outward-looking mission.

Although monasteries are by nature places of self-denial and self-discipline, those that sprang up as the Roman Empire was crumbling tended to be purposefully missional, embodying the character of Jesus in communal life. Alongside the rigorous spiritual disciplines flourished scholarship, the arts, craftsmanship and innovation in agriculture and technology.

Among the Celts, when a group of monks founded a new monastery, it was often close to a village—neither in the middle of town nor in the middle of nowhere. There they would establish a compound and begin to live out their communal ways of life according to a rule.

Engagement with the townsfolk might be through the trading of necessities, through conversation or through extending hospitality and care to those in need. Monasteries became centres of medical care, refuges for the traveller and the destitute, and places of recovery and discovery for seekers.

Celtic monasteries maintained an explicit pathway by which sojourners and seekers could be integrated into the communal and spiritual life of the monks. A seeker or sojourner entering the compound would be shown to a specially designated room, separate from the main group, and assigned a spiritual guide, who would help them navigate the unfamiliar ways of monastic life. They were welcomed into some of the spiritual practices and to share the abbot's table. Since the Celts sought to acknowledge the presence and beneficence of God in even the most mundane routines of life, newcomers could not help but be exposed to the monks' spirituality, expressed in prayers at set times of the day and over simple daily activities.

As monasteries grew, their capacity to serve their surrounding populations developed and diversified. Monasteries became centres of education, instruction in arts and craftsmanship, and centres of 'best practice' in agriculture. Monasteries did a great deal to relieve the suffering and enrich the lives of the nearby townsfolk. And at each point of interaction between the monks and the common people, there was opportunity to observe and to some extent participate in the everyday spirituality of the monks.

Those who wished to travel on could do so, those that wished to stay and learn more about the spirituality of the monks progressed though stages of formation that were later formalised as postulant, novice and oblate. In turn oblates would lead pilgrimages into the unknown, often resulting in the formation of a new monastery beside another village.

In this way, the gospel spread across the British Isles and Northern Europe, bringing civility, learning and improved quality of life.

Fast forward to the 19th century and a series of upstart movements began out of compassion for the underclasses that lived, struggled and often died too early in the back streets of British cities.

Much is made of the preaching and brass bands that were often the visible features of the Salvation Army. However, what fired the passion of William Booth was his deep compassion for the women who suffered, the children who went hungry, and the men who were caught in the endless cycle of petty crime and incarceration.

Booth devised a model of ministry illustrated in a series of concentric circles, from those being reached and served by acts of compassion, through those who made professions of faith and on to those who signed a covenant commitment as 'soldiers'.

Notable in both the example of Celtic monks and the Salvation Army is that practical, compassion-based ministry was dynamically integrated with what we would more commonly call 'evangelism'. Concern for the welfare of the whole person fuelled mission, not just the desire to gain prayers of commitment or to grow church membership.

As in Jesus' ministry, in both these examples people could freely benefit from the compassion of Jesus' followers without any obligation to embrace his teaching or become a disciple. However, compassion with no strings attached apparently led to a great deal of spiritual interest, which in turn led to a trickle and then a flood of new disciples.

Church is more than 'church' and not less
Church is not just a public worship service. The fact that you've read this far suggests you already know this. However, the fact that so many churches (right across the ecclesiological spectrum) put almost all their effort and resources into their Sunday worship services suggests that for many, it's a 'penny' that's yet to 'drop'.

In the 1980s and 1990s the idea of worship services geared to seekers became the strategy *du jour*. Seeker-sensitive services sought to make the worship gathering accessible and comprehensible to those with no church background. And for churches like Willow Creek and Saddleback, they worked. But then came the rub. Seeker services stopped 'working' for those who were already well-entrenched in church culture. So large, attraction-based churches began other services for those well established in the faith. It's hard to provide a worship experience and teaching that serves those yet to believe and those who already do at the same time.

More recently churches have developed a worship service model of 'meaningful for believers and accessible to seekers'. Some, like Tim Keller at Redeemer Presbyterian Church in New York (a gifted scholar, brilliant speaker and able missiologist), seem to be making it work; others much less so. And the less church-oriented the surrounding culture, the more this is true. (The culture in most of the US seems to maintain at least a vague association with Christianity. When the planes hit the twin towers, Americans—even hard-nosed New Yorkers—flocked into churches. When disaster strikes Australia, the change in service attendance is barely noticeable.)

The central challenge is trying to make one environment serve the discipleship needs of people at a variety of discipleship stages. In my experience, Keller's brilliance notwithstanding, it's an uphill battle. More recently Andy Stanley, Reggie Joiner and Lane Jones at North Point Community Church in Atlanta have developed a model based on a house, where each environment (foyer, lounge room, kitchen) is geared to people at particular stages. After taking hundreds of churches through the Pathways workshop, it has become apparent to me that those with ministries that attempt to span more than one stage of development tend to be consistently effective in only serving people at one stage, or they simply annoy and disappoint everyone. The North Point team seem to be onto something.

For the church to be a disciple-making community, we need more than just a worship service. Leaders of burgeoning home-based church networks like Neil Cole and David Garrison would likely chime in that you don't need a public worship service at all. The effectiveness of their movements in making disciples suggests that they might just be onto something too.

Another recent development, particularly in the UK, has been the emergence of 'Fresh Expressions of Church'.[3] This movement sets out to create worshipping communities that are more adapted to the surrounding culture and less bound by traditional forms. Some of these projects have been quite effective in reaching the unchurched, introducing them to Jesus and forming them into maturing disciples. Others have been more a case of starting a program that serves a felt need in the community and labelling it 'church'.

It's common for these new churches to attract unchurched people because various 'fresh expressions' have served people's need for food, or community, or a safe place to play. Given their intended 'market', they've needed to keep explicit gospel teaching, participating in the sacraments and overt worship of God fairly minimal and at a very basic level. And that's just fine for those newly exploring the Christian faith. However, it won't serve to form mature disciples. For that, another context with different process and content is required. If 'next step' environments are provided, there's a good chance a fresh expression will serve as a discipling community. If a 'seeker-friendly' environment is all there is to it, chances are very few genuine disciples will be formed.

---

[3] www.freshexpressions.org.uk

Church is not just the service, and it's not just other 'stand-alone bits' like alternative services or playgroups. These can serve as valuable parts, but they're not the whole unless they begin with 'soil' and finish with reproducing 'fruit'.

Case study: 'Lunch Church'

St Chad's Anglican Church meets in an unremarkable, white-painted brick building sitting in a side street in Chelsea, a south-eastern suburb of Melbourne. While a house in bayside Chelsea will cost the purchaser about ten years' average salary, there are a surprising number of poor people in the area, living in caravan parks, boarding houses, public housing and on the streets.

For several years St Chad's has run a meals program. People can walk off the street and be welcomed into a large dining hall where they will be greeted, seated, waited upon and listened to. During the meal there may be a testimony given, but little more overtly Christian content.

A couple of years ago the assistant minister offered Youth Alpha over a meal at the same time in an adjacent room. About thirty people participated, and many made first-time commitents, insisting on being baptised in the chilly waters of Port Philip Bay.

The Alpha group has since morphed into Lunch Church, where all the basic elements of a worship service are practised (except congregational singing), albeit in modified form.

From time to time Youth Alpha is offered again, and more people are added to Lunch Church. Meanwhile, the meals program continues as it did before. A few of the original Alpha participants now serve on the meals team, while others have taken up responsibility for aspects of Lunch Church.

The meals program isn't church. All of this taken together is church.

Programs serve people, not vice versa

I'm guessing that some of you reading this will be stroking your beards knowingly and thinking, 'Ah, he's falling into the programmatic church fallacy.' Others may not have a beard to stroke, but may be thinking the same thing.

This fallacy is so-named because it believes that programs can in-and-of-themselves turn people unchurched people into fully devoted followers of Jesus Christ. It's easy for large churches (and some not so large) to drift in this direction. And it's even easier for outsiders to look from a distance and accuse large churches of sausage-machine discipleship.

The tendency of church members to serve programs rather than vice versa has led some like Neil Cole to eschew formal programs altogether, preferring a simplified, organic form of church.[4] Neil's work with Church Multiplication Associates has been remarkably successful among people groups considered to be highly gospel-resistant. While organic church is an approach that has proven effective, I'm not sure it's a mandate to abandon the idea of large churches altogether, nor is it a reason to abandon programs.

Making disciples tends to be a life-on-life process. Churches large and small are more likely to be effective in making disciples when their activities—structured or spontaneous, formal or organic—facilitate 'Christ in me rubbing off on you'. This means personally serving, attending, praying, listening and bearing witness (more on the importance of these later). To the extent that programs facilitate these relational processes, they can serve as disciple-making contexts. When programs fail to facilitate relational processes, they get in the way.

Jesus came as a human and not a publication or an iPhone app because relationships are the basic transformational unit of ministry. Effective churches use programs to support and facilitate life-transforming relationships. Programs can provide process and environment where people can exercise their gifts. But the programs in themselves don't do the heavy lifting.

Large church leaders tend to be extroverts (not always, but often). Extroverts draw their energy from interaction with people, and most extroverts have a high capacity for interaction. They're attracted to opportunities to interact, and will start conversations whenever they have opportunity. Introverts, who may make up as much as half the population, are just as happy to let others make the relational running.[5] To help

---

[4] You can check out Neil's thinking at www.cmaresources.org
[5] Buettner, Dan. 'Are Extroverts Happier Than Introverts? Insight into differences between two personality types'. *Thrive*, 14 May 2012.

introverts be disciple-makers, it's useful to provide context and process. Relational ambiguity usually ranks fairly highly on an introvert's list of anxieties.

About a decade ago Bill Hybels produced a helpful book and video series called *Just Walk Across the Room*.[6]. Introverts do much better when they're provided a 'room to walk across', be it a playgroup, a homework club or a sporting club. While introverts struggle to initiate relationships, they tend to do the longer-haul discipling work once the relationship is cemented. A well-designed program can be just the kind of environment where an introvert can bring their best to the discipling process, whether it's with the totally unchurched or seasoned Christian leaders.

Making disciples on purpose—it's a team sport

'I planted, Apollos watered, God gave the growth,' says Paul in 1 Corinthians. People have used this verse to validate a host of questionable ministry practices, from 'hit and run' evangelism to cheesy signs outside churches. Paul's point is not that we should just do whatever we want and let God cause the 'seed' to 'germinate' some other time. Rather it is an acknowledgment that each person has a different and equally important contribution to make to the growth of the kingdom (and no one should get an inflated sense of importance about their little bit). Each must recognise that their ministry is a small contribution in a bigger process. Going on, Paul switches metaphor and says we should be careful how we build. Part of being careful means understanding your contribution to the bigger process, and acting with consideration and cooperation with others who are also contributing. When all the various 'trades' work from the same set of plans, the result is more likely to be a useful and durable building.

Much of the writing and training in evangelism has been about individuals and how to communicate content. Just as important is the idea of evangelism as a community sport, and thought must be given to what this means in terms of process and context.

---

http://www.psychologytoday.com/blog/thrive/201205/are-extroverts-happier-introverts

[6] Hybels, Bill. *Just Walk Across the Room: Simple Steps Pointing People to Faith* (Zondervan, Grand Rapids, 2006).

In my workshops I frequently ask the participants if any of them came to faith during a conversation with a stranger. Out of the couple of thousand people who have come to Pathways workshops, I've had just one hand go up (it happened last year and spoilt my perfect theory). That's not to say that such conversions can't happen. It's just that they're uncommon—or more precisely, it's uncommon for such a convert to hang around in a church long enough to get to one of my workshops.

I also ask people to raise their hands of they knew one Christian or less at the time they made their first prayer of repentance and faith. Hands do go up, but it's usually less than ten per cent of the room. Conversely, more than eighty per cent of hands go up when I ask if people were in the company of two or more Christians when they made their first prayer of repentance and faith.

Most people come to faith in the Christian community, having been embraced by the Christian community. I'm for working with the approach that is more commonly effective.

The culture of a discipling community is perhaps the most effective missional dimension of a local church. In an increasingly postmodern and post-rational society, evangelism is shaping up as more of a socialisation process (as it largely was prior to modernity) than an educative one. People are more likely to be curious about the gospel as a set of propositions, and more apt to grasp its meaning, when it serves as an explanation for their experience of participation in the Christian community.

A person who has experienced the love of Jesus expressed through the compassionate action of his followers is more likely to find credible the idea that 'God loved the world so much that he gave his Son'. Further, a person who has shared life with those who are experiencing some of the 'abundant life' that Jesus promises will be more likely to be curious about its source. The truth is, communities of disciples make disciples, and no program or course will serve as a substitute.

Jesus' primary invitation to would-be disciples was simply to 'come with me'. For those who did, the character of Jesus proceeded to rub off on them. Jesus created a certain and attractive culture among those who followed him, fuelled primarily by his mere presence. There is an unassailable power in tactile interaction with which mere information can't compete. If the message and the culture are at odds, people will believe the culture. If, however, the message and the culture are congruent, the potential is powerful.

Disciple-making on purpose: thinking like a farmer

I've already mentioned that before I started working as a church growth consultant, I worked as a human resources manager for a large agribusiness. My office was smack-dab in the middle of a fruit farm. Growing up in the suburbs, I knew almost nothing about farming and farmers. I was on a steep learning curve.

One thing I knew was that farmers are people that grow things on purpose. They invest, organise, and work toward profitable production. While strictly speaking orchardists can't control the growth of an apple tree and its fruit production, they can do an awful lot to influence it. And they do.

Farms run on seasons and lifecycles. In Australia apples are harvested from late January through to late May, depending on the climate and the variety. Pruning kicks in soon after and goes through to August. Come spring it's all about nutrients, water and pest management. In summer you can add crop load and light management to the springtime priorities.

Apple trees will produce almost nothing of commercial value in the first two or three years. They reach optimal production after about seven years and once they hit twenty years old they become difficult to manage profitably. Successful orchardists are diligent students of their location, their trees and their crop. The better they understand, the better they can cooperate with the trees' natural process and interaction with the environment.

Everything you find on a farm somehow contributes to the production cycle—its purpose and meaning is understood in the context of that cycle. While large, powerful tractors make broadacre farms more efficient, you won't find them on an orchard, where smaller, narrow tractors are required to operate between rows. Picking bags and ladders are useless for farming wheat but indispensable for farming apples. Every activity and piece of equipment is tailored to the type of farming being engaged in.

Farming is the hard work of intentionally applying technical knowledge to an organic process in order to maximise an outcome. The farmer exercises management (not necessarily control) through the whole lifecycle of the crop.

As we've seen, in Mark 4, Jesus used farming as a metaphor for the kingdom of God: 'What's the kingdom of God like? Well, it's like a farmer who scatters seed.' Jesus spent most of his time in the largely rural territory of Galilee. His audience were mostly primary producers, so they understood his stories. They would have taken for granted that his stories were not instructions on farming, but analogies. No farmer would just walk out and randomly scatter seed on unprepared soil. Jesus didn't detail this because it was redundant information to his audience. In this and similar stories he was making a point, not setting out a procedure. The absent information is not a mandate for us to be simplistic about disciple-making.

Farmers can wander about scattering seed at random if they like and they may or may not see some kind of a crop. Wiser farmers will be more thoughtful and more intentional, and will in all likelihood see a much greater crop. Disciple-making is not that different.

Making disciples is the hard work of intentionally applying knowledge to a spiritual process in order to maximise an outcome. Disciple-making gives diligent oversight (not control) to the entire discipleship journey, from stranger and unbeliever to devoted follower and minister.

Every activity in an effective church somehow contributes to the discipleship journey—its purpose and meaning is understood in the context of the kingdom of God. Every activity and piece of equipment is tailored to the surrounding community that is being engaged in becoming devoted followers of Jesus.

Starting with one kind of crop: focusing mission on a demographic slice
'Tell me about the last ten people to come to faith in your church.' It's a pretty standard consulting question. The answer tells me a lot. Usually, the minister can't name ten people who have recently come to faith (sometimes they can't tell me about any), which is a telling fact in itself. But of the stories they can tell, there will usually be some degree of commonality about most of them.

In one large church, most of the first-time commitments were made by parents of kids in the playgroup. In another, all of the first-time commitments in the prior year had been made by people for whom English was not their first language. Ask for the backstories on the commitments and you'll know who the church is reaching and how.

My point is this. In the churches I've studied and served, most new believers have come from a small number of defined people groups. Some may not fit with one group or another, but the majority do. They might be defined by a particular life stage (for example, having a toddler at home) or a particular need (for example, improving their English) or by particular association (for example they are students, parents of students or staff of a local school).

Some churches have identified specific 'mission focus groups' and so this clustering this is intentional and expected. For others it's apparently accidental. It's uncommon in my experience for churches to reach a significant number of people who seem to appear at random with no common characteristics.

Research by George Barna and more recently by Thom Rainer and Eric Geiger indicates that churches trying to reach everybody all at once tend to reach no one at all.[7] When I suggest to client churches that they identify a specific mission focus group, it's common to get some push-back.

'But we're called to reach everyone in our parish. Do you mean to say we should reject a person who doesn't fit some kind of target group?' It's a natural reaction. For some the idea of focusing mission on a particular group for people implies excluding others. I'm not talking about exclusion. I am talking about focus of attention and resources.

Sometimes I hear the objection, 'But Jesus didn't have a mission focus group—he reached out to everybody.' I'm not sure that's the case. Let's take look at the gospels.

Jesus claimed he was sent only to the lost sheep of Israel (Matthew 15:24). In fact, this verse comes in the context of him defining his mission focus group. The event takes place in Tyre—non-Jewish territory where Jesus has 'withdrawn'. He is there on vacation, not a mission trip. A desperate Gentile woman recognises him and begs him to heal her daughter. Still grieving the

---

[7] Barna, George. *User Friendly Churches: What Christians Need to Know About the Churches People Love to Go To* (Regal, Ventura, 1991): Rainer, Thom S. & Geiger, Eric. *Simple Church: Returning to God's Process for Making Disciples* (B&H, Nashville, 2006).

death of his relative John the Baptist, exhausted by the events around the feeding of the five thousand and the relentless pursuit by the crowds, Jesus is seeking some downtime. Performing a healing would blow his cover and bring people running from all over.

Out of compassion Jesus heals the girl, then immediately leaves, heading north to Sidon (Mark 7:31ff). Then he doubles back, crosses the Sea of Galilee and cools his heels in the Decapolis—again, not country frequented by the lost sheep of Israel. Someone recognises him and sends a deaf and mute man his way. Jesus takes the man out of the village, heals him on the quiet and (incredibly) tells him to keep his newly opened mouth shut.

Jesus crosses the lake again, and no sooner arrives back in Jewish territory then another crowd gathers, hungry for miracles, teaching and, eventually, for bread (Mark 8:1ff). This is back among his mission focus group, so the teaching and miracles flow. Then Jesus darts off again, ending up hiding out in Caesarea Philippi, another Gentile region where it seems he's finally afforded some peace and quiet (Mark 8:27). No miracles are recorded in this region, only important discourse with the Twelve.

The synoptic gospels are set predominantly in Galilee. Jesus, being a good Jewish man, travelled down to Jerusalem a few times a year for festivals. You'll find a lot of arguments and discourses are recorded from there. Because Jerusalem at the time was the centre of rabbinic teaching, we find him in debate with the religious leaders while he's in Judea for a festival like Passover or Tabernacles. Otherwise he spent most of his ministry time criss-crossing the region to the north of Samaria, where he grew up. Even when he sparked a revival in Sychar in Samaria (John 4), he only stayed a couple of days before returning to his home patch.

Now let's narrow it further. Early in his ministry Jesus went on a recruiting drive, calling Peter, James, John, Andrew and Matthew to follow him. While the four fishermen left their businesses (complete with a huge catch of fish) to their relatives in order to follow Jesus, Matthew left a lucrative and probably not-entirely-above-board tax collection enterprise. He threw a going-away party and invited his friends—the low-life of his neighbourhood (Matthew 9:9ff).

The religious professionals tried to coach Jesus in the fine art of religious professionalism, advising him that he was hanging with the wrong crowd.

Jesus clarified his position beautifully: 'I'm not here to call the kind of people you guys seek as followers—those earnestly righteous religious types who suspect they're a wee bit better than common folk.' (Well, that's my rough translation anyway.)

Instead Jesus was after the outcasts—those who were probably excluded from the synagogue, the social circles, the economic cycle. His teaching was directed straight at these people. 'Be happy if you're hungry, sad, despised, longing to be made clean and righteous,' he paradoxically declares in the Beatitudes. 'If you're happy, popular, full and fulfilled—be afraid, be very afraid,' he continues. It's hard to argue that the target audience here was the middle class. He went on with parables that used very simple similes, suited to a concrete-thinking, unsophisticated audience. Then he put a sting in their tails to aggravate the religious leaders. It's pretty obvious that his teaching was designed to appeal to the poor and oppressed while risking the resentment of the wealthy, well-liked and influential. He even seemed to go out of his way *not* to appeal to the religious set (see Luke 11:37ff).

To summarise, Jesus' mission focus group was disadvantaged Galilean Jews. He focused on these people, tailoring his time and method and message to them. Yet he reached quite a few outside that group as well.

Churches that get intentional about mission seem to have a happy knack of reaching people who don't fit their mission focus group. I can't explain why except to say that churches that are intentional about mission will usually have some process for people to follow in participating in the community of faith, making a faith commitment and beginning to mould their life to the teaching of Jesus.

By narrowing the mission focus to a particular demographic slice we gain the possibility to tailor activities to the needs and characteristics of the group. This applies to scheduling, location, supportive services like childcare, language, format and more besides.

Choosing a mission focus group does not preclude a church from welcoming and showing compassion to whoever comes their way. It simply recognises the unavoidable reality that every decision we make will suit some people and be less suitable for others. So we will make decisions about resources, strategies, schedules and style with this particular group in mind, in order to reach and make disciples among them.

Case study: Why tailoring to a mission focus group matters

Let's compare two churches. The first runs playgroups on Monday to Thursday mornings each week. About a hundred families with pre-schoolers are represented, most of whom don't attend church. On Friday, in the same timeslot the playgroup occupies on other days, they run a program called 'Christianity Explored' where people interested in faith can learn about the message of Jesus and how to become his disciple. At the same time, small groups for new believers operate, all on the church campus. High quality childcare is provided on Fridays, in the same location that playgroups run on other days of the week.

The second church has playgroups and equivalents running five days a week, reaching a little over a hundred families. On Wednesday night they run an evangelistic course called 'Reason for God'. No childcare is offered.

It doesn't take a brain surgeon to figure out which church is more effective in making disciples (and the difference has little to do with the relative effectiveness of Christianity Explored and Reason for God). The first example church sees about seven faith commitments a year (not stunning, but not insignificant). The second, unsurprisingly, has had none. A little more tailoring of their program to the particular needs and constraints of families with pre-schoolers would lead to greater mission effectiveness.

Why 'local' makes sense and attraction is attractive

There has been a lot of conversation of late about workplace-based mission. At the same time, I get some degree of blow-back when I talk about somewhat structured, church-based programs like playgroups as a mission context. The narrative goes something like this: 'You're still about come-to-us kind of ministry (which is so, like, 1980s) when Jesus told us to go.' Others might use the terms 'attractional' (implication: bad) and 'missional' (clearly good). More sophisticated types will describe programs as centripetal when mission is centrifugal.

I'm not convinced such binary categories are all that helpful. Jesus told us to 'Go make disciples', the sense being '*As you go* make ... ' or 'Make disciple-making your way of life.' Whether the people from which disciples are drawn are found in a church-based program or a workplace is not really the issue. Making disciples is the issue. Let's measure our effectiveness against the outcome Jesus commanded (that is, disciples who obey his commands), not the context in which we connect.

I'm not against the idea of workplace ministry; it's just that it faces a couple of significant hurdles, especially in a country like Australia. The vast majority of Aussies live in large, spread-out cities. It's not uncommon to travel an hour to work. The person at the next desk (or the next checkout, or driving the next forklift) may have travelled an hour from the opposite direction. It's a big call for them to come to Alpha (or anything else) at your church. Now I can hear the objections: 'There you go, thinking attractional again.' So here's the nub of the problem. The vast majority (my straw-polling suggests eighty to ninety per cent) of people who make a faith commitment make it *after* they've developed a sense of belonging in the Christian community. It's unusual for a person to commit their life to Christ having only known a single believer. I challenge you to poll you own church community and see if you get a different result.

If you're committed to workplace ministry, you should consider planting a church in or near your workplace, and find some other believers to form community into which you can invite your unchurched friends. Then meet at lunchtime or after work.

If you're not up for planting a workplace church, helping a person feel like they belong in the Christian community is much easier if they live somewhere near where the church meets. Local churches can do a great job reaching local people, with a little thoughtful missiology.

Modality is not a dirty word

A few decades ago Ralph Winter observed that church in the New Testament took a couple of forms.[8] Paul wrote letters to locality-based communities in places like Ephesus and Corinth. These have their analogues in the local or parish churches we know today. They meet at a set place, tend to create their own routines and rhythms, and can be effective in reaching those who live nearby. Winter labelled these 'modalities'.

Winter also observed a second form of church. It was generally smaller, more highly specialised and demanded a higher degree of commitment. Paul travelled with a band of supporters and apprentices, and had learned his missionary trade in a similar band led by Barnabas. The missionary band travelled from city to city, staying anything from a few weeks to a couple of

---

[8] Winter, Ralph D. 'The Two Structures of God's Redemptive Mission.' http://frontiermissionfellowship.org/uploads/documents/two-structures.pdf

years, pioneering new churches or strengthening ones they had planted previously. Some modern 'para-church' groups and missions agencies follow this pattern. Winter calls such bands 'sodalities'.

The important lesson is this. Both of these are forms of church (I'm guessing Winter wouldn't go for the term 'para-church'). The two forms are both valid, but they don't roll the same way. This is important when we think about the book of Acts as a model for mission.

Some of the missional literature that's emerged in the past fifteen years has looked at Paul and his ways and advocated that local churches pattern themselves after him (perhaps they're drawing on Roland Allen's missiology from the beginning of the 20th century). The problem we find is this: Paul operated in sodalic mode—narrow focus, high commitment, small and nimble like a commando unit. Your average local church member, even if they're a keen disciple, probably doesn't have the freedom and flexibility to operate in sodalic mode—they have jobs and partners and kids and all the rest of it. That doesn't mean we can't be in a missional mode in a local church, but we can't expect the kind of commitment a sodalic band demands.

Local church, or modalic mission, tends to be a slow-burn (recently the term 'slow church' has gained wider use, illustrating the point). The advantage of the local church is that it tends to be pretty stable, and it's likely to be around for a while. It can serve the unchurched people in the surrounding community in a steady, consistent way, demonstrating the kingdom of God and allowing people to get as close as they like without forcing a crisis of decision. That doesn't mean we won't preach the gospel or at the right time challenge people to a faith commitment—but we'll be patient and thoughtful about it.

Further, because local churches are geographically stable and tend to have more people, there is opportunity for a somewhat more diverse ministry, where people with less ministry skill or less confidence (for example, the kind that freeze solid at the thought of explaining the gospel to people) can find a place to serve and be useful in the kingdom. Their special contribution may be cooking or pastoral care or fixing things. They get a place on the team, confident they can invite an unchurched friend to hear the gospel explained by someone else (like a preacher or an evangelist).

Felt needs and discipleship needs

Jesus' ministry was pretty much equally divided into meeting two kinds of needs—what we might call as 'felt needs' and 'discipleship needs'. People came from all over Galilee and Judea to hear Jesus speak. But they came even from the surrounding *countries* to experience his healing power. The Jews were intensely curious about Jesus, because at the time there was an almost fever-pitch anticipation of the appearance of the Messiah. Rumours of this authority-wielding, parable-talking miracle man spread like wildfire. You can almost hear the whispers in the crowd as you read the gospels: 'Maybe he's *the One*!'

Those outside the Jewish people (that is, Gentiles) did not share the Jewish anticipation of a Messiah. They were attracted by the possibility of their diseases being healed—so much so that they would travel for days to get to Jesus.

And here's the point: people with little or no spiritual curiosity will gladly come and hang out with you if your community does something to meet their felt needs.

To jump to an aside that I simply can't resist, we often wonder why we don't see miracles in the Western world such as those reported in the gospels. You may take the view that there were no miracles, and opt for some other explanation. My personal belief is that there were miracles—spiritual power dealing with physical problems. If Jesus and the apostles had miracles happening all around them, why don't we?

Ever noticed that in the story of the feeding of the five thousand, the disciples present Jesus with an expression of compassion: 'Send them away to get food—they're all hungry'? (It's likely the disciples were hoping to pull up stumps and head for the local hamburger joint themselves, but never mind.) Jesus responds, 'You yourselves give them something to eat.'

'What? But look at them! There's gotta be, well, I dunno, thousands of them. That's more than a years' wages, just for a snack!'

'Hang on, this kid's got a handful of barley cakes and a couple of fish.'

'Yeah, great! To feed this crowd?'

With the most meagre of resources, Jesus fed the crowd. Once the disciples' resources were exhausted, his power kicked in.

When the crowd on the other side of the lake asked for a repeat performance, Jesus told them that the main course was his own flesh. That freaked them out and they left. Jesus was not in the business of bread and circuses for the proletariat.

When we get to the absolute end of ourselves and our resources, God is more likely to intervene (no guarantees—there's more to it than that). Jesus had only the clothes on his back—he was perpetually at the end of his tangible resources. And he was full of compassion, full of faith and highly attuned to his Father. No wonder miracles happened.

Back to the main point – the 21st century, post-Christian West is not first-century Galilee. Christianity is lampooned in the Australian media (and in social media). The church's stocks are not trading so well. Secular people are not expecting a Messiah per se (although a small but visible-on-new-release-day minority venerated Steve Jobs as if he were one). The poor and sick in Jesus' time were probably less interested in a Messiah than they were in basic survival. Like the outcasts of the first century, our first point of engagement is likely to be around felt needs: something people want, appreciate, like or hope for, and generally something more immediate than eternal life.

In churches I serve, people have come to faith because the church has first put a meal in front of them, or provided a group to improve their English, or provided a place to socialise where their kids could play safely, or helped them apply for a visa, or visited them after a funeral, or just given a socially awkward, difficult young kid a place where they could belong when no one else would. Any one of countless possibilities for kindness and thoughtfulness represent opportunities for mission.

Turning our attention to discipleship needs, Jesus' approach is again noteworthy. He led with the idea of 'Repent and believe the good news' (Mark 1:15). Through his life and teaching he made it clear that the repentance of which he spoke was not about 'Stop being naughty boys and girls, and obey the law!' Instead he taught 'Turn around your thinking and believe the wonderful news I am announcing.' As we study the rest of Jesus' life, he set about turning upside down the common understanding of what it meant to live under God's reign (or, as Dallas Willard argues, perhaps it's more accurate to say he was turning the prevailing understanding right-way up).[9]

Jesus was not simply about social welfare (meeting felt needs). He was also about discipleship: challenging people to turn their thinking, values, priorities and behaviours right-way up. Effective proclaiming of the kingdom of God must address both felt needs and discipleship needs. In my experience, churches that are growing through disciple-making are paying attention to both.

Invite, invite, invite

One the key concepts of the Pathways process is that of invitation. Michael Harvey of Back-To-Church-Sunday fame has been the voice of one calling in the wilderness, 'Invite people to church'.[10] I'm absolutely in agreement—so long as your definition of church is not confined to a worship service.

If by 'church' you mean a few believers are hanging out together (they need to do more than that, but bear with me) then you could invite an unchurched friend to a camping weekend, to a barbecue, to coffee, to a bridge group, or to whatever might be helpful and appealing and attractive to them. Then you could keep inviting them to similar things, and then maybe to a Bible study and then maybe even to a church service.

Whatever your pathway, it will work most effectively when Christians develop a habit of invitation. It may only take six invitations for a person to walk the journey from complete unbeliever to Christian leader—or it may take hundreds. It's not a numbers game. But if you don't invite people to take steps toward becoming a fully committed disciple, my research suggests they almost certainly won't take them.

Work hard and pray

Let's return for a minute to the metaphor of farming. Farming is a faith-based enterprise. Farmers invest a lot of capital, effort and emotional energy in their enterprise, knowing they only have so much influence. With the benefits of science we can shorten the odds of success, but we can't

---

[9] Willard, Dallas. *The Divine Conspiracy: Rediscovering Our Hidden Life In God* (Harper Collins San Francisco 1998)
[10] www.unlockingthegrowth.com

guarantee that every seed will germinate, every cow will conceive or every tree will set fruit. Given the right conditions they should, but the farmer can only do so much. Ultimately it's up to God's design, printed on the DNA, to come through. Then there are the variables of weather, pests, diseases and the like. Sooner or later, it's up to forces beyond human control.

The farmer must have faith to make the investment. They can't 'wait and see' for very long. When the farmer judges the time to be right, they sow, or plant, or buy livestock, and then hope.

Making disciples is ultimately a spiritual process. And like farming it's a cooperative process—humanity does their bit, and God must do his. While farming relies on God's design, disciple-making relies on the active work of the Holy Spirit in the heart of the disciple-to-be.

The fact that Jesus commands us to make disciples indicates that there is work for us to do. The church is not a jungle where disciples grow spontaneously without human involvement. But neither is it a factory where humans can manufacture disciples by force of their own will and effort. When God created humanity, he put them in a garden, and that provides a metaphor for all our endeavours in the kingdom: humanity in cooperation with God.

The discipleship farm requires both our effort and the action of God to germinate the seed of the gospel. And this is where the importance of prayer kicks in. Our best effort and thinking will only get us so far. In prayer we submit ourselves to God, recognising that we need his guidance to inform our effort, and also to work in both ourselves and those we're serving so that Christ may be formed in us and others.

I've worked with churches that pray a lot but don't do much. In general, they don't grow.[11] I've also worked with churches that work hard and don't pray much—sometimes they grow, occasionally they grow quickly, but they're vulnerable to spats and splits and it's common for them to shrink just as fast. Sustained growth over the long haul is a partnership, and we invite

---

[11] There are a few historical exceptions to this, where concerted prayer sparked revival, but this book is not about that. Sustaining revival like the Wesleyans in the 18th and 19th centuries takes discipline and hard work. The Welsh revival came and went in the space of a couple of years for lack of organisation.

God into the partnership through consistent, humble and, dare I say it, disciplined prayer.

Behave your way to a new culture

Pascale, Sternin and Sternin wrote a wonderfully provocatively titled book called *The Power of Positive Deviance* (you'll need to read it yourself to find out whether you might want to begin your own quest for positive deviance).[12] In their counter-intuitive and ground-breaking work, they found an interesting contradiction to the conventional (classical Greek) belief that thinking determines action. While I'm not about to throw out all that Plato, Aristotle and the Enlightenment may have to teach us, newer research suggests that we can also act our way to a new way of thinking.

The majority of church growth books assume the best approach to change is what might be called a 'rational-comprehensive approach'. In this, current reality is thoroughly appraised, the environment analysed, a case made for change, a vision cast for a new tomorrow, a strategy devised and a plan designed. With determination and optimism, the march into the better future begins. (Can you hear the strains of *The Battle Hymn of the Republic?*)

Rather than seeking to change everyone's thinking and implement root and branch transformation, you could opt for an approach based on Everett Rogers' theory of the diffusion of innovations.[13] Rogers first proposed this idea in 1960s and it's since been popularised by Malcom Gladwell's *The Tipping Point*.[14] A host of other writers have contributed to what is now a fairly well formulated and validated theory.

Applied to organisational change, the idea goes like this. Begin with a few who might be willing to try something new and look at implementing a small initiative to see if it generates the desired result. Do your very best to make it work, applying all your best thinking and sustained effort. But don't try to change the whole organisation at once, and don't bet all your resources on it (Pathways is a helpful paradigm, but it's not the pearl of great price). Treat your project as an experiment. See what you get. If it's effective, try to figure

---

[12] Pascale, Richard, Sternin, Jerry & Sternin, Monique. *The Power of Positive Deviance: How Unlikely Innovators Solve the World's Toughest Problems* (Harvard, Boston, 2010).
[13] Rogers, Everett M. *Diffusion of Innovations* (Free Press/Simon & Schuster, New York, 1962).
[14] Gladwell, Malcolm. *The Tipping Point: How Little Things Can Make a Big Difference* (Little Brown, New York, 2000).

out why and try another experiment based on what you've learned. If it fails, try to figure out why and try another experiment based on what you've learned.

The whole idea is to generate what the theorists call 'social proof' — generalised anecdotal evidence that what you're doing actually works. In the case of Pathways, you would want to see some new faith commitments, increased participation in 'belonging' activities (more on that later) or whatever the desired outcome of your experiments might be.

While social proof is not sufficient for the registration of a new pharmaceutical product or the publication of your work in a peer-reviewed journal, it's generally enough to generate some wider interest, so you can get more people involved in initiatives to bring more change.

Over time, you can align all of your church's activity into discipleship pathways while avoiding too much blood on walls.

The beauty of the diffusion of innovations approach is that each small change represents a fairly low risk. Because you're only experimenting, small failures don't lead to a broad collapse of the change process.

Part 2
Seven Stages Explained

Chapter 3
Clarify Your Mission Focus

Before I outline the stages that make up the pathways model, let me stress the importance of clearly identifying a *mission focus group*. You'll remember that a mission focus group is a certain demographic slice of your community that you have thoughtfully and prayerfully chosen as the kind of people you're going to organise yourselves to reach. For one church it might be families with pre-schoolers, for another it might be the local arts community, while yet another could choose students at a nearby university.

I've set out a process in Appendix 1 that will help you choose a mission focus group if you're yet to identify yours.

If yours is a small or family-sized church (that is, less than fifty people average weekend attendance), you would do best to choose just one mission focus group for now. As you reach them, other related possibilities will open up, but if you try to reach two or more unrelated groups at once, you will likely run thin on human resources and either be ineffective or burn out your most willing workers.

If your church is larger than family-sized and up to around 150 people average weekend attendance (that is, a pastoral-sized church), you might have capacity for two or three mission focus groups. If your church is larger still, perhaps a few more. To reiterate Thom Rainer and Eric Geiger's advice, least is most. You're better off doing a great job reaching a narrower slice of the community than doing a poor (or exhausting) job in an effort to have something for everyone. Their advice to 'say "no" to almost everything' is not exaggerated (well, perhaps only a little).

You can slice a community every which way along a hundred different fault lines. You may want to go a little broader than focusing solely on middle-aged, divorced, alcoholic males for whom English is a second language. However, specialising on any one of those categories might be just what God is calling you to do.

If your church is over-programmed (and most are), perhaps you could apply Pathways to the ministries around a single mission focus group while you manage the resources around all the rest.

I can't over-emphasise the importance of a clearly identified mission focus group. It makes much of the planning and decision-making around various ministries so much easier.

Church planters and missional communities
If you're church planting, you would do well to begin with a single mission focus group. If you're part of a missional communities network like 3DM or SOMA, you may have already thought about your mission focus group.[15] If not, I encourage you to identify as clearly as possible who your community is best positioned to reach, and figure out how you can get as much overlap of time and effort between the majority of your community members and your mission focus group.

A bunch of the church plants I've watched have used the 'gather and scatter' model, where the team gathers for worship, teaching and encouragement, and then scatters so that each is a missionary in their own sphere. If the spheres overlap significantly so that unchurched people get to experience relationship with a number of Christians, this can work. However, in large, spread-out cities like Melbourne where I live, the spheres seldom overlap. Christians finds themselves as lone missionaries in their work, sport or neighbourhood contexts, and find themselves being a good witness but usually not making disciples. Mission, in the overwhelming majority of cases, is a team sport. It generally takes a community to make a disciple.

Further, when it comes time to begin a public worship service (and most church plants do eventually), having your primary mission focus group in mind will help you figure out some of the criteria: time, location, support services (for example, kids' facilities), the language you use, the printed or multimedia communications, the duration—you get the idea. There will be different answers to these questions for a uni-student church than for a church reaching families with small children.

---

[15] www.3dmovements.com, http://wearesoma.com

Chapter 4
Potential Contact

Assuming you're clear on your mission focus group, let's work through each step on the Pathway in detail. The examples set out in the following chapters are by no means exhaustive—they're just there to help illustrate and clarify.

We begin with the stage '*potential contact*'. This is the stage in your pathway where you seek to engage your mission focus group presuming they are total strangers to you. That is, this step is about engaging the people you are called to reach but don't know by name, and for whom you don't have contact details.

'Potential contact' activities are those designed to connect with people in your community who don't necessarily know anybody who attends your church. These activities may include your website, Facebook page, signs, printed fliers and advertisements. They also include intentional choices on the part of congregation members, like frequenting a particular café or pub in order to meet people who are part of your mission focus group, or engaging forums or other digital spaces where your mission focus group might be found.

The whole purpose of activity in this stage is to let people know you exist and are interested in whatever interests them.

Let's think about some examples. One church I know of is located in the wealthiest suburb in Melbourne. Their 140-year-old building is classic bluestone surrounded by mature trees, and looks like the perfect venue to a fairy-tale wedding. In fact, the church hosts about 150 weddings a year. While weddings make money, they're seen primarily as a ministry opportunity. So the church has a website geared to be 'hit' by couples seeking to be married (and they have the Google analytics to prove it). The church maintains an active Facebook presence and seeks to engage (pardon the pun) and maintain contact with couples who will be and have been married there.

In another church, people involved in the playgroup connect with other parents through a community buy-swap-and-sell website. Given that their mission focus group is parents of toddlers, frequenting a site where baby and toddler clothing and paraphernalia make up the bulk of the merchandise exchanged is a smart move. Purchasing a car baby seat offers a chance to make a new friend when you go to pick it up!

A church plant I coached was located in a mining town in outback Queensland. Their primary 'potential contact' device was a regular newsletter they stuck under the windscreen wipers of every car in the car park of the local shopping centre. I have to admit, I was as sceptical as you probably are as you read this. Yet the community response was phenomenal. The mission focus group for this church was the isolated wives of men working in the mines. The newsletter always included an invitation for women to connect at a lifestyle (fitness, nutrition and spirituality) group held in the church. For this mission focus group, it was perfect. A number of women called to make inquiries whenever a new edition of the newsletter was published. You might be asking, 'Why not letterbox drop?' The answer: a significant number of people lived on properties out of town, or in smaller neighbouring towns, and only came into the larger centre to shop. Some came into town a couple of times a week just to 'be around people'.

As you can see from these three examples, the 'potential contact' activities were relatively simple, but thoughtfully designed with the needs and lifestyle of the mission focus group in mind. To understand your mission focus group, you'll need to do your homework, and perhaps try a bunch of different activities until you hit on one that works. Essential to effective 'potential contact' activities is to design them from the perspective of the outsider.

Workin' the web

I've already given a couple of examples of kinds of internet-based 'potential contact' activities. One was a church website. Another was committed believers making friends with unchurched people in an online community space.

Let me go out on a limb here. I can't see any valid reason why a local church would not have a thoughtful and well-presented website. Even if a church is simply interested in picking up the Christians that move into their neighbourhood, or those de-churched believers that are looking for whatever reason to re-engage with church, the web is the number one place people go to find a church. A church without a website is like a business without a phone.

While more than half the churches with which I work have websites, most of the ministers I've coached tend to have awkward answers to the question, 'Who is your website for?' There is usually a bit of a blank-face response until the penny drops and they realise the question is about target audience. Very, very few church websites are designed for their mission focus group— and to be useful as part of your mission strategy, your website should be. Let me put it another way. The primary target audience for your website should be people who don't belong to your church but whom you hope to reach.

And this is nowhere more important than your home page/landing page. Members of your mission focus group should be able to clearly see buttons that represent their interests on your home page. For example, if you're trying to reach families with primary school kids, your home page should include at least one picture that suggests families with primary-schoolers come to your church. A big button labelled 'Kids' Stuff' or something similar would be worth thinking about (make sure the button takes them to a page with information on your activities for kids and their parents).

Web design with the outsider in mind also applies to aspects like language. If you're reaching people whose English is limited, having some basic information or a button for each of the common non-English languages spoken in your area sends a powerful message of thoughtfulness and welcome.

Think also about socio-economics. Choose language, images and a design theme that suits the surrounding culture. Keep the religious jargon off your homepage, unless it's meaningful for your mission focus group.

You might want also to consider search engine optimisation around the known needs of your mission focus group. That means ensuring your site is easily found in searches your mission focus group might make. If you run a playgroup, you want your playgroup to turn up in the top three search results that combine 'playgroup' and your suburb or town. Given that people now use a range of devices to surf the web, it's worth ensuring your site is optimised for the most common devices and platforms.

For example, a church that had a steady stream of parents bringing kids to be baptised figured that this group would make a good mission focus group. So they had a suitable button on their landing page labelled both 'Baptism' and 'Christening'. They organised their search engine optimisation around those terms combined with their suburb and municipality. One of the images on the landing page was of a baptism service.

Don't underestimate the value of other websites that serve your mission focus group. One church that commenced a playgroup struggled to attract participants until they discovered that the local council website has a listing of all the playgroups in the area. The playgroup coordinator at the church contacted the council and arranged for the church playgroup to be listed and linked. Three weeks later, the playgroup was full with a waiting list.

In short, an outsider who represents your mission focus group should find your church first go if they search for any kind of activity that you offer them. On hitting your page, they should get the impression from your website that your church would be a place where they would feel right at home.

There's good reason to have your church rosters and calendar and all sorts of stuff that's useful and informative to insiders on your site—but not on the front page. A tab that leads to a page for regulars is all you need on the homepage.

All of the above is beginning to sound a little technical, so engaging the help of a digital specialist is probably a good investment for any church that's looking to improve its online presence. Going into the technicalities and details is beyond the scope of this book, but for starters, you should be thinking about things like:

- a look and language geared to your mission focus group
- landing-page access to activities that serve your mission focus group
- optimising for criteria that your mission focus group is likely to search
- ensuring smooth running and clear presentation across a variety of platforms and browsers
- making the most of other sites that serve your mission focus group.

Social media

Most of the above pertains also to social media, although the interactive nature of social media, where users generate content, means there are all kinds of added complexities.

It's worth considering separate social media pages for the various groups around your church. For example, you might want separate pages for your homework club, playgroup, seniors' ministry, youth group etc. You might want to put these on different platforms too, based on your research as to which platform your mission focus group is most likely to use.

Thinking about access and visibility for each page is important, as each may have differing privacy and security considerations, leading to differing access and moderation considerations. It also means you can assign a specialist to moderate and curate each page rather than it all coming back to one person.

Before you go creating a bunch of different Facebook pages, remember that these require work. While a website can be reasonably static, social media needs near constant updating, and, if users can post content, constant moderation. Think carefully.

Also think about searchability within the social media environment. Some social groupings tend to limit their online experience to activity within a social media platform (some research I was shown found that mothers of toddlers were highly likely to spend the majority of their time online within the Facebook environment. So if you want to reach them, you'll probably need a Facebook presence).

One of the most useful features of social media platforms like Facebook is their segment-specific advertising potential. This allows you to target your ad to an amazingly narrow group limited by age, gender, location, beliefs. And the cost is surprisingly low. However, be aware that some ads can have unintended consequences. Open invitations to youth group activities could attract a slice of your mission focus group for which you're not prepared.

Signs

Signage is a common 'potential contact' initiative—just about every church has a sign out the front. Signs should be most interesting to the kind of people you're trying to reach.

One church with which I worked sported a sign declaring the efficacy of the blood of Christ to redeem us from our sins and the inerrancy of the scriptures as the Word of God. While this is all very theologically orthodox, it won't make much sense to an unchurched person. Signs like these send a message something akin to, 'You're only welcome if you understand and agree.'

While you should advertise your service times on your sign, it's just as important to advertise the activities that will be of most interest to your mission focus group. So if you're reaching people for whom English is a second language, you might even advertise your conversational English group in several common languages.

You'll remember the huge real estate-style signs I mentioned in the story about Julie and Nelson in an earlier chapter. Signs still have a place.

And always, always make the next step inviting, obvious and easy. Include phone numbers (extroverts want to call and talk to you immediately) and an email address (introverts want to be anonymous until they have a little more information and you've removed a little of the ambiguity for them). Make sure enquires are followed up very, very promptly.

Inhabiting as a 'potential contact' activity

A common 'potential contact' activity is to inhabit the spaces your mission focus group might inhabit. I currently serve on the board of a community organisation that provides housing support and foster care. The church I attend at present sets out to be a church for those who serve the local community. The board is a context that put me in touch with the mission focus group for my church.

Some of the church planters I coach hang out in coffee shops or pubs just to be around the unchurched. Neil Cole and Hugh Halter are both masters of making such 'third spaces' the lounge room for their planting teams.[16] If places like cafés and pubs are a good place to meet your mission focus group,

---

[16] Hugh has written a bunch of inspiring and accessible books on mission. Check him out at www.hughhalter.com, Ray Oldenburg in his book *The Great Good Place* (Marlowe & Company New York: 1991) identified home as the 'first place', the place of one's occupation and the 'second place' and 'third places', or 'third spaces' as social environments such as cafes, coffee shops, community centres, beauty parlours, general stores, bars, and hangouts.

prayerfully choose just one and be there often—multiple times each week. Don't spread yourself around; make one place the habitual haunt for your team or missional community. The first friends you'll make will be the staff, and then perhaps some other 'regulars'.

Whatever you do, remember that activity in this space, whether it's a habit, a program or a communications medium, is all aimed at helping members of your mission focus group to become aware of you, either personally or as an organisation, and to see that you have something on offer that may be valuable to them: be that simple kindness toward café staff, friendliness to an isolated person or a program that meets their felt needs.

Once you know a person's name and how you might connect with them again, they've begun their journey on the pathway, whether they're aware of it or not. It might be a conversation in a café, a response to their email or a handshake at the door, but that contact means your new acquaintance is 'in touch' with your church.

Chapter 5
In Touch

'*In touch*' activities are intentional efforts to foster relationships, helping acquaintances get to know you a little better, and you them. A person needs only know one person from a church to be in touch. 'In touch' activities could very quickly move a person forward. It might be as simple as answering their phone call, inviting them to a program that meets their needs and introducing them to a few of the other participants. In touch work can also stretch over a long time. You may be friends with someone for many months before they move to the next stage.

At the 'in touch' stage, a person will have just one person, couple or family who links them to your church. Technically, you could draw a huge circle to encompass all the friends, relatives and colleagues of everyone in your church and consider them to be in touch with your church. While that's true, there will be a huge variation in the potential of any of these people to move further along the pathway.

Because the 'in touch' stage involves a person only knowing one Christian, or one Christian family, activity at this stage is often informal rather than programmed. It can be conversations over coffee or beer, chatting in the park while watching the kids, chatting with parents at the school gate or those staccato conversations that stop and start among (mostly) blokes as they labour over a car engine or the construction of a deck.

An 'in touch' activity can be the first conversation with a person making a phone inquiry, or the first greeting at the door of a weekday program or a weekend service. While these first contacts should quickly lead to introductions to more people and therefore a transition to the next stage in the pathway, it's important to remember that first impressions count.

Another example of 'in touch' activity is the contact people make with local churches for pastoral services (christenings/baptisms, weddings and funerals) or the cold calls ministers receive from people looking for pastoral care or practical assistance.

Sometimes people just want to get what they came for and not enter into dialogue. But often people outside the church contacting the minister will welcome ongoing engagement if the minister (or a person introduced to them by the minister) is willing to invest time and effort into the relationship.

One of my friends saw significant growth in his church on the Northern Beaches of Sydney through thoughtfully engaging every 'census Anglican' couple that came to him to 'get the kids done' (baptised). I encourage pastors and church planters to make the most of pastoral service inquiries by seeing them as a step in a discipleship pathway.

A further example of the 'in touch' stage is the work of pastoral care and chaplaincy. This may mean being part of a visitation or pastoral care program at a local hospital or to isolated people in their homes. It could mean being a chaplain (whether paid or volunteer) in a school, a sporting club, a military base or a prison.

In some Australian states, religious organisations have a 'right' to offer a small amount of religious education in local schools (as society in Australia becomes increasingly suspicious of organised religion, this 'right' is meeting with some stiff opposition). The religious education teacher may be the only Christian the kids in the classroom know, and therefore their only contact with the church. That makes those kids, however tenuously, in touch.

In Australia, World Vision partners with local churches to assist vulnerable children in schools through a volunteer support program called Kids Hope. In this program, adults spend regular time one-to-one with a child that could use a little extra attention and encouragement. That adult may be the only Christian the kid knows. In Pathways thinking, it's an 'in touch' activity of the church.

The critical task at this stage is to build connection so that an increasingly warm and trusting relationship forms. Whether it happens in a few minutes or over months, your mission with a person who is 'in touch' is to build the conviction that they matter to you. You can't fake this. The heart of mission is genuine love, whether it takes the form of interest, admiration or compassion. The person who's in touch must be getting the message, 'I'm interested in you. I think you're important.' If they get the impression they're your evangelism project, they will likely keep their distance.

Qualities of relationship

As you read you'll probably become a little wearied of the theme, but I can't overstate the importance of believers representing the love and compassion of Christ to those yet to meet him. While I'm writing about mission in terms of function and process, if we reduce it only to these we miss the point. Content and process are the containers for extending God's love, in acts of compassion and in helping people to become disciples of Jesus.

Bearing this in mind, let's talk a little more about the qualities of relationships that help a person move through the 'in touch' stage to 'belonging', which is the subject of the next chapter.

Frequently activities in the 'in touch' space have similar characteristics to 'helping professional' relationships. Many churches provide counselling services for people with various challenges such as relationship issues, emotional difficulties or financial problems. Counselling centres were common in Australian churches in the 1990s and were seen as an opportunity to 'reach out' to people.

Slowly it emerged that not only were counselling services generally ineffective in helping people become disciples and join the church, they actually served to motivate church members to leave that church and go elsewhere. As it turns out, people don't want to sit in church with someone who knows all their most personal secrets—not even the pastor or a trained counsellor.

To borrow Eric Berne's terminology from his theory of transactional analysis, some efforts to serve people take on a kind of parent-to-child characteristic: the idea that the helper is coming from a position of greater knowledge, mastery or power.[17] The person helping takes a 'one-up' position, and the person being helped finds themselves in a corresponding 'one-down' position.

These relationships are in a way asymmetrical. The person being helped talks a lot about themselves, makes themselves vulnerable and is open about their need. The person helping discloses little of themselves of a personal nature,

---

[17] http://www.ericberne.com/transactional-analysis

protects themselves from being vulnerable and is supposed to gain nothing from the relationship lest they fall into transference.[18]

This is all very well if we're simply setting out to provide a service to assist people as an act of compassion. I'm not dismissing such activity—indeed, Jesus' healing had an inherent 'one-up' characteristic by dint of his power. The difficulty lies in the idea that mission involves both compassion and disciple-making, or in the hope that serving people from a dispassionate, one-up position might create opportunity for disciple-making.

It's not that an inherent one-up relationship can't provide the beginnings of a discipleship journey. It's just that it seems, in the Western world at least, to make it more difficult. Perhaps we in the West are socialised to gain what we need from people providing a professional, dispassionate service and then walk away with no expectation of relationship (I'm guessing most of us would find it weird if our urologist invited us over for a barbecue.)

Of course, ministry to children will always have an inherent parent-child posture. But the process of maturing and individuation in the child includes the process of moving from a parent-to-child posture with adults to a more adult-to-adult basis. In fact, relationships where this is not achieved are generally regarded as problematic.

Someone once described witness as 'one beggar showing another beggar where to find food'. It's a case of one person stumbling upon salvation and eagerly telling a friend where they too can get their fill. I know it's a little simplistic, but the image conveys the idea of an open and equal relationship.

The more our relationships with unchurched people take the form of open and equal friendships, the less likely those people will feel that they're giving up their sense of self in order to consider the possibility that your belief about Jesus might just be valid.

---

[18] This is a term used in the psychotherapeutic disciples that describes how a person, - usually a 'client' or 'patient' associates feelings from a significant earlier relationship with a current one. Usually it's a case of feelings about a parent being 'transferred' to the therapist. In the more cognitively-based therapies it's usually seen as problematic.

This is not to say we shouldn't go out of our way to use whatever means we can to show kindness to unchurched people—perhaps even outrageous kindness. I won't bore you with the war stories, but some of the happiest times of my life have been when I've set out to use whatever resources I've had at my disposal to show a sort of extravagant, going-out-of-my-way-to-be-kind type of love to my friends. But here's the kicker: on every occasion they want to reciprocate, and if ours is an open and equal relationship, I'll gratefully accept.

This kind of love often takes a relationship to a new level of appreciation and openness - an environment of greater trust where I can be open about my faith without my friend feeling like I'm trying to sell them a used car (or a used worldview).

Without some kind of reciprocity (that is, the kindness and openness goes both ways), relationships can either suffer from the 'professional distance' we discussed before, or descend into a kind of fused dependency where the one-up/one-down roles become entrenched.

Churches tend to be suckers for these kinds of relationships, simply because churches by their very nature attract both people in need and a higher-than-usual proportion of people who desperately need to be needed. To use terms borrowed from family systems theory, church seems to be the place where chronic over-functioners and chronic under-functioners go to meet. And we usually draw our clergy from the former category.

When relationships get stuck in an over/under-functioning kind of reciprocity, they're pretty much useless for making disciples, and indeed have good potential to cause over-functioners to burn out or develop other symptoms, and under-functioners to descend further into blaming and dependency. These outcomes don't fit our definition of mission, but plenty of churches seem committed to achieving them anyway.

Jesus was never going to get suckered into over-functioning or fostering dependency. In fact, he saw it coming. In John 6 he noticed a wave of human hunger approaching (v. 5) and made a compassionate response by feeding them (vv. 10-11). Some things never change, and this kind of bread and circuses (together!) will always win a presidential nomination. Sensing this (v. 14) Jesus beat a hasty retreat (v. 15). On the other side of the lake, the crowd tried to manipulate him into becoming the man-with-the-manna

(vv. 30–31) despite Jesus categorically calling out their motives (vv. 26–27). Unfazed, he announced that he himself was the bread from heaven, which was enough to dull the crowd's enthusiasm for a second feast.

A further complication of service-driven activity in the 'in touch' space is the tendency for the helpers to be significantly outnumbered by those being helped. While this is a problem at any stage in the pathway, it's fairly common to see small teams of people providing relational support or food or practical assistance to many, many people. Indeed this was the case with much of Jesus' ministry, and as Jesus demonstrated in John 6, when there is no help on offer, or there's a call to take responsibility for yourself, the hungry crowds look elsewhere. It was only those who were personally committed to Jesus and who shared a deep relationship with him who stuck around.

One-among-many relationships
This brings me to one-among-many relationships such as chaplaincy. Let me say at the outset I am a fan of chaplaincy, and count among my friends those who are both spiritually and physically alive because of the faithful ministry of prison chaplains.

That said, inherent in the structure of a priestly kind of person in the midst of a bunch of people busy with other things is the challenge of engaging people from the chaplaincy context with the community of faith.

I've heard more stories than I can count of chaplains forging relationships with people and—often in a time of crisis—helping them to make a faith commitment. However, because the chaplain has acted largely alone, they've found it difficult to integrate the new believer into a local church, and thus the believer becomes dependent entirely of the chaplain for their spiritual companionship. Sooner or later circumstances change or the chaplain runs out of capacity, and the new believer's faith becomes vulnerable because their supportive environment is gone. If we are the one-stop-spiritual-shop in someone's life, we're in danger of them conflating their relationship with God and their relationship with us.

While I would not want to discourage witness and evangelism (I'll talk more about these in the next two chapters) among our friends and those we serve, it's imperative that we look for ways for our unchurched friends to become friends with our friends from church.

The rapid evangelisation approach

At this point it's probably time to say that Pathways thinking does not sit all that well with the rapid evangelisation, rapid mobilisation approaches that have emerged over recent years. While I have good friends who have jumped into this mode of mission, I confess that I am bothered by the transactional nature of the approach. When Jesus sent out the seventy-two, he did tell them to shake the dust from their feet as a warning to the towns that would not welcome them (Luke 10:11). But I'm not sure that's a basis for cold-call, take-it-or-leave-it evangelism.

It's important to look at context before taking a verse as a proof text. Jesus had just set his face toward Jerusalem (9:51) and was sending out the seventy-two as kind of advance parties (10:1). Jesus was famous, and now he was making his final journey toward his death. People from all over the region had flocked to hear him and be healed. These were largely Jewish people who expected the imminent appearance of a Messiah and had no doubt heard about (and possibly witnessed) astounding demonstrations of power. The disciples were sent to preach and to heal, the miracles bearing witness to the nearness of the kingdom.

This is not analogous to a 21st-century, Western-world university campus or workplace, where the average Joe or Joanne has no idea about Jesus the Messiah, healer or king of a spiritual kingdom. Conversely, they are likely to have heard plenty of propaganda about the evils of the church. In a post-Christian culture where people are very suspicious about the church, I think we need to give people a little more time and space to disagree.

While Paul and Barnabas did their own bit of dust-shaking in Pisidian Antioch, it was in protest against being expelled by the leaders of the city, not because the people of the city were slow to show interest (Acts 13:13-52).

Chapter 6
Belonging

Whatever in touch activity you find yourself undertaking, you can only consider it part of a pathway if you are mindful of inviting your new friend to take the next step. And that next step is toward '*belonging*'.

'Belonging' activities are those where unchurched people can begin to feel like they belong among the Christians. In the main, churches in Australia are reasonably good at this. Most churches have a playgroup or a Mainly Music group or a kids' club. All of these are regular activities where people can come along and 'fit in'.

Unchurched people feeling like they belong is the key idea:. The possibilities for 'belonging' environments are almost endless: sporting and hobbies clubs, service groups, book clubs and homework clubs.

In general, 'belonging' activities meet a felt need. It may be explicit, like a homework club, or it may be more implicit, like the need for social interaction through a book club. 'Belonging' activities might be highly structured, like the Boys' Brigade company I spoke about earlier, or as informal as a bunch of blokes with a habit of going to the footy together every couple of weeks.

One of the church planters I coach is quite the musician. He plays a regular gig in the back room of one of the local pubs on a Sunday afternoon, and he encourages a handful of people from his church to come and bring their friends. These gigs happen often enough (every couple of weeks) that people who keep coming along get to know the others, both Christian and non-Christian. Between sets, conversations and introductions happen. Community forms.

'Belonging' activities generally have little or no religious content in a formal sense. They're geared to be accessible to people with no religious experience, and generally with no felt need for a religious experience. That said, spiritual content is not necessarily out of bounds. The Moot community in London runs a 'de-stress' meditation class that's identifiably spiritual—but it directly meets a felt need and requires no religious priming.

Earlier I mentioned Bill Hybels' resource called *Just Walk Across the Room*. More than any other environment, 'belonging' activities are a 'room to walk across' – especially for us introverts for whom initiating social interaction is easiest if there is minimal ambiguity. Christians 'walking across the room' is an essential success factor for 'belonging' environments. To serve their purpose in the mission pathway, a 'belonging' activity must be a context where Christians make friends with unchurched people. Remember, most people have a number of Christian friends before they themselves become a Christian, and it's in these kinds of environments that those friendships are most likely to form. Therefore, 'belonging' environments need to have a number of Christians present with whom unchurched people can relate. The importance of this can't be overstated.

It's also essential that the Christians who inhabit these activities have sufficient opportunity to cultivate relationships. If it's all about being a passive audience, or if the Christians spend all their time and effort running the formal, structured components of the activities, the conversations won't happen, the relationships won't form and the opportunity to help people feel a sense of belonging will be lost. Christians simply must get out of the kitchen and make friends with the 'strangers'.

Too often the church makes a great effort to make people feel like guests when people actually want to feel like they're home. At my place, guests get the best food served on the best crockery with the best silver. They don't get asked to help and at the end of the occasion they go home. Those who live here get whatever is on offer, served on any old plate (if you're lucky) and take their turn washing up. When you belong somewhere, no one is waiting for you to leave before they can relax. It's this kind of belonging that best serves as a precursor to believing.

Conversely, a lot of activities around church are labelled 'outreach' when the real story is that the only people who turn up are the same ones that turn up on Sunday. The activity might be the kind of thing you could invite an unchurched person to attend, but if no unchurched people come, the activity is only helping those who already belong to keep feeling the love.

Listening as a gift
I am constantly amazed at the explosion of social media in the last decade. I realise some people use social media as a convenient adjunct to their social lives in the real world—kind of a complimentary technology to actual

connections. Meanwhile millions of younger people are posting some kind of show-reel of their lives in order to get 'liked'. I might dismiss the endless angst and trivia and pictures of lunch as shallow and inane, but I would be missing that underlying cry, 'Will someone please *notice* me?' What are people missing in the real world that a little 'thumbs up' on a social media post could be their source of hope and validation?

So how do we cultivate the kind of connection that people so deeply crave? James provides a clue: speak little, listen much (James 1:19).

Being validated by being noticed is about feeling I'm worth something. I love to talk. I love to have the attention of others. It's almost too good to be true when people laugh at my jokes or show appreciation for my teaching (or buy my books!). I feel *validated*. Being listened to is balm for my soul.

I know all the theology about being valuable because I'm created in God's image and redeemed by the costly sacrifice of Christ. But that doesn't always filter into my fragile inner child that frets about being okay. The validation I experience in a positive response is more immediate and—it pains me to say—more influential on the state of my heart. I suspect I am not alone in this. Perhaps God is loving me through the attention of others.

People feel valued when others pay them appropriate and tolerable attention. In short, we bless people when we listen to them. There's no shortage of people blurting out their stream of consciousness online. Yet people willing to pay careful and respectful attention to others is rare. Given the rarity and desirability of a listening ear, willingness to put aside our own need for attention and putting in the effort to be genuinely interested in another presents a powerful opportunity to help people feel like they belong.

Counter-intuitive and counter-cultural as it may be, in contemporary Western society listening seems to be more powerful than speaking for building the kind of community to which people will want to belong. Let me unpack that a little more.

In a society where everyone seems to be vying for attention, when we take time to listen with genuine interest and give another person our undivided attention—when we're genuinely present to them—we send profound message of respect and validation. As a coach, I've lost track of the number of times people have said to me, 'I've never told this to anyone.' It's not that I am pastorally gifted or have unusual compassion. It's just that coaching is a discipline of shutting up, putting aside my own stuff, paying thoughtful attention and asking questions.

Try for a moment to juxtapose these two ideas: the World Health Organization projects that by 2030 depression and related disorders will be the leading cause of the global burden of disease[19] while psychiatrist Scott Peck makes the bold claim that anyone can be a therapist if they're prepared to love deeply enough.[20] Peck goes on to state that a means of expressing love is to offer sustained, undivided attention.

Even if Peck's claim is not *absolutely* true, the church has an opportunity to at least offer *some* meaningful response to the ballooning incidence of depression simply by being sufficiently connected, available, interested and self-forgetful to listen carefully to people and give them the gift of our attention.

In the upper room discourse that takes up about a quarter of John's gospel, Jesus emphasised over and over the centrality of the disciples loving one another. Earlier in his ministry Jesus taught his disciples that self-denial was an essential quality of following him (Luke 9:23). Love and self-denial correlate pretty strongly. We can exercise self-denial by putting aside our impulse to talk and our desire for attention and genuinely attending to another. When someone receives another person's interest and attention, they feel loved. 'By this will everyone know you are my disciples' (John 13:35).

When giving respectful interest and attention becomes part of the culture of a community, it's easy for people to feel valued, wanted, perhaps even loved. When the currency of such a community is the Christian faith, it's conducive to faith formation. You start to be like the people you hang around.

A listening community has a good chance of being a loving community, especially in our content-saturated, look-at-me society. And a loving community will foster curiosity as to what might be at its centre.

---

[19] http://www.who.int/mental_health/management/depression/wfmh_paper_depression_wmhd_2012.pdf

[20] Peck, M. Scott. *The Road Less Travelled: A New Psychology of Love, Traditional Values and Spiritual Growth* (Touchstone, New York, 1978).

Fellowship is a tough nut to crack

While fellowship is a valid thing as far as it goes, groups that have a relatively stable, longstanding membership (like the mothers' group that's been together so long they're all grandmothers) are notoriously difficult for outsiders to join. There is just too much shared folklore. Some of the churches I've served have their calendars so filled with 'fellowship' activities that there is no time or energy left to serve those yet to belong. It's a tough call to make, but for such a church to grow, some of those cherished times of fellowship will need to give way to fresh activities designed specifically for outsiders.

Typically, 'belonging' environments for women are much easier to create than those for men. Women seem to naturally gather just to talk – more so than Men. While men do talk (about half as much as women according to the research), it's usually while they're doing something else—whether it's watching sport or sampling whiskey or riding bikes or erecting a cubby house.

So reaching men usually requires some kind of activity that's attractive and trusting that the conversation will happen around it. Men seem reluctant to seek any kind of help or assistance that suggests they have a need. So running courses or seminars that imply they're somehow deficient is less likely to be attractive to them. However, asking men to contribute their knowledge, strength and skill is usually music to their ears. Sometimes the best way to engage men is to ask for their help.

Non-Christians may be unchristian

At this point I need to stress the importance of acceptance. Before a person makes a faith commitment, they may have little or no interest in obeying Jesus' teaching or conforming to the behavioural norms of the Christian community. That means (health, safety and other risk management considerations notwithstanding) that the Christians who create and participate in 'belonging' activities will need to be robust enough not to be freaked out by some 'unchristian' behaviour: from swearing to getting upset to being impolite, inconsiderate, intoxicated or perhaps even a bit reckless. This doesn't mean such behaviour goes unaddressed, but we need to be calm and understanding in how we define and enforce standards and expectations.

Further, the people you're seeking to reach may have very different personal moral standards to yours. Jesus hung out with people who had very different personal and professional ethics to his own. I personally have my own standards on smoking, alcohol, drug use, divorce, homosexual behaviour and gender identity. By and large, my standards are quite conservative. However, when creating an environment where people can feel God's love by being welcomed into a community, I must be prepared to come face-to-face with people who have very different standards to me.

This causes some internal discomfort. The challenge is to show the love of Christ to those with whom I disagree and to those who make me uncomfortable. Jesus himself said words to this effect: 'Why should you be rewarded for loving only those who love you? Terrorists and drug dealers do that. The real test is to love your enemies, to show the compassion of God to those who make you squirm' (Luke 6:32ff).

While policies and practices will be very context-specific, the main idea is that judgment (explicit or implied) and expectations that unchurched people will behave like believers do in church on Sunday will kill off the effectiveness of a 'belonging' environment. Change in behaviour may not happen until a change of heart on the other side of a faith commitment. Expecting people to behave 'like us' before they are welcomed to spend time among us is getting things the wrong way around.

'Belonging' activities are an opportunity to make friends with people who are not the same as us and who might hold beliefs and values very different to ours. And unless such friendships form, the possibilities for mission are limited. The quality of those friendships will determine the effectiveness of the 'belonging' environment. It's important for the unchurched person to form a network of trusting relationships, where the conversation can get beyond polite conversation (or, in the case of blokes, bluster about sport, cars, computer games or whatever else they're into).

Witness before evangelism
Generally speaking, it's the believers who should take the initiative in leading the conversation to meaningful spaces. This is where witness kicks in. You'll note I used the word 'witness', not 'evangelism'. The terms 'witness' and 'testimony' are commonly used in the legal system, but in the church setting they've taken on quite distinct—and in my view unhelpful—nuances.

Jesus declared that believers will be his witnesses (Acts 1:8). A witness is simply one who experiences something (sees it, hears it, smells it, feels it) and then relates their experience to another. It doesn't necessarily mean telling a life story, and it doesn't mean entering into an argument. Witnesses in a court of law are there to simply tell the truth—not to try to convince anyone.

Witnesses give 'testimony'. In court, witness testimony is simply relevant evidence. It's not necessarily rehearsed, structured or designed to be persuasive. It's not a person's complete story—just the relevant information. It's given entirely from the witness's point of view. It's most often in response to a question.

Yet in church we've come to think of 'witnessing' as persuading a person to adopt a set of beliefs. In court, such efforts would undermine a witness's credibility, perhaps even render them unreliable. The same goes in 'belonging' environments. In church we think of testimony as our life story or at least our conversion experience. In court this would only be relevant if we were asked about it.

So with our unchurched friends, particularly in 'belonging' environments, sharing testimony is no more than the habit of talking about our spiritual life and experiences in much the same way as we would talk about any other aspect of our lives.

If I bought a new guitar, I would want to tell my friends about it. If I've completed some aspect of my latest car restoration or house renovation, I would tell my friends in the process of ordinary conversation. I might even offer to show my friends said guitar, car or house if they seem interested. In the same way, if I've had a spiritual insight or experienced an answer to prayer, I'll talk about that in the course of ordinary conversation.

My 'testimony' is simply a meaningful account of how God is at work in my life, in a way that links with the flow of the conversation. It's going to be of more interest to the other person if it connects with their story. My musician friends are more likely to be interested in my guitar, my petrol-head pals will be more interested in the car, and my building buddies will be more interested in my nifty tiling work. Other parents might take interest in my prayers for my kids, and a stressed-out friend might be curious about my meditation habits.

I have introduced people to Jesus using a 'set play' like a rehearsed presentation or a tract. But witness seems more credible if it's responsive and from the heart.

To be able to do that you need to cultivate a living and growing relationship with God. This is perhaps the best example of the integrated nature of the Pathways philosophy. The activities in the early steps of the pathway will be more effective in helping people move toward Christ if those environments are inhabited by people who have a deep and vibrant spiritual life. Cultivating that kind of life is the task of later steps in the pathway.

Fostering spiritual interest

The habit of witnessing is mostly about fostering a spiritual interest, a sense of curiosity, perhaps even a sense of 'I want what you've got'. Too much 'evangelism' is driven by anxiety on the part of believers to get their gospel presentation off their chest in order to assuage their guilt and sense of obligation.

Spiritual interest, I believe, is at least partly aroused by the work of the Holy Spirit in the heart of my unchurched friends. While God works by his own volition and in his own time, I believe he works also in response to our prayers. Let me reiterate that the essential and underpinning power of Pathways is the work of Holy Spirit, and I believe that work comes about through prayer.[21] All of this is to say, for your friend to become interested in the gospel, I encourage you in the strongest possible terms to pray—hard and often. Be a persistent widow (Luke 18:1-8) and nag God on behalf of your friend.

To summarise, 'belonging' activities are the contexts where unchurched people can feel part of the Christian community (be it on church 'turf' or not). They're contexts where unchurched people can make some solid friendships and develop some spiritual hunger or curiosity. This comes both through Christians sharing enough of their story for people to be interested and through the work of the Holy Spirit to foster spiritual desire.

---

[21] I really like the way Dutch Sheets explains the function of intercessory prayer and I recommend his book *Intercessory Prayer: How God Can Use Your Prayers to Move Heaven and Earth* (Bethany House, Bloomington, 1996).

Chapter 7
Embracing the Gospel

Now that our friends are interested, they're ready to take the next step. They're only an invitation away from 'embracing the gospel', which is the next stage in the pathway.

At the outset of this section, I feel it's incumbent on me to warn you that we're about to dip our toes into some theology, history and sociology, with a dash of neurobiology thrown in. You'll need to do a bit of conceptual work with me in order to understand why I land where I do. Hopefully it's coherent enough to follow.

The aforementioned theology etc. is what I call 'quick and dirty'—partly because I freely admit being fairly perfunctory in my scholarship (my students will nod furiously if they read this) and partly because it doesn't make for good readability to comprehensively cover really big ideas in order to make my argument absolutely, indisputably watertight (that is, I'm not going to re-write Wilmington's Systematic Theology just to support a point). Hopefully you'll get the idea, decide whether you think it's valid, and read on.

To become a disciple of Jesus, I believe it's important to undergo a conversion experience. And in saying that I'm aware some of you may find that idea unpalatable. I'm not saying you need to go back to tent crusades and thirteen repetitions of 'Just as I am'. Neither am I saying people can't become believers, or even disciples, by something resembling osmosis—just that it's not the pattern we find either in the scriptures or in the history of discipling movements: from the early church, to the Syrian missionaries, to the Celts, the Moravians and the Wesleyans. And further, becoming a believer without a definite point of decision—or more specifically, a definite point of repentance—tends to lead to problems later on.

Let me explain. Being a disciple of Jesus means following Jesus as a way of life. Following Jesus means his cause becomes your cause, his ways your ways, his commands your code. If you're not seeking to do that, you may be an admirer of Jesus, but you're not a follower.

People who are not following Jesus are, by definition, living by some other philosophy, be it a religious system, instinct or the zeitgeist. At some stage I believe it is important for a person to consciously renounce all other ways of life and to make a primary commitment to follow Jesus.

In the New Testament record, this primary commitment was marked by the rite of baptism. I should point out that the culture that forms the background for much of the New Testament was highly communal, so 'conversion' of the head of a family would mean conversion of the whole household, meaning everyone in the household, even infants, was probably baptised at the time that the head of the household was. I'm not going to get into a debate about paedobaptism here, other than to say that traditions that baptise infants have recognised that a person reaches a time when they must make a discipleship decision of their own, and so the rite of confirmation was introduced.

Regardless of the theological arguments about the point of regeneration and whether that is synonymous with conversion, almost all Christian traditions have a rite where a person makes a firm commitment to follow Jesus. Those rites exist because that commitment is important. Paul spends a fair bit of time talking about the old self and the new self (for example, Romans 6:6; 2 Corinthians 5:17).

Repentance and the nature of sin

Embedded in the idea of conversion is the concept of repentance—a change of mind, and a turning around. While a point-in-time conversion is important, it marks the beginning of a journey of 'being converted', or living a life of repentance. This is the essence of discipleship, a continual renewing of one's thinking to better mesh with the thoughts of God, and a continual renewing of behaviour to more closely reflect the character of Jesus.

This brings us to the nature of sin. If we take the narrative of the fall of humanity in the garden (Genesis 3) as the origin and the archetype of sin, it seems to me that one way to look at sin is as a rejection of God's revelation (given by whatever means) and his counsel, and doing whatever appeals to you (Paul's argument in Romans 1 follows a similar vein). Sin is not in its essence about falling foul of a list of banned behaviours, so much as a posture of being a law unto oneself. (I know some of you are quoting question 14 from the catechism in your heads. Let's just do a little theology together and see where you land).

The Greek word translated 'sin'—*hamartia*—carries the idea of an arrow diverting from its true trajectory and missing its target. In developing his theology in Romans, Paul states that 'all have sinned and fall short of the glory of God' (3:23). When Moses asked God to show him his glory, God revealed his character (Exodus 33:18ff). Sin means straying from God's intended way for us and so failing live up to the character of God.

In that great prophecy of the coming Messiah, Isaiah observes, 'We all, like sheep, have gone astray, each of us has turned to our own way; and the LORD has laid on him the iniquity of us all' (53:6). For me, that sums it up.

Conversion is a defining act of repentance—an acceptance of God's revelation and counsel as true; an admission of being guilty, of being a law unto oneself; and a commitment to a change of heart, mind and behaviour. Conversion is a change in one's philosophy of life.

I can hear my fellow evangelicals protesting that I have not addressed the sacrifice of Jesus as the all-sufficient propitiation for sin. I'm not implying that the idea of atonement is unimportant or that salvation is just a matter of 'being good'. And I can hear my less theologically conservative friends accusing me of denying God's grace. I'm not discounting that either. I'm simply stressing the need for repentance.

Jesus' opening announcement was 'The time has come. The kingdom of God has come near. Repent and believe the good news!' (Mark 1:15). We need to hold true to this announcement—the way to embrace the good news is to repent.

And believe the good news
All that notwithstanding, there is good news that must be believed. This begs the question: what exactly is the 'good news'? This is yet another theological minefield, the exhaustive study of which is beyond both my pay grade and the purpose of this book. Yet the Christian gospel is what differentiates mission from mere philanthropy, so at the risk of being accused of heresy and/or reductionism, I offer my attempt to pin down the idea of the good news.

Sometimes the first step in defining something is to put a fence around it by saying what it's not. The good news is not a public worship service. While church services often include words and actions that point to Christ and sometimes even give instruction about following Christ, just getting a person to church is not synonymous with giving them the good news.

I know a lot of liturgically minded people will want to disagree with me here. I appreciate, for example, Cranmer's gospel intent in the structure, order and content of the Anglican Prayer Book. And I suspect sacramentally inclined people will protest just as loudly that the sacraments themselves are a proclamation of the gospel. All I can say is this: in the field testing of lived experience, the overwhelming majority of churches that rely on liturgy and sacrament alone to proclaim the gospel are in decline. That is, in the business of making disciples, liturgy and sacrament don't, by themselves, seem to be effective modalities—but more on the importance of sacraments later.

Neither is the gospel any kind of activity, group or ritual like meditation. While people need to experience the gospel, and often 'belonging' activities serve to illustrate what the kingdom of God is like, at some stage the good news of Jesus must be set out plainly and a person needs to make a conscious response to it.

Put plainly, the gospel is some rather specific information about Jesus of Nazareth: who he is, what he has done and why that is significant. My attempt at an irreducible minimum might go something like this:

- Jesus of Nazareth is God incarnate, the second person of the triune God.
- Jesus of Nazareth died to take upon himself the punishment for the sin of all humanity. He rose from the dead and ascended to the throne of the triune God.
- If a person acknowledges that they are estranged from God because of their sin and that Jesus' death makes way for their sin to be justly forgiven, they can be reconciled to God and be in a loving and eternal child-father relationship with him forever.

Those who have studied soteriology in depth will probably want to put it differently and chide me for attempting to get it down to such a simple set of ideas. We had some mighty hard-fought councils in the first few centuries of the church trying to do just that, and the creeds they devised are much longer. Chastisement accepted.

Those who hold to the doctrine of limited atonement will take issue with my phrase 'all humanity'. Duly acknowledged.

And anyone reading these statements (or the creeds for that matter) will protest that they raise more questions than they answer. For example: 'Who is this Jesus of Nazareth guy?' 'How do you know about him?' (If you answer 'the Bible', all sorts of questions about its origins, inspiration and reliability emerge. And that gets you into the long story of Israel.) Then there are questions about the triune God, which leads you to the idea of the Trinity (good luck making that easily comprehensible). Then there are questions about sin and righteousness and judgment: 'What exactly is sin (my discussion above notwithstanding)?' 'And life after death—is heaven real?' 'How about hell?' 'Will everyone who does not pray the silver-bullet prayer and attend church end up there?' And on it goes.

In a kind of oblique way, that's my point. We need to be clear on the central ideas of the gospel of Jesus Christ. And we need to recognise that for those ideas to make sense, there's a whole bunch of other questions that may or may not need answers.

Before I go on, let me be clear that I'm not arguing for arguing—that is, I don't think introducing a person to the gospel of Jesus is about winning an argument. Neither is it about having all the answers (God is infinite, so you're going to get to the end of human understanding before you get to a comprehensive definition of the Almighty). There will always, at some level, be unanswered questions.

However, we do need to be able to provide a comprehensible account for what is a radically alternative worldview to the one prevailing in the Western world. Embracing that worldview may not necessarily be a prerequisite for a person to come to the point of repenting and believing the good news, but it will become important for their formation as a disciple. And there are those who will ask a whole bunch of questions before they're ready to become a follower of Jesus.

Either way, conversion—becoming a follower of Jesus, becoming a Christian or whatever term you like to use—means embracing a particular set of core ideas as true and entering into a reconciled relationship with God.

Just becoming a regular at church and vaguely subscribing to the content of liturgy and sermons is not really adequate—and my experience of churches that rely on such a process for the formation of disciples is that their effectiveness in making disciples is rather poor and their disciples rather unsure of what they believe. You can't make disciples without some solid, basic, orthodox doctrine and an effective process for its integration into life.

Rediscovering catechesis

All of this leads me to the rather ancient idea of catechesis. It's not a word we use much anymore. Its Greek origin carries the idea of 'echoing' verbal instruction, and at times took the form of candidates learning rote responses to a set of questions.

By the time the church had settled it's basics of operation and management somewhere in the second century, a fairly standard pattern had emerged for a person to convert to the Christian faith. Prior to baptism (which functioned as the rite of regeneration and the marker-point of conversion in the early church), a seeker was instructed verbally in the fundamental doctrines of the faith (early formulations of the Christian faith such as the Apostles' Creed likely arose as frameworks for catechesis).

In the lead-up to the Reformation, the emergence of printing seeded a rediscovery of catechesis, and throughout the Reformation period considerable attention was given to forming inquirers and new believers in the orthodox faith. Orthodoxy—right teaching and, by extension, right belief—was very important to both the early church and the Reformers, and should, for the health and growth of the church, be important still.

Before you reach for your long-treasured copy of the Westminster Catechism, we need to apply a little missiology. David Bosch, in his landmark book *Transforming Mission*, observed, 'The Christian faith never exists except as translated into a culture.'[22] This means the gospel in its original form was carried in the medium of culture, and it comes to us usually in a cultural mishmash of the first century, the 16th century and each century from then to now.

---

[22] Bosch, D. J. *Transforming Mission: Paradigm Shifts in Theology of Mission* (Orbis, New York, 1991), p. 458.

The translators of modern editions of the English Bible generally work with highly reliable Greek texts and do their best to turn first-century common-use Greek into fairly standard modern English. The face-value meaning of the words is not so much the issue—it's the conveyed meaning in their original culture that's tricky. And it's trickier still to make sense of the biblical message when it comes to us all dressed up in our various traditions.

While your good old Westminster Catechism is available in fairly comprehensible English, it dates from a particular time and culture. As an organising set of ideas for catechesis circa 1647 it was probably as good as it gets. It was the church's best attempt at that time to translate the gospel as it came to them into 17th-century English culture.

Catechesis and subjectivity

Fast forward 360-odd years from Westminster and the world has rotated a few times. The Enlightenment idea of empirical and discoverable truth has been rattled somewhat by the proliferation of views, opinions and peer-reviewed journals all scrambled together on an internet that carries mind-boggling volumes of data. On the issues of life, consensus is hard to find. If the truth is out there, nowadays it's impossible to have any empirical certainty that you've got it. No one can stand back far enough to be able to claim objectivity. The idea of *the* truth is being eroded by the more appealing notion of *my* truth.

Rather than beginning from a defined and broadly accepted common ground and building upon that foundation proposition by proposition, people are increasingly seeking what can be held as true *for them*. Twenty-first century Westerners tend to seek answers to their questions and longings not by scientific method or by logic and rhetoric but by experience and emotional resonance. This has profound implications for mission in contemporary Western society.

Twenty-first century Westerners are increasingly diverse, culturally fragmented and building their sense of what's what from a grab bag of their past, pop culture, their emotions and their social setting. Educated to form their own views, make their own way and create their own morals, it can be a tough ask to present them with a pre-formed creed and say, 'Take it or leave it.'

The difficulty lies not in the propositions of the old catechisms but in the how and why they're offered. It's not that the Westminster Catechism is no longer true; it's just that the questions it poses and then answers are not the top ten questions unchurched seekers are asking today—at least not at the outset. And while FAQ might be a handy page for a cell phone plan or installing some software, the gospel as FAQ from three centuries ago is unlikely to hold the interest of too many 21st-century seekers of spiritual truth.

Here's the dilemma: catechesis is important—the truth is important—but the classic catechetic process of set questions and correct answers from centuries ago is unlikely to be the best way to help someone explore faith in a contemporary setting.

All, however, is not lost. Catechesis has more or less taken on a new form and a new name. Most people have come across process evangelism tools like Alpha, Christianity Explained and the like. They're not quite systematic theology boiled down to a series of questions, but they are processes that are useful in helping people with little or no grounding in the message of the gospel to begin to get their mind around it.

A couple of important features of process evangelism are these. First, it tends to take place in thoughtful social settings. You can run Alpha in a lecture theatre if you want, but it's much more effective around tables, with food and coffee (or beer or wine or whatever your mission focus group prefers) and lots of opportunity for interaction. Process evangelism tends to be more effective if the dynamics of the 'belonging' environment (the previous step in the pathway) are carried over into the 'embrace the gospel' step.

Second, process evangelism allows people time to think things over, weigh things up and perhaps even count the cost (as in Luke 14:28ff). There is opportunity to ask questions and time for a bit of research (by the 'seeker' or by the facilitator!) without the pressure of the 'today-only-while-stocks-last-you-could-get-hit-by-a-bus-tonight' type of pitch that was once commonplace in crisis evangelism methods.

Time to think and wonder and question is important, especially for well-educated people. Nowadays the young of the educated middle class tend to hold their options open for a long time. They might try several courses at university before settling on completing one. They might try several long-term partners before finally marrying one. In short, the younger middle class are increasingly slow to commit themselves to anything. Given that following Jesus is a whole-of-life commitment, rushing people to a decision simply to alleviate our own anxiety is generally unhelpful.

While less-educated people will generally make commitments more quickly, they're also more likely to break them. In my experience, rapid conversion-type evangelism methods seem to get quick results in welfare-class settings. It's not universally true, but people in this socio-economic group are more likely to make faith commitments on the spot, just as they are more likely to move in with someone they've just met. And in both cases, the new commitment is pretty fragile and likely to have a lifespan measured in weeks.

Whether the faith commitment comes quickly or slowly, fairly intensive discipleship around the time of the faith commitment is important if a person is to be genuinely converted and not just inoculated.

Emotion and decision
This is not to say that conversion ought to be seen as entirely cerebral, rational, thoughtfully weighed-up decision (any more than choice of a marriage partner is). Recent advances in neuroscience have called into question Aristotle's idea that humans are primarily rational beings. Even René Descartes' declaration 'I think therefore I am' is looking a little shaky.

Without going into too much detail, it turns out that humanity is much more driven by emotion (both the emotion consciously experienced as feelings and emotion of which we are unaware). It's probably more accurate to say that the human being is a rationalising creature—one that seeks both to moderate and to explain instinctive urges and behaviours.

Our big cerebral cortex distinguishes human brains from those of other mammals and is the locus of our ability to reason. But as you've probably experienced, it doesn't always win the battle for control. The much smaller, faster, more viscerally connected limbic system drives a fair bit of our responses and behaviour, including some of what we might categorise as spiritual and even religious.

Steve Addison, in his work on movements, draws on Finke and Starke's study of the spread of the gospel through the Baptists and Methodists on the

American frontier.[23] Addison points out that the dry intellectualism of the educated clergy in the established churches was no match for the somewhat emotional, subjective testimony of barely trained frontier preachers, both in drawing a crowd and eliciting a response. It seems that it's not just the postmoderns who make emotive decisions.

It's no surprise then, that Christian traditions that embrace the sensory and the experiential seem to be attracting more people than those that deny the emotionality of humanity and seem to understand people as entirely rational. (Almost nobody was ever argued into a Christian commitment, C. S. Lewis being the most notable exception.)

I remember a very sincere lecturer back when I was an undergraduate (oddly enough at a college that was, at the time, unmistakably Pentecostal in outlook and teaching) drawing a little train with 'truth' as the locomotive, 'obedience' as the mid-carriage and 'feelings' as the caboose. This expressed a worry that emotional, unthinking people blown about on a tide of emotions would make unwise and irrational decisions. It seemed plausible, even noble at the time—after all, any kind of appeal to the emotions is surely some form of manipulation, is it not?

As it turns out, there is a case to be made that emotion is essential for decision-making. Recent research into the psychological trait of alexithymia—that is, where consciousness and reasoning are disconnected from feelings—has found that people with the trait find decision-making difficult, or tend to make poorer choices than those without the trait. Without some modicum of hope, desire, fear or some other emotion, decisions seem to lose their meaning and motive.

Let's relate this to catechesis. While traditionally catechesis has been a process of information, better understanding of how humans function should help us to think more holistically. That means thinking about the entire experience of catechesis, which goes beyond content to include the seeker's interaction with the social environment and the emotions they

---

[23] Addison, Steve. *Movements That Change the World: Five Keys to Spreading the Gospel* (IVP, Downers Grove, 2011); Finke, Roger & Stark, Rodney. 'How the Upstart Sects Won America 1776–1850', *Journal for the Scientific Study of Religion*, 28:1, March 1989.

might experience through participation in the 'embrace the gospel' environment.

Just to be clear: remember my earlier statement that the gospel is some rather specific information about Jesus of Nazareth. The content is important. And so is how you translate it into the setting in which you find yourself. And so is the seeker's experience of engaging that rather specific information. If you're beginning to think, 'Boy, there's a lot to consider'— well, you're right.

Learning versus education

At the risk of over-complexifying the matter to an even greater degree (and thanks to Tim Dyer for that word), let's throw a bit of learning theory into the mix. You'll be glad I did, because it might just come out simpler on the other side.

The work of educational theorist David Kolb on human learning has revolutionised the ways I teach.[24] In fact, outside of the university setting (where I occasionally find myself giving pseudo-formal discourses to hapless undergraduates), I try to think more in terms of *learning facilitation* than teaching. If we can think of catechesis as an interested person's involvement in a learning environment, we'll possibly make the process a lot less pressured, more enjoyable and hopefully more effective.

While so much of the education system in Australia confuses learning with the delivery of content (you've probably heard teachers lamenting the struggle to 'get through the curriculum'), Kolb argues that genuine learning takes place through discovery and experience. I would go so far as to say, in contrast to the kind of educative processes Kolb advocates, most educated people in the Western world are actually inoculated against learning. So much of our schooling experience involves engaging with content that we only need to retain for a short but intensive time: cram it in, vomit it up on the exam paper and promptly forget it.

As a teenager I spent years labouring over unit circle trigonometry. Back in 1982 I was quite good at it. Thirty years later my daughter came home with her maths homework wanting some help with—you guessed it—unit circle

---

[24] Kolb, David A. *Experiential Learning: Experience as the Source of Learning and Development* (Prentice-Hall Inc., New Jersey, 1984).

trigonometry. I know it's back there in the musty and mouldy recesses of my brain, but when I needed it, I could not pull it out in a way that made sense. My daughter now works in healthcare, and she has no need for trig. Neither do I. Being good at trig got me an A for maths in Year 10, but it has been of absolutely no use until now (when it's good for illustrating how useless it is to teach people stuff they won't use—and nothing more). And now I've got all the maths teachers offside.

We've been socialised to sit and soak up information, with no consideration being given to integrating it—because integration means putting learning to use, and so much of what we are 'taught' at school has no scope for application in any immediate sense. And that, it seems to me, goes a long way to explain why all those sermons we preach see so little fruit—we're effectively taught to disconnect what we hear from how we behave, even if we give our nodding agreement to what we hear.

If Kolb has anything to teach us (and if we actually learn by integrating it—see what I did there?), then genuinely effective catechesis will be a facilitation of discovery and experience that leads to putting learning to fairly immediate use.

Got all that?

Let's go back to the idea of process evangelism as catechesis. From a theological perspective, objective truth is essential. From a sociological and pedagogical perspective, subjective truth is what people engage. And truth that can be quickly integrated into lived experience is what people retain. Effective process evangelism is not about choosing one over another so much as making sure objective truth becomes a person's subjective truth and their lived experience.

A finer-textured missiology
Let me add one more layer that gets back to Bosch and his idea of translation. We translate the gospel by taking it from one culture to another, which includes language, behaviours and values. It's a tricky missiological task, but it means that when we think of helping people to embrace the gospel through a process of catechesis, it is important that we pay attention to the way the content is presented and the process by which it is delivered.

Let me give an example or two. A church planter I coached was working in a suburb of a city that was a 1960s industrial centre. The suburb had once housed the families of twenty thousand men who had worked at the steelworks. Fifty years later, the steelworks were a shadow their former self and generational unemployment had become the norm in the surrounding neighbourhoods. With generational unemployment came welfare dependency and all the familiar social problems that correlate with it.

Needless to say, most of the people living in the area had not finished high school, and in general their experience of education was not fondly remembered. Many of them were functionally illiterate. When the time came to think about introducing people to the gospel, it was clear the content would need to be pitched at a very basic level and in a non-literary form. Further, the context would need to feel more like a lounge room or a public bar than a classroom.

In contrast, another minister I knew worked in a well-to-do area where the average person in the street had more degrees than a thermometer. Stock answers with 'because-the-Bible-says-so' apologetics were just not going to cut it. Catechesis in this context looked a lot like an MBA tutorial.

Let's draw it all together. The 'embrace the gospel' step is the intentional introduction of a person to the good news of Jesus Christ. It's more a process of formation than mere 'information', including understanding, experience and response. It's most effective if the process and the content are tailored to the unique needs and characteristics of mission focus group.

More an environment than an event

What might be called a 'crisis' model of conversion came to prominence through the revivalist movements of the 18th and 19th centuries, and persevered well into the 20th century, finding its zenith post world war 2 in the ministries of evangelists like Billy Graham. In my home town of Melbourne, Billy Graham still holds the record for pulling the biggest crowd to the Melbourne Cricket Ground (143 750 people on 15 March, 1959). While large scale revivalist-style crusades are still conducted, and still attract huge crowds in non-western contexts, it's probably safe to say that their day is done in the west.

I refer to this model of conversion as 'crisis' because it seems to understand the way of salvation as a single, climactic decision, often made in an a context where the life of the unbeliever and the believer are sharply contrasted: the former culminating in eternal destruction, the latter in eternal life. A crisis of decision is created, and those yet to 'make a decision for Christ' are urged to do so, lest their life end suddenly and they find themselves eternally cut off from God.

I'm not rejecting this way of thinking as invalid, so much as suggesting that the church at various times though history has been quite effective in making disciples by taking things a little more slowly. Examples include the early church under persecution and the monastic missionary movements of the medieval period. It's my conviction that in the 21st Century western world, taking things more slowly is likely to be more fruitful.

By my observation, most churches that are effective in growing by making new disciples understand the context for conversion more as an environment than an event. That is, an environment is created in which a process of interactive catechesis can occur, usually over a period of several weeks.

Before I jump into describing such an environment, I would like to have a quick conversation about the transition process: that is, helping people make the transition from a 'belonging' environment into an 'embracing the gospel' or catechesis environment. In my experience, this is the most important and probably the most difficult transition in the Pathways model. It's the transition where most churches struggle.

The first difficulty has to do with invitation. Our invitation will be far more effective if it's couched in terms of 'Would you like to come with me to ... ' rather than 'You should go to ... ' These people are our friends – we care about them. They're not spiritual widgets on a convert-making assembly line. We don't send people on to the next stage, we walk with them.

Second, we should be prepared to make several invitations before one is accepted. I think we wait too long for 'just the right moment'. You probably can't tell when a person is 'ideally prepared to hear the gospel'. Declining your invitation is not the end of that person's spiritual journey. Ask again sometime later. Err on the side of 'going a little early'.

Having said all that, let's take a look at some examples of process evangelism.

The gospels as catechesis
If you're not into off-the-shelf tools, the gospels themselves provide a pretty handy starting point for catechesis. After all, the whole Christian enterprise is founded on Jesus of Nazareth. Both Luke (1:4) and John (20:31) candidly state that their purpose in writing their accounts of Jesus' life was so that people would believe.

On a purely common-sense level, when a person expresses a degree of curiosity about the Christian faith, it seems a natural response to invite them to read the most ancient accounts of the founder's life. From a discipleship perspective, the sooner a person can read the scriptures for themselves and begin to grasp God's revelation, the better.

I use the term 'revelation' advisedly. While I acknowledge there is a spectrum of positions as to the nature and authority of the Bible, almost every Christian tradition holds the sixty-six books of the Christian scriptures to be sacred and most believe that, at a bare minimum, they *contain* revelation. For both the germination and ongoing formation of faith, it seems that revelation is essential.

I'm not sure how to give a rational explanation or some highly developed theological theorem for the following observation, but let me say this: the Holy Scriptures and the Holy Spirit seem to make a rather potent team for people at every stage of their journey toward Christian maturity. I am continually surprised and delighted at how quickly people develop a degree of spiritual insight and how theologically orthodox people seem to become just by habitual reading and reflection on the scriptures.

A number of the newer missional discipleship movements (for example, 3DM) use inductive Bible studies around the gospels as their primary method of catechesis. My former colleague Phil Graf would invite the barely literate gang members of East LA to read Mark's gospel with him (Phil is about 6' 4" and looks like a marine, so he has some street cred). His 'there is no wrong answer' approach had these kids discovering the truth for themselves and coming to faith with surprising speed.

It's possible that the gospels provide as much content as you need. Alternatively, you could try one of the growing number of process evangelism tools available.

Alpha, Christianity Explained and a cast of thousands

Best known in Australia (and probably the UK) is Alpha.[25] Alpha has been used as an effective embrace-the-gospel tool for all kinds of churches, from plants to mega-churches, among Catholics, Presbyterians, Pentecostals and the good old Church of England from which it originated.

Alpha uses a relatively modern medium (usually video presentations, but not necessarily) and intentionally injects opportunity for group interaction. People get to bounce the presented content off their own thoughts and experiences. All this happens in the context of a meal. Generally the course goes over 10 weeks, which means the content is delivered over time, with opportunity to think and interact during and between sessions. Each session occurs in the context of an intentionally welcoming group who serve participants some (usually rather nice) food.

Toward the end of Alpha is a weekend retreat, where participants have the opportunity to experience the ministry of the Holy Spirit through healing and receiving gifts such as speaking in tongues. Whether that sits well with your theology or not, it demonstrates Alpha's effort to take objective truth (the person and work of the Holy Spirit) and enable people to interact with it in a personal and somewhat subjective manner.

Alpha has its critics, but it's been an enormously useful resource for helping people to embrace the gospel.

Another popular process evangelism tool has been the Australian-developed Christianity Explained.[26] This comes in the form of a workbook and is designed to be used one-to-one (that is, by a Christian helping a yet-to-become Christian). It takes six sessions using the gospel of Mark to introduce the person and work of Jesus, the way of salvation and how to become a Christian. It covers those fairly specific ideas about Jesus of Nazareth (mentioned earlier) rather neatly.

Because the context is one-to-one or a small group, there is plenty of scope for interaction, asking questions and having time between sessions to think, reflect and wrestle. It works best if the Christian who's using the course is

---

[25] https://www.alpha.org/
[26] http://www.christianityexplained.com/

warm, non-judgmental and patient with questions and objections. The interactive process allows the objective truths to be subjectively engaged.

While Christianity Explained is not intentionally experiential in the way Alpha is, it seems to work well if the 'seeker' experiences the kindness of Jesus in the Christian community where they're beginning to feel like they belong.

Until recently, Christianity Explained was the first choice process evangelism tool among the church planters I've coached, probably because it's easy to use with minimal logistics. You can do Christianity Explained with a friend in a café or pub.

There are a bunch of other process evangelism tools, some I've only heard about and others that have been road-tested by church planters and pastors I've coached. I've even co-written one myself. While they each have their unique features and benefits, they're not all created equal.

In choosing a means of catechesis for your context, you'll need to take into account all the criteria above, and think carefully about which one will best communicate with your particular mission focus group. Further, it's vital that the person learning about Christ and the way of salvation is given a clear opportunity to make a faith commitment. Put another way, it must answer the question, 'What must I do to be saved?' and clearly invite the participant to do it.

If your church tradition is other than one generally conceived as evangelical, you may find my insistence on a faith commitment characterised by acknowledgment of sin, a requirement for repentance and built on the concept of 'salvation' to be harsh or even judgmental.

I would like to gently encourage you to think about what I've actually written and keep it distinct from the more fundamentalist positions of which it might remind you. I would also like to refer back to my earlier discussion about the value of repentance and defining choice to embrace a new worldview. And let me further encourage you to follow the example of the Bereans (see Acts 17:11 to decode my attempt at being cryptic) and then make up your own mind.

Evangelism by confrontation

Conversely, by now I suspect there will be another group entirely who have either stopped reading or are bristling with objections—not the least those who prefer 'tract' or 'set presentation' evangelism.

Particularly popular in the 1980s and 1990s, this approach often uses either a literal printed tract (such as 'The Four Spiritual Laws' or 'Two Ways to Live') or a memorised presentation that follows a formula. The content is pretty much those important ideas about Jesus of Nazareth to which I referred earlier. One could ask, 'Why go through a drawn-out process of catechesis when you can simply tell someone the essential facts and they can take it or leave it?'

First, let me say there's nothing wrong per se with having a clear presentation of the gospel on hand (or in head) to be used when appropriate. Neither am I implying we should not talk to strangers about our faith.

I simply want to point out that a single crisis does not a disciple make, and in anxiously seeking to do our duty of going and making disciples, our attempts at evangelism may be more about us alleviating our sense of obligation and less about loving our neighbour enough to share the gospel with them.

I've already mentioned how few stories I have heard of lasting disciples being made from a one-off encounter with a stranger, and how the vast majority of conversions come through relationship with family member or friends who invite the person into the embrace of the Christian community.

I've also heard far too many stories of people being deeply offended by well-meaning Christians 'confronting people with the claims of Christ' (or some such phrase). I've both engaged in this kind of evangelism and been on the receiving end, and I've found it unpleasant and unproductive on both sides. I think the net effect of confronting strangers is to dissuade more people than it persuades.

It was love that motivated the Father to send Jesus. Until a person can sense the love of God in us for them, I'm guessing they're more likely to feel like a sales prospect than someone loved by the Father.

I've already discussed those contexts that seem receptive to rapid evangelism and I want to reiterate that, where people are quick to respond to the gospel, they're likely to need a lot of care and attention in follow-up formation. If we're prepared to hang around and work through the tough stuff with them, modelling the ways of Jesus and helping them to develop the habits of a disciple, let me express my wholehearted encouragement.

I'm just very wary of the hit and run. And that leads me to the next step.

Chapter 8
Following Jesus

Following Jesus is the discipleship stage where the new believer (or the person beginning to believe, if that's the way you want to look at it) begins shaping their life—their beliefs, values, thinking and behaviour—to the life and teaching of Jesus of Nazareth. While it begins with what was quaintly called 'follow-up' back in the era of crusade meetings, it goes well beyond an eight-week Bible study on Christian basics.

Following Jesus is a step from which we never truly graduate, although we may progress by adding further stages to it, as we will discuss later. It's about embracing the journey toward Christlike maturity (Ephesians 4:13; Colossians 1:28) as a way of life—or as Eugene Peterson put it, pursuing 'a long obedience in the same direction.'[27]

Profession rites

For the new believer, doing this step well means beginning it well. As I discussed earlier, it begins with an initial act of response to the gospel—believing and accepting God's generous offer of salvation and repenting of a way of life that is astray from the ways of Jesus.

Most Christian traditions mark the occasion of conversion with a rite. In the New Testament the rite was baptism, as it is in many churches today. Other churches baptise infants and perform a rite of confirmation, when people baptised as infants make a conscious choice to follow Jesus. Once a person has made a profession of faith, it's important that the profession rite according to your tradition be performed as soon as reasonably possible.

If you're wondering why I'm being so direct about baptism (and confirmation, if that's your tradition), there's an article in Appendix 2 that unpacks my thinking about it. You may want to read it before you read the

---

[27] Peterson, Eugene. *A Long Obedience in the Same Direction: Discipleship in an Instant Society* (IVP Downers Grove 2000)

rest of this chapter. If you're happy to take my word for it on profession rites, read on.

Discipleship is about obedience

Obedience in faith is absolutely essential to the life of discipleship. Let me remind you of my earlier discussion about conversion being the beginning of a lifestyle of repentance, and being transformed into the character of Jesus.

As soon as I mention obedience, I can feel people screwing up their faces and protesting a gospel of salvation by works, or a faith based on fear and guilt and shame. So let's get this idea of obedience nailed down.

John's gospel, especially the upper room discourse, developed the theme of obedience and linked it to 'abiding' in Jesus' love so that our joy may be complete (15:10-11). The central idea to which we're called to be obedient is to love one another (15:12). Much of the rest of the teaching of the New Testament is an explanation of how we go about abiding in Christ and loving each other.

We obey Jesus—not in fear to avoid negative consequences, but in faith that he knows what will be life-giving and joy-producing for us. Obedience to Jesus is not a means of earning God's favour in some kind of quid pro quo arrangement—it's about embracing the good life that God in his love wants us to have.

I wouldn't 'obey' a dietician because I'm scared they will curse me with bad health if I don't. I do what they say because I trust they know what's good for me. It's not a perfect metaphor, but you get the idea.

Faith, then, is at least in part the belief that God loves me and knows what's best for me, so I'll do as he commands (or I'll seek to live according to my best understanding of his character), even when all of my instinct points the other way. I don't need to understand all the causes and effects of why one way of life is life-giving and the other detrimental—in faith I can simply trust that God knows best.

Now let's more closely examine the step in the pathway that I've called *following Jesus*.

Formation beyond education

Let me frame all that is to follow with this basic premise: forming new believers into followers of Jesus—that is, the process of discipleship—bears a much closer resemblance to the relationship between a craftsman and their apprentice than that between a professor and their students.

My father has a copy of his grandfather's indenture, or contract of apprenticeship, dated sometime in 1890s. The young William Morgan was to live with, eat with, serve and obey his master, a local bricklayer. During this time he was not allowed to drink alcohol or to marry (two of society's great vices). From a 21st-century perspective is seems almost like bond-slavery, and I'm not advocating we indenture new believers to mature disciples (although, now I think about, the idea is not without its merits!). I'm seeking to emphasise that forming a craftsman was a whole-of-life undertaking, not just the transfer of some knowledge and skill. The apprentice was formed as a craftsman by modelling himself on his master: his habits, his values, his standards, his priorities. It was about the craft and about the man. The curriculum was largely the master's life and whatever challenges were thrown up in the undertaking of his trade.

Similarly, the greatest resource you can offer a new believer is your own life, your example, your stories, your struggles and the methods, habits, ideas, writers and other resources that have served you. More than anything else, making disciples is the art of letting your life do the talking, or a Paul said, 'Imitate me as I imitate Christ' (1 Corinthians 11:1).

As I said earlier, becoming a disciple of Jesus is the switch to a worldview that puts Jesus and his cause at the very centre of one's life. The 'following Jesus' stage is about the difficult task of reorienting our thinking, priorities and behaviour from whatever worldview we were operating under to the new worldview that, put simply, says 'Jesus is Lord.' This reorientation process has technically been dubbed 'sanctification', or the process of making one's life sacred.

This can lead us into some tricky territory. The death and resurrection of Jesus accomplished our sanctification—that is, his work has made us sacred, which we enter into by faith (Romans 1:17). In terms of our eternal status, we have been marked as set apart, adopted as children of God (John 1:12). Our 'sanctified' status before God is received by faith, not achieved by compliance with standards.

However, in terms of our lived experience, sanctification is a process brought about by our 'abiding in Christ' (John 15:5ff) or 'walking by the Spirit' (Galatians 5:16) or living for the will of God (1 Peter 4:2). The fact that Jesus, Paul, Peter and the writer to the Hebrews spent so much time exhorting believers not to live according to the old ways but to live according to the character of God is *prima facie* evidence that believers have a choice to live according to the character of God ('by the Spirit' to use Paul's terms) or according to their ungodly instincts ('in the flesh' as Paul puts it).

The stage of 'following Jesus', in Pathways parlance, is all about developing a lifestyle of 'putting off the old self and putting on the new' (Ephesians 4:22-24). Let me emphasise that the very fact that this is a major theme of the New Testament indicates that the church needs to be taught, reminded, even commanded to do this. It's an ongoing process of becoming mature, or Christlike (Ephesians 4:13).

Continually putting off the sinful and putting on the sacred is another way of describing the lifestyle of repentance I described earlier. I'm not advocating some kind of worm theology or living life out of fear, guilt and shame. Rather, I'm advocating living in acknowledgment that the best life to be lived is the life that the God of Love invites us into.

The terms 'guilt' and 'shame' have become super-contentious in recent times and there has been a collective societal reaction to the church's use of shame and guilt as a means of manipulation. While this is an important issue, it's also somewhat of a sidebar to my main narrative here, so I've put some more developed thoughts about guilt, shame and judgment in Appendix 3.

So assuming that a new believer has begun the journey of repentance as a way of life and has accepted their ongoing need for transformation, both inward and outward, how exactly do we intentionally cultivate Christlikeness in them?

I'm so very glad you asked.

Formation in prayer
Before I head into a more detailed consideration of doctrine and engagement with scripture, allow me to emphasise the centrality of prayer. If you've read this far you're probably sufficiently committed to making disciples that prayer should be as reflexive as breathing.

If we're committed to making disciples, the most basic action we can undertake to serve them is to pray. Paul was a spiritual giant, yet he frequently implored the churches to which he wrote to pray for him and his apostolic band. Flip it over and most of his letters contain several detailed prayers for the recipients. It seems he was always praying for and thanking God for the churches under his care. We would do well to follow his example.

It follows that we should provide an example to the new believers by modelling, sharing and encouraging prayer. As a disciple-maker, you must ensure that prayer underpins every activity and is a prominent feature in devotion, worship, planning and pastoral care. I'm almost assuming you know this. In forming the life of a disciple in a new believer, praying for them and with them is fundamental.

Whole books have been written on prayer (or, in the case of writers such as E. M. Bounds, a whole series of books that have become devotional classics). I don't want to just gloss over it—prayer is the single most important devotional activity in which a human can engage. But neither do I want to give it a half-baked treatment when you can read Dutch Sheets or Peter Wagner (and you should).

Suffice to say, what you're about to read about formation of spiritual disciplines is as much (either explicitly or by implication) about the formation of habits of prayer as it is about habits of engaging the scriptures. I've focused a little more on engagement of scripture because it seems the more difficult habit to form. It seems to me that those who are daily in the scriptures will usually be consistent in prayer—yet it seems less likely to flow the other way.

Formation in the scriptures
As we discussed under the heading of catechesis, it's important that disciples experience sound teaching. Paul emphasised to Timothy in the strongest possible terms the importance of teaching sound doctrine (2 Timothy 4:1-2). That of course leads us to thinking a little about the efficacy of the Sunday sermon for discipleship.

Be prepared for some thoughts that I know will ruffle a few feathers. As a young man just starting out in my ministry, I very quickly became disillusioned with the congregation of which I was a part. I had preached several sermons by this stage, and to my dismay there had been no Whitfield-style revival in response.

One thing is certain: it was not due to the inferior quality of the preacher's hermeneutical skill or delivery style. These were, in my humble estimation, simply awesome. No, it had to be something about the stubborn and smug congregation. Or perhaps there was something problematic about the notion of preaching a Sunday sermon in itself.

I wrote this question and stuck it to my desk lamp where I would see it every day: 'Why don't sermons revolutionise lives?' The question remained taped to my lamp, unanswered, for several years.

Preaching sermons has been the staple of Christian ministers for centuries. It seems to be the primary skill set we seek to develop in Theological colleges. Thousands of sermons are preached across Australia every week by an increasingly skilled and scholarly class of clergy. Yet the church is still not experiencing the Whitfieldian revival I expected back when I started out in 1987.

Yet with preaching we persist. We hold conferences, workshops and masterclasses on the subject, and still it does not—on the whole—produce more or better disciples. And so we try harder and harder to perfect what clearly is not delivering what is expected.

A mid to late 20th-century psychologist would look at us putting in more and more effort yet seeing no more result and confidently diagnose us all with a classic case of cognitive dissonance (an idea developed by American psychologist Leon Festinger in 1957). While the term has fallen into disuse as psychology has moved on to newer and more exciting pathologies, it's worth stopping to wonder why, for all our effort, we're not seeing much result.

This has not always been so. Jonathan Edwards seems to have singlehandedly sparked the First Great Awakening in the 1730s using only the pulpit as his point of influence. In 1739 Whitfield travelled to the US and held crowds spellbound, his theatrical and emotive style a contrast to Edwards's stern scholarship.

Edwards's sermons are still in print. Preachers still preach them. Preachers study Whitfield's delivery style and seek to emulate it. There has been no corresponding contemporary awakening.

While we're in the 18th century, let's take a look at another seminal Christian character. John Wesley actually mentored the young Whitfield, and while his preaching was never as impressive as that of his protégé, it was Wesley's movement that was to be the conduit for a revival that burned for three generations on two continents.

While Wesley was also a famed open-air preacher, his legacy lies in the hundreds of ordinary laypeople he discipled and deployed in mission. We'll talk more about deploying people in ministry in the next chapter, so for now let's take a quick look at the method that gave rise to the Wesleyan movement being dubbed 'Methodist'.

Participation in the Wesleyan movement took place at two or three levels simultaneously. Familiar to most of us is the 'society', which roughly correlated to what we would nowadays call a congregation. As Wesley's movement dispersed into the towns and villages with smaller populations and smaller venues, societies became regularly sized at around fifty people. These gathered once a week to learn from scripture, pray, sing and care for each other (yep, not too different to a Sunday service today). It was in this context that the scriptures were expounded to an often illiterate audience. Note that the preached word was an essential part of Wesley's model.

Here's where it gets interesting. The next level was the class—a group of about a dozen people who met to give account of their spiritual experience and condition. Because literacy was not widespread, these were not Bible studies but primarily a means of accountability. Each member would be asked to describe the condition of their soul. Trained leaders would facilitate the groups, give counsel to members and report to church leadership. People found to be lax in their discipleship were expelled. Interestingly, membership in class was prerequisite to membership of the society. One could not attend the larger public meeting without a three-monthly ticket issued by the class leader.

The smallest unit in the Wesleyan system was the band, a device Wesley adapted from the Moravians. While classes were mixed and geographically based, bands were formed of people of the same gender and marital status. Bands were not compulsory, and focused on dealing with temptation and confession of sin. Although bands as a method of discipleship were introduced earlier, they were in time de-emphasised in favour of classes.

Let's get back to preaching. As we have conceived of it, preaching in the contemporary setting is seen as a kind of public lecture or oration—and what people do with it is their own business. And as I observed, the outcomes are largely disappointing even though we put more and more effort into it. Thom Rainer, in his research on US churches that were effective in growth through evangelism, found that preaching was a very important consideration.[28] Preaching is important, perhaps even vital. But it is not sufficient by itself to form committed, resilient disciples. In Wesley's method, society members were held accountable for putting into practice what they had heard in sermons (that is, for living a life of repentance). It seems we need a multifaceted approach.

Let me put it another way: By all means encourage new believers to come to church—and we'll talk about that some more soon. But the idea that sermons alone will form disciples? Well, the evidence for that notion is patchy to say the least.

Think about any effort of human development and you'll probably be able to identify some intentionality around content, process and environment. Indeed, we've touched on these already in both the 'belonging' and 'embracing the gospel' steps.

You'll also remember that I spent a fair bit of time earlier discussing adult learning, and how our Western education systems seems to develop in us a habit of thinking that divides ideas from behaviour. I also talked about Kolb's assertion that people learn by discovery and experience.

Now let's pull some of this together.

First off, let's hear Paul's counsel again: doctrine is important. More specifically, his counsel was to 'preach the Word' (2 Timothy 4:2). What does he mean? Not the sixty-six books of the yet-to-be-completed canon. More likely he meant the gospel of Jesus Christ and the doctrines that flow from it. So what do we make of that?

In a mostly literate society, we can do much by cutting out the middle man and getting new believers into the scriptures for themselves—specifically the gospels. Given that the Old Testament provides the historical context for the

---

[28] Rainer, Thom S. *Surprising Insights from the Unchurched and Proven Ways to Reach Them* (Zondervan, Grand Rapids, 2001), p. 150.

gospels and the rest of the New Testament is a kind of *midrash* (commentary) following them, it's my conviction that we should encourage new believers to spend a good chunk of their time in the gospels. Sometimes I worry that we see Jesus as the warm-up act to Paul, because Paul—particularly his letter to the Romans—looks more like systematic theology that we can analyse and categorise. Jesus is the main event and Paul a kind of exposition thereof.

Returning to an earlier theme, the scriptures and the Holy Spirit seem to do a pretty good job of formation, that is, the transforming of a person's life by (among other things) the renewing of the mind. Reading the scriptures is imbibing authoritative revelation. What could be better for straightening out one's thinking? When we as disciple-makers over-mediate by insisting on interpreting the scriptures on people's behalf, we run the risk of building unhealthy dependence on us and interfering with their connection to God.

The same goes, dare I say it, for devotional materials. Sure, I grew up on Quest Notes and I'm grateful for them—but I really started to develop my spiritual life when I simply engaged God in the scriptures for myself. I'll talk about reading other literature in a minute, but I want to clearly and strongly emphasise the importance of encouraging believers to read the scriptures for themselves.

I'm not saying we shouldn't teach doctrine, I'm just saying we should beware of substituting teaching by religious professionals for personal reflection. Why not encourage both? Regularly hearing a well-crafted sermon teaching doctrine as an exposition of scripture, coupled with a daily diet of reading the scriptures, is a pretty useful base for forming a new believer.

How do we encourage engagement with the scriptures? Now that practically everyone can read, we tend to tell people what to do and send them off to implement what they've 'learned' (which almost never works—not for prayer, Bible study, dieting, budgeting, exercising, time management, sobriety or any other discipline you care to name).

Cast your mind back to Kolb's ideas about discovery and experience. Telling a person what they should do has been demonstrated to be one of the least effective modes of influence—unless you have the aid of some extrinsic reinforcer (that is, 'If you do as I say you'll get what you want or avoid what you don't'). And too often the thing we hold out as the thing to avoid is guilt.

I would rather build a discipling culture based on the biblical ideas of faith, hope and love. Helping a person discover biblical truth and inviting them into an experience of revelation offers them the possibility of gaining the benefit of spiritual exercises, which in turn opens the possibility of developing an intrinsic motivation—faith that God loves them and is full of grace, and hope of knowing and experiencing his love (which is what Paul prayed for the Ephesians in chapter 3).

The most important influencer of a new disciple in developing a devotional habit is your own life. If you can share with them the benefit (maybe even the joy) that you experience through your devotional life, you may just inspire some interest and motivation in them to do the same.

One of the most helpful ways to start someone off in their devotional life is to do the process with them. Before the Industrial Revolution and universal education, townspeople were encouraged to join the local priest for the morning and evening offices—a simple liturgy of scripture and prayer to open and close the day. The monastic orders created daily communal rhythms for worship, prayer and reflection on the scriptures.

The Celtic monks were masters of this. Seekers coming into the monastic community were enfolded into some of the spiritual rhythms of the community, where discovery and experience were possible. When a person joined the monastic community as a baptised member, they knew the way of life for which they were signing up.

How could this work if you're not a sixth-century Irish monk?

Through most of history, well-developed lives of *individual* spiritual discipline have flowed from the experience of *shared* spiritual disciplines (not the other way around). Recently, movements like 3DM have been advocating a less deductive, more inquiry-based approach to the scriptures, conducted in pairs or small groups.

Generally referred to as 'discovery Bible study', this approach focuses less on getting a person's propositional theology straight and more on helping them develop habits of engaging with God in the scriptures and immediately putting their discovery into practice. This method can be used both for catechesis with a seeker and for formation of a new disciple.

Since this approach is more caught by sharing than learned by instruction, it works best one-to-one where a disciple-maker and a new disciple sit together and read the scriptures by whatever pattern they choose (there are a bunch of different patterns and processes around). The new disciple is invited to reflect and share, and the disciple-maker offers thoughts and observations as appropriate.

Discovery Bible study in its various forms allows new disciples to experience discovery of truth in the scriptures for themselves. You may not have to do this with them every day for the rest of your life, but starting a new disciple in their devotional journey by being their companion in their spiritual practices—as regularly as life permits—will serve to establish their devotional habits.

There's a broad variety of discovery-style approaches around—a web search will yield enough to get you off to a good start.

If you're of the more contemplative type, *Lectio Divina* is an ancient approach to scripture as prayer that encourages listening for a subjective encounter with God in the scriptures. It's a favourite of mine because it's both simple and experiential.

Other approaches to formation through spiritual disciplines include Tony Campolo's challenge for people to read the gospel of Mark over and over for a few weeks. Not a bad way to start.

Neil Cole, in his classic *Cultivating a Life for God*,[29] encourages reading thirty to thirty-five chapters a week. That will get you going as well, although just about everybody baulks at the sheer volume of reading—I think they complain it eats into their TV-watching time.

Wayne Cordero advocates SOAP[30]—encouraging people to read a passage of scripture, make some observations, consider how to apply the insight gained to everyday life, and then pray.

---

[29] Cole, Neil. *Cultivating a Life for God: Multiplying Disciples Through Life Transformation Groups* (CMA Resources, 1999).
[30] SOAP: Scripture, Observation, Application, Prayer. http://www.enewhope.org/nextsteps/journaling/

Whatever approach you favour, for the reasons I stated earlier, the gospels are probably the best place to begin for the new believer.

An inspected life
As a younger leader I thought discipleship was largely—if you're working with literate people—a matter of finding a simple method and getting people into it. I've tried to make a case for the power of example and experience in forming devotional habits, and using shared devotional experience to shape and motivate personal devotional practices.

However, while seeing and experiencing the power of a regular and intentional devotional life can serve to motivate, disciples in contemporary society seem to struggle to maintain personal devotional habits over the longer term.

We're talking about what the contemplatives call 'spiritual disciplines' or 'spiritual exercises'. The idea of 'exercise' gives us a clue. And using what we know about success and failure in the realm of physical health might just be helpful in thinking about developing spiritual health and maturity.

While mail-order companies have made untold billions out of people's good intentions to get fit at home, most of the miracle exercise equipment that promises killer abs or a bikini body fails to deliver—not because the machine is defective or the promise hollow but because the result requires effort and self-discipline.

The same goes for dieting. I'm astounded by the continual stream of diets (often advocated by celebrities with Photoshop-quality physiques) pushed by magazines and sidebar ads on social media. Also proliferating in the aforementioned sidebars is a succession of pills, tips, tricks and hacks to make weight loss easy. Achieving health and fitness is not about getting some newfangled device or knowing some obscure trick. We fall for this stuff because we want to avoid the simple, unpleasant truth that, all other things being equal, health and fitness is a question of consistent effort and discipline.

Being fit and well feels good. The benefits are well documented and can spill over into mental health, career success and a range of other aspects of life. Going for a run or pounding out some laps in the pool releases endorphins that produce a sense of happiness and wellbeing that can carry us through a good portion of the day. If the benefits are so good, why do people struggle for motivation?

While I'm sure there are countless peer-reviewed studies giving incisive neurobiological insights into the complexities of human emotions, we all know the simple summary explanation. We don't do what's obviously good for us because we just don't feel like it.

If doing what's physically good for us is hard even though the benefits are tangible and can easily be measured, building the disciplines to be spiritually healthy, where it's difficult to directly measure the benefit, is even harder (although there have been quite a number of studies on the health benefits of prayer).

To work the metaphor of physical training a little more, one of the most effective ways to get fit and improve your health is to get a coach or trainer— that is, someone who will help you set goals for yourself and then hold you accountable for sticking to your commitments. As it turns out, people do better with a bit of accountability.

Let me get personal for a minute (this will give you rare insight into the oddball way my brain works). As I write this, it's 9.00 pm and I still have another seventy words to go to meet my quota of two thousand for the day. Once I've written my quota (only fifty to go now), I can go and eat 600 kJ worth of food (probably an egg on toast) before bed. Why these exact numbers? Because I have a coach who will literally charge me $210 if I fail to meet my objectives for the week (the $210 is her coaching fee—if I hit my goals the coaching costs me a cup of coffee, if I fall short I have to pay full whack). And for this week that means not exceeding 8400 kJ for six out of seven days and hitting the two thousand-word quota for the two writing days I've set aside (and the good news is, in explaining all that I hit my word count for the day).

As I write I'm expecting ninety per cent of readers to have a 'What the ... ?' type of response. Yeah, I know, it all seems a bit legalistic and contrived. And I'm the first to acknowledge that it is. But here's the important point. The goals I'm pursuing are my own. They don't come from the Bible, the church or my coach. The deal about paying the coaching fee is a little incentive I freely and willingly entered into. This is not about sin, or duty, or guilt (and only a tiny smidgeon of shame). It's about me getting a little help to live up to my own hopes for my life.

You see, for the first five months of this year I carried six kilograms more than I wanted to and got no writing done. Sick of missing my personal goals, I got myself a coach to hold me accountable. I don't need someone making me feel guilty, but I do need someone who wills my success and keeps an eye on my progress.

Centuries ago, Wesley was dismayed by people falling away from the faith commitment they had made in response to his sermons, so he devised small groups (the bands and classes I described earlier) for accountability, or as he called it, 'discipline'.

Let me reiterate—accountability is something we willingly enter into in order to gain the benefits of a disciplined life. We can't make it on our own, even if we want to. That's why people have personal trainers, Jenny Craig and Alcoholics Anonymous. We need people who care enough to keep watch on our souls. And we need community (more on that in a moment).

It's my conviction that all of us should be in accountable relationships for our own good. Centuries ago, humans lived in small villages and everyone's business was everyone's business. If someone was going a little astray, the community tended to knock them into shape (sometimes literally).

Nowadays humans increasingly live in big cities where we can be pretty much anonymous, autonomous and accountable to no one. Most of us are so familiar with being a law unto ourselves that the idea of someone else inspecting our life seems like a massive intrusion.

And that intrusion is not something we can impose. But it is something we can model, encourage and invite. For two years I met on Saturdays for breakfast with two young men at the local Maccas. (I know you hipsters will be turning your noses up, but it was one of those end-of-the-line suburbs—literally, it was where the train line ended—and it was Maccas or nothing!) When we met I confessed my sins to them, to model being accountable and transparent. And they in turn confessed theirs to me. We prayed for one another and talked over what we had learned in the scriptures. We got to some fairly raw and real issues—much more than we could have in the larger group of young adults that gathered at my house during the week. This leads me to talk about community.

Formation in community
I recently read a study which found that people adopt the social norms of those they hang around (see, your mother was right). Older studies (focusing, oddly enough, on biker culture), coming out of the World War 2 experience, have found that powerful and amazingly durable bonds and social norms are built when people share in tight community and deep struggle together. I know that sounds obvious, but when you think about it, it has some significant implications.

If these studies and the theories that flow from them are correct, the corrections system is Australia is actually geared to produce more and better criminals (let's get the crooks together in community and give them a cruel enemy whom they will band together to resist). The predictable result: deeply committed and well-networked crims.

The corrections story is instructive. On the inside (I count a number of corrections graduates as my friends) there are all sorts of courses run to help inmates reform: courses on anger management, respect for women, dealing with addictions and more besides. These courses tend to run on an *education* model (and we know how well that works with unit circle trigonometry). Meanwhile, there are powerful forces of *socialisation* working in almost direct opposition to the reform courses. And we wonder why we have a recidivism problem.

Let's think about making more and better disciples instead of more and better crooks. Paul, when writing about the possibilities for the church growing up into maturity in Christ, uses a series of collective terms like 'we' and together' (Ephesians 4:9-16). Becoming who we're called to become— who God has imagined us to become in Christ—is really only possible in community.

In the grand laboratory of human behaviour, it seems that socialisation will eat education for breakfast. You become like the people you hang around. Which means that, along with developing a deep devotional life, a deep communal life is critical for the formation of disciples (which further explains why the Celtic monks and the Wesleyans were so enduringly effective).

The writer to the Hebrews was on to this: 'Don't give up meeting together, but encourage one another' (10:25). The Jerusalem church was facing persecution, and some of its members were avoiding Roman and Jewish attention by avoiding meeting together. This tactic was probably good for keeping a low profile, but bad for keeping the faith.

I've lost count of the number of times I've heard the protest 'Going to church doesn't make you a Christian.' Technically true. However, from a purely practical standpoint, not going to church is a pretty reliable recipe for making you a non-Christian (or at least a lapsed one).

I'm not going to hold up the average Christian public worship service as the most edifying experience ever to be had, but I will say this: meeting with other Christians to offer a loving response to God for his goodness, affirm the faith to which we hold, beseech God to intervene in this broken world and intentionally fix our attention on Jesus is good for the soul.

As a young adult I found singing songs of worship a profoundly uplifting experience (and thank you, Geoff Bullock, for putting words of worship into the mouths of a generation). In my early thirties church began after church, talking with young adults and encouraging them in their journey with Jesus. For about five years from my late thirties I attended the church where Allan Meyer was the senior minister and I found his sermons a regular tonic and challenge to my battered soul (thanks, Al). At close to fifty the highlight of my week is to hold a crumb of unleavened bread and a shotglass of grape juice and contemplate the enormity of what Jesus has done for me (I'm tearing up as I write this).

And this leads me to touch once again on the sacraments: this time on the ritual variously termed the Eucharist, the Lord's Table, the Lord's Supper or simply 'communion'.

Eucharist—receiving 'good grace'
Jesus rather audaciously reimagined the Passover, transforming its bread and wine into a memorial ritual commemorating his body broken and blood shed for the forgiveness of sins (Matthew 26:28). He re-cast the meal as sealing the new covenant between God and humanity (Luke 22:20).

I spoke earlier of the inherent power of sacrament to confer grace. It's not that we can't access God's grace without sacramental ritual, but that entering into the physical ritual puts us in a posture to experience God's grace.

Here's my best understanding of how it works. When the elements of the sacrament are set before us, and the words of one of the last supper narratives read out, we are reminded of the meaning and significance of the ritual. As we receive the elements, perceiving what they represent, we symbolically take Jesus' death upon ourselves and into ourselves in much the same way that a Jewish family would take the death of a sacrificial lamb upon themselves and into themselves by eating it.

I'm not saying that the Eucharist is a literal sacrifice (or the table an altar for that matter), but rather a memorial of the once and for all sacrifice of Jesus. It's significant that Paul warns his readers that taking it lightly and not perceiving what the sacrament represents is to eat and drink judgment upon oneself (1 Corinthians 11:29)—a stern warning indeed.

Jesus took the cup and described it as the new covenant in his blood. Our participation is a kind of recommitment or renewal of our covenant with God. By this we acknowledge once again the death of Jesus as sufficient for our redemption; we respond to the gracious gift of life; and we re-commit to living a life of faith, hope and love in response to God's generous and costly love for us.

Participation in the Lord's Supper acts as a re-centring of our faith: retuning to first principles, examining our hearts, responding to God's kindness, committing afresh to the way of discipleship. Entered into thoughtfully, it's like a periodical recalibration for our souls.

In forming disciples, such a recalibration and opening of the heart to receive afresh the grace of God serves to renew and strengthen the faith of the believer. I don't think this is by any means automatic—remember Paul's insistence that we examine ourselves before taking part (1 Corinthians 11:28). Like any other religious practice, it can become an empty ritual stripped of its meaning and power.

Conversely, approached with appreciation, reflection and faith, this sacrament serves as a powerful nutrient in the formation of the believer, and we would do well to encourage disciples to participate in it fully and expectantly.

To sum up my thoughts on attending church services: different aspects of the gathering speak to different people, or to the same person differently at different stages. When church is entered into humbly and sincerely, one is usually blessed. Modelling, encouraging and inviting participation in the Christian community in worship is an important part of forming new believers into followers of Jesus.

The fellowship myth

'Fellowship' with our 'fellow' followers of Jesus is, according to many songs and poems, a sweet experience. In church as in cuisine, sweets are not wrong in themselves; they're just not all that nourishing. They are comforting and pleasurable, making us feel good in the short term, but will lead to our untimely demise if they're indulged in to the exclusion of more nourishing experiences.

I've visited churches where the congregation is made up almost entirely of people who have been there a long time and show plenty of evidence of over-indulgence in sweet stuff (in both of the senses above). Without exception, such churches are getting older, numerically smaller and increasingly insular, meaning new people feel a palpable sense of being outsiders and very few return.

Allow me to challenge you with the contrast between 'sweet' fellowship and genuine fellowship. Every year on April 25, Australia's serving and former soldiers march to commemorate Anzac Day. That day you see old men gather in small quiet groups to remember their experiences of war, and to remember those who didn't come back or those who have passed on since the last Anzac Day. There might be beer, a game of two-up and a few other trappings, but the connection between these men is fellowship: the common experience of striving together in the pursuit of a noble cause, the shared experience of hardship, mortal fear, unspeakable loss.

Real fellowship is never a goal in itself—it's a by-product that you might experience while you're working together in the pursuit of something that's bigger than just yourselves. It's forged in struggle, interdependence, risk and hope. It's not just war that produces fellowship; it might be experienced working long and hard together to create a stage play, or to rescue an injured hiker, or to build a medical clinic in rural Zambia. It might be kind of sweet, but not like sugar.

Any activity designed just for fellowship has no real place in a mission pathway. I'll talk a little later about how you might proceed if your church is blessed with activities designed for 'sweet fellowship'.

The gift of being known

Back to the idea of socialisation. In terms of the gathered community there is a single factor that, in my observation and experience, outweighs all of the welcoming programs and efforts at integration we may make, and is an essential part of forming disciples that persevere and mature in the faith. That factor, quite simply, is being known.

In his landmark book *Connecting*, psychologist Larry Crabb asserts that therapists would be redundant if we could learn to connect deeply.[31] As someone with close connections to a number of people who earn a good living out of psychology and related disciples, I'm not sure it would be prudent of me to agree entirely. However, studies in the field of psychology have established that a significant proportion of the benefit derived from counselling comes simply from the formation of a trusting relationship with a person willing to give the client a substantial slab of undivided attention.

You'll remember I spent some time talking about the value of listening in the chapter on 'Belonging'. The same goes in this context. There seems to be a deep craving inside the heart of humanity for connection—not just superficial, and not necessarily physical, but connection where we can be genuinely open about ourselves and have what is revealed acknowledged and accepted, perhaps even loved.

We can't plumb the depths of this on a Sunday morning—or even in a Wednesday night cell group. We may get a little closer in a life transformation group (read Neil Cole's *Cultivating a Life for God* for more on these) or an accountability triplet.

But getting to the absolute depth of connection is not the point—it's getting some way along the journey. How far you get depends on a bunch of variables, not the least each individual's capacity for intimacy. For some, even the possibility of being exposed is utterly terrifying. For others, their capacity for over-sharing can leave the hearer wincing.

---

[31] Crabb, Larry. *Connecting: Healing Ourselves and Our Relationships* (W Publishing, Nashville, 1997).

Connection is somewhat of a dance. Some find it easier than others—but to the extent that one can tolerate the discomfort it may arouse, connection is balm for the soul and holds out enormous possibilities for people to find hope and develop maturity.

A listening community is likely to be a loving community, and also more likely to be a learning community—learning in the broad sense of people putting new thinking into tangible action. What do I mean by that?

Let's go back to Kolb for a minute. He maintains that translating learning into behaviour (that is, 'doing') through active experimentation is an essential part of the learning cycle. And change in behaviour is a key outcome of discipling. According to Kolb's theory, 'doing' is preceded by forming new ideas or modifying existing ones. These two stages are preceded by reflective observation—the learner thinking about and seeking to understand their learning experience. It's pretty hard to accomplish this while absorbing more and more content. Conversely, understanding and insight often come when the learning facilitator (in our case the disciple-maker) asking thoughtful questions that invite reflection.

When people thoughtfully engage a question, they don't just tell you their answer; they tell themselves, often for the first time. But they won't even engage the question if they don't believe you are listening.

To summarise my thoughts on community: socialisation beats education as a formation process, so hanging around in the community of believers is essential for the deepening, continuance and maturation of faith. Going to church, if approached in the right spirit, is generally good for you, because the experience of sung worship, or the preached word, or the Lord's Supper, or conversation afterward (or a combination of these) will bless you. In order for formation by socialisation to take place, a person needs to be heard and known, so building a culture of loving by listening is very important.

You will have noticed I did not spend a lot of time on the content of the worship service other than the Lord's Supper. This is intentional. I'm assuming most of my audience comes from traditions where worship in song and/or the preached word are given prominence. Much has been written on these two issues by deeply committed, knowledgeable, competent and insightful people. Leaders of churches that make either or both of these a priority will likely have gone to considerable effort to develop these aspects of their services. Frankly, I don't have much new or helpful to offer.

Conversely, for those of us who inhabit these traditions, the sacraments seem to have taken a back seat and I wanted to emphasise their importance.

Speaking of what's been written by people much smarter than me, let me take a paragraph or twelve to talk about the value of books and other resources for the formation of disciples.

Resource thyself

At Discovery Church where I was a member before a recent house move, senior minister Rohan Dredge introduced an eleventh commandment: *Resource thyself.* As we think about forming new believers into followers of Jesus, helping them into the habit of resourcing themselves is pretty important.

It has been said that the one who does not read is no better off than the one who cannot read. Although that's clearly not true in an absolute sense, it does make an important point about the value of engaging with the thinking of other people through books, and nowadays through dozens of other media.

I know I've spent a fair bit of time on adult learning theory, particularly David Kolb, and worked hard to convince you that content alone does not a follower of Jesus make. We've been journeying together now for nearly forty thousand words, so hopefully my point has been made. I feel it's safe to confess that, all of the foregoing notwithstanding, I think reading good books is extremely important. The fact you've got this far in this book indicates you place some value on reading too. (Whether this qualifies as a good book is for you to judge!)

Anyone who has been coached by me will quickly get sick of the question, 'Have you read … ?' I encourage people to read. For forming disciples the scriptures are central, but reading Christian writers and engaging Christian thinkers is also important.

I've already made the point about our media-saturated society, and the Christian quarter is no different. There are thousands of sermons on YouTube, hundreds of thousands of Christian books in stores and online, whole cable channels dedicated to 'Christian' TV, and enough MP3 files of sermons circulating to keep us all entertained all of the time (and maybe for most of eternity).

The environment is resource-rich. The real question is: how do you navigate it, and how do you encourage an apprentice follower of Jesus to engage solid Christian thinkers?

Let me begin with you. Who are you reading (and from here on, take 'reading' as shorthand for engaging by whatever media you choose)? Who have you read that has shaped your thinking? What's your own personal list of resources for new believers?

As far as is relevant, you could begin by introducing your disciples-in-formation to the thinkers who have influenced you. Or you might want to talk to the people you respect and see who they're reading.

As I talk with other Christian leaders about forming disciples, a couple of titles come up in the conversation. The first is *The Purpose Driven Life* by Rick Warren.[32] This works well as a basic orientation to aligning your life with God's purpose. It's sold a gazillion copies for a good reason. Another is *A Passionate Life* by Mike Breen and Walt Kallestad.[33] This is foundational reading for anyone in the 3DM movement, and covers the basic habits and principles of the Christian life. It uses the rubric of eight shapes to anchor the learning.

A helpful approach is to form small reading groups that work a bit like a strung-out book club. Read a chapter per week and meet each week to talk it over: a mix of socialisation, reflective learning and accountability. With coffee thrown in, what's not to like?

Some churches with which I've worked have developed a kind of discipling curriculum, which could be books, video resources, audio files or a mixture geared to form godly thinking and behaviour in their congregational members. Small groups can work though them book-club style.

Another church used to send out cassette tapes (remember those?) of sermons and speeches from the best Christian leaders they could find. They would mail out a few dozen each month and encourage people to listen to

---

[32] Warren, Rick. *The Purpose Driven Life* (Zondervan, Michigan, 2002).
[33] Breen, Mike & Kallestad, Walt. *A Passionate Life* (Nexgen, Mumbai, 2005).

them as they drove around in their cars, then pass them on to someone else. The church had hundreds, perhaps thousands, of tapes in circulation. As the tape went the way of the dinosaur, they moved to CDs. Now it's as simple as texting everyone on their database a link to an MP3 file. The idea is to keep the congregation turning over helpful, godly thinking in their minds. Given everything else coming at us nowadays, being transformed by renewing your mind (Romans 12:2) is a pretty momentous task.

Before you jump online and order a bunch of books, consider a couple of missiological caveats. Books are fine for people who read, or who, with a little encouragement, could get into the habit of reading. For some people, especially those who didn't exactly relish school as a kid, books can be a real psychological barrier. You might want to think about video resources or some other form of learning materials instead.

Think also about the cultural symbols contained in the resources you use. And make sure they really connect with the life and experience of the kind of people you're reaching. For example, I love Billy Hybels and appreciate his ministry—but when he tells stories about yachting with his buddies, sailing boats that cost as much as my house, he loses me. I know the yacht is not the point of the story, but the mental image of the expensive boat seems to trip me up. It may seem silly and inane, but those sorts of sensitivities run deep and can cost you your credibility.

I encourage every church to take ongoing resourcing seriously and cultivate habits of learning between Sundays. But first take some time and perhaps do a little testing to ensure resources are a fairly close cultural match.

Before I get to the final idea in this section, I want to give a gentle warning about over-resourcing disciples. At some stage, it's important for the disciple to make the transition from apprentice to colleague. That means them taking full responsibility for cultivating their own faith.

I'm not advocating we just cut them loose, but I am saying we shouldn't spoon feed people, or even do all the 'food preparation' and serve it for their consumption. Part of this means making the subtle transition from the traditional mentor role (my life speaking into yours) to peer mentor or peer coach (our lives speak to each other's and we hold each other accountable to maintain our individual integrity). Developing the habit of asking questions and being transparent will make this transition easier.

Fruitful witness
The final concept I want to address in this section is that of sharing faith. By this I mean two things: bearing witness to God's goodness as we go about our daily lives, and becoming disciple-makers ourselves. This has two important implications.

The first is the issue of fruitfulness. Working in the fruit growing industry, I learned that fruit grows on young wood. Apples grow on two-year-old wood, meaning a shoot that emerged last year will set fruit this year. When pruning, the orchardist is thinking about retaining enough older wood to maintain a framework for the tree while stimulating enough new growth to maintain productivity into the coming year or two. Sustainability and productivity.

Too often we concentrate so much on building a strong disciple who will be well established in their faith that we neglect to cultivate fruitfulness in their lives—that is, we don't help them become disciple-makers themselves. We end up growing ornamental trees.

The real opportunity of a new disciple is that they will probably be at their most productive as witnesses in the first couple of years of the faith journey. A little like apple trees, new fruit grows on young wood.

There's a clear and simple sociological reason for this. At the point of conversion, there is (or should be) a fair bit of reorientation going on in the new believer's life. Their family and friends should notice, or at least hear about the difference. A new believer inviting their family and friends to their baptism or confirmation opens up conversations and piques curiosity. It's not unusual for one person's conversion to set off a chain of faith commitments in their family and social circle.

This is why people who have radical conversions tend to make the best evangelists (the apostle Paul, for example) and why people whose conversions make a visible change of life in their teens or later tend to be more fruitful in their witness than 'cradle Christians'.

That doesn't relieve us 'converted as kids' Christians of our call to bear witness to Jesus. It just means that when a person has a conversion experience that makes an obvious difference (and many do), we should help them make the most of the possibilities.

Perseverance

The second implication of fruitfulness early in the discipleship journey is that of perseverance. It may seem paradoxical, but the person who shares their experience of faith and encourages others on the same journey is more likely to persevere in their faith than the one who waits until they have all their sanctification ducks lined up before uttering a peep (or quack).

This was borne out most clearly to me when working with the Church Army. Our head office and training facility was co-located with a church plant and a sixteen-bed residential rehab unit. Our staff and students ate, worked, learned and worshipped alongside a bunch of guys in various stages of recovery from addiction to alcohol and other drugs.

Working on an old-school 12-step model, we discovered that residents in the rehab program made better progress when they were mentoring someone else through the program. A person who was working on Step 4 (making a searching and fearless written moral inventory of themselves) could be helping a newcomer to settle in and make the honest assessment of the state of their lives for Step 1 (admitting powerlessness to overcome addiction and the unmanageable state of their life).

A quick sidebar: if you think the 12-step program looks a lot like a conversion and discipleship process, you're right—so long as the idea of 'Higher Power' is clearly defined as God in Christ. It's sad that AA has lost its original centre and has de-emphasised doing 'step work' in favour of more and more meetings. The step work of rigorous self-examination, repentance, taking responsibility and depending of God for the grace and power to persevere is a solid discipleship framework that I believe everyone would benefit from working through. And remember, according to Gerald May in his brilliant work *Addiction and Grace*,[34] we're all addicts. We're wired for it.

The groups that have been most effective in helping new believers to be fruitful in witness tend to be those that enfold new disciples into small, highly accountable groups. These include Neil Cole's concept of life transformation groups and the 3DM idea of 'huddles'. You don't have to be a small, submerged, house-based movement to make these groups work. Large churches like Gateway in Austin, Texas, have adapted the idea in a

---

[34] May, Gerald G. *Addiction and Grace: Love and Spirituality in the Healing of Addictions* (Harper Collins, New York, 1988).

program they call 'Running Partners'. A fairly big outfit closer to home (curiously, also called Gateway—but in Melbourne's south-east) has adapted Neil Cole's ideas into a program called G3.

The common thread in all of these is concern for people who are yet to profess faith in Christ, and a commitment to pray for them, bear witness appropriately with them (which explicitly or by implication includes expressing love in a way that is meaningful to them) and inviting them to an environment that is helpful in their journey toward Christ.

The way they generally operate is with a short list of accountability questions. The groups meet and work through the questions giving account of their behaviour. Some groups discuss scripture. Then they pray for each other and kaboom! Launched into another week!

You'll remember a couple of chapters ago I made a passing comment about the integrated nature of Pathways. Before we jump into the next chapter, let me pick up that thread again for a minute. If new disciples are well-formed, they become high-potential workers at other steps in the pathway, particularly in the 'belonging' and 'embracing the gospel' steps. When I say 'well formed', I mean they are:

- developing strong spiritual practices that transform their character;
- connected in a listening community to support and challenge them; and
- committed to being fruitful in their faith.

Leaders of growing churches tend to think in terms of reaching people and making disciples who can in turn reach people and make disciples. While Pathways is diagrammed as linear (for simplicity), it's actually systemic—effectiveness in the later steps fuels effectiveness of the earlier ones, just as effectiveness in earlier steps enables people to progress toward the later ones.

And thinking about involving people to serve at all steps of the pathway is the essence of the next chapter.

Chapter 9
Serving in Ministry

'Serving in ministry' is pretty much self-explanatory. So why a whole chapter on it? Because I think there's more to this than meets the eye.

But first, let's establish a working definition.

As a discipleship step, 'serving in ministry' is both a way of lovingly responding to God and a way of embracing the good and abundant life God has prepared for us. I read somewhere that a simple definition for the meaning of life is 'figuring out what God wants us to do, and then doing it'. It might also be a simple recipe for happiness and fulfilment.

While some might say we owe a debt of gratitude to God, expressed in service, I prefer to think in terms of Ephesians 2:10, which suggests that God has for a long time imagined the kind of life I could live and the kind of contribution I could make, and he invites me into it.

To think more broadly, and in line with George Eldon Ladd's theology of Jesus as the inaugurator of the kingdom of God, serving in ministry is moving beyond the idea of simply being redeemed and becoming like Jesus in character, to joining in with the mission of Jesus in the world. Serving in ministry is about taking up God's great redemptive cause in Christ.

It follows that the *Missio Dei* ('mission of God') becomes the lens through which we understand our lives in Christ and our service in the church, both for disciple-makers and disciples-in-formation. This means there's some specific theological formation required in the life of the disciple—that is, a theology of mission. Without a sense of the purpose of God's activity in the world across space and time, we can reduce the idea of serving in ministry to rosters and budgets and the survival of our own little local expression of God's kingdom. Without a theology of mission we end up with a mentality of maintenance.

It's not that we need to be thoroughly theologically formed (and whoever is?) before we can serve. It's just that without understanding the big picture of a redemptive metanarrative, we can get caught up in a very small and ultimately self-defeating picture of the church as a social grouping that exists primarily for its own perpetuation.

From the perspective of formation, it's important to think over how, as a disciple-maker (and as a discipling community), you will form disciples in a missional theology. *Perspectives on the World Christian Movement*, a reader edited by Ralph Winter and Steven Hawthorne, is a superb and accessible resource.[35] But whatever resource and process you decide on, it's important to pay attention to the 'why' of church activity, otherwise the 'what' gets reduced to personal preferences.

Thinking more developmentally, serving deepens a sense of belonging. In my household, if you live here, you get responsibilities. You take your turn to cook and clean up (because no one wants to do that job all the time). You get allocated a job like emptying the bins, or cleaning the floors, or shopping (glad I didn't get that one). If you belong here, you have responsibilities.

Frequently in Pathways workshops, people question the order of the steps, pointing out that many people—especially men—serve around the church before they even consider the idea of following Jesus. And that, of course, is undeniably true (we thought about this a little in the chapter on 'belonging'). People serve for a bunch of reasons, not the least because it feels good to give your effort and resources to something you think is worthwhile; it feels good to be needed; and it's satisfying to use your skills.

The aspect that sets apart serving in ministry from serving-to-belong is that serving in ministry is a response to Jesus and a contribution to his cause. It's never purely that, of course, and there will always be at play the sense that we benefit from serving.

The 'why' aspect is important because ministry at every stage of the pathway needs to be clearly aligned with the mission of Jesus. And remember at the beginning of the book we defined mission as continuing the work of Jesus in the world: acting with compassion and making disciples. Lose sight of that and we fall into activity for its own sake or for the perpetuation of what has always been.

---

[35] Winter, Ralph D. & Hawthorne, Steven C. (eds). *Perspectives on the World Christian Movement: A Reader*, 3rd edn (William Carey Library, Pasadena, 1999).

All of that said, participation in ministry helps to cement the disciple's commitment. We commit to the thing is which we participate, not the other way around. Let me emphasise this: involvement generally comes before—and generally leads to—commitment. We date before we marry (usually). Involvement asks of us a series of small commitments that tend to be self-reinforcing and cumulative. And many of those small commitments are actually good for our development as disciples.

A quick bit of autobiography. Like most young couples, my wife and I struggled to cope with the adjustment to parenthood, especially when the kids were really tiny. To be honest, just getting through the week seemed like a major achievement. Some Sundays, getting the family out the door looking nice, being nice and smelling nice (that's an issue with babies!) in time for church at 10.00 am seemed like a bridge too far.

Yet most weeks I was there (even if my wife and the kids were there perhaps one week in three). I was there usually because it was my turn to preach, or to lead worship, or to play bass or rhythm guitar. I was there because I had a responsibility, and while that responsibility sometimes seemed like a bit of a drag, it got me to church, and in the end I was always glad I was there.

Another snippet of my backstory, this one slightly more ancient: the church in which I grew up was a pretty typical outer suburban 1970s Baptist church with heaps of young families. By the late '70s and early '80s there were heaps of young teens. But here's where it was slightly less typical: by the late '80s there were heaps of older teens and young adults—that is, we kept the majority of our youth, including me.

Why was that? A big part of it was this: the youth served in ministry. The person greeting you at the door, the person taking up the offering, the musicians in the band, the worship leader, the sound guys (why are knob jockeys always guys?) were all more likely to be under twenty-one than they were to be over.

People commit to what they're involved in, not the other way around. If you want a more committed congregation, get people serving (it works better than preaching at them—it really does). If you want to retain young people, get them involved in every single imaginable role they may be able to learn to do. If you want people to feel like an 'insider' who really belongs, give them a job.

Summing up? Getting people involved in ministry, increasingly for the right reasons, is good for them, good for the church and good for the advancement of the mission of Jesus in the world.

Teams versus rosters

One of the things that surprised and bemused me as I began working in the Anglican system was the apparent preoccupation with rosters—for everything! In fact, 'doing the rosters' is a major undertaking in many churches. I had no idea.

I sometimes say, half seriously, that my mission in the Anglican Church is to abolish rosters and see teams replace them. Why would I say that?

I've just made the point that getting people involved in serving helps them feel they belong. But getting people to do all kinds of stuff just because it has to be done can elicit a range of far less desirable responses, from fatigue, to feeling unappreciated, to demotivation, to eventually feeling exploited.

The problem with rosters is that they can quickly become a set of expectations that come with an ever-decreasing sense of the joy of belonging, balanced by an increasing sense of feeling more negative emotions, like resentment.

Teams work a little differently. You might still be on a roster, but as far as possible you serve in community with a bunch of other people. There's a sense of doing stuff together. If the team culture is healthy, you'll help each other out, thank one another and have small celebrations when you do well together.

You can't necessarily group all the roles in a church community into sets of team responsibilities, but you can do it with most of them. Although larger churches are harder to manage due to their complexity, and in larger churches it's easier to be a stranger in the crowd where no one really knows you, a significant upside is the possibility of functional specialisation: that is, people can narrow their contribution to the things they like and/or are good at. That means more tasks can be handled by specialised teams. With a team-based approach, people find themselves doing fewer jobs but more often, and forming community with the people with whom they serve.

People also have a chance to think about service according to their gifts. Christian Schwarz identifies gift-based ministry as one of the eight quality characteristics by which church health can be measured.[36] This means serving in ministry according to the peculiar gifts that God has given you (how you define gifts and giftedness will vary depending on your exegesis of passages like Romans 12, I Corinthians 12 and Ephesians 4, which I'm not going to elaborate on here). The theory goes that if you're serving according to your gifts, you'll be more effective, feel more satisfaction, be less inclined to feel you're being exploited and be less likely to burn out. Certainly I would rather play guitar in church every week than count the offering once a month.

Schwarz is probably right (and his exhaustive research is hard to argue with). But let me add a few qualifiers, which apply especially to church plants in their early stages and small churches (regardless of age).

First, sometimes gifted apostles, prophets and evangelists should still stack chairs. Church plants generally launch public worship services with barely the resources to pull them off. Some small churches maintain their program of services with even less. Small churches simply can't afford the luxury of everyone being a specialist.

In the corporate world I was an HR manager. I did HR work: no line management, accounting, marketing, product development, distribution or any other function outside HR. Someone else cleaned my office. It was a big company and HR was a big enough job to keep me busy.

When I went out on my own as a consultant, I was everything from CEO to janitor. Small businesses require generalists, and so do small churches.

Big churches organise like corporations and you can specialise according to your gifts (mostly—there's still a time to jump in and help when a big task requires all hands to the pump). Small churches organise like families and we all do whatever it takes. Most small churches try to do way too much, but I'll get to that later.

Second, sometimes a gifted preacher or counsellor just drives the sound desk. It's not okay for someone to just sit back and do nothing because they can't do what they love or are gifted to do. Where there are a number of

---

[36] Schwarz, Christian A. *Natural Church Development: A Guide to Eight Essential Qualities of Healthy Churches* (Institute for Natural Church Development, 1996).

people with similar gifts, some people may need to be content with working with their mere competencies for a while.

Third, sometimes a gifted worship leader or bible study teacher will need just to sit down and shut up. Robert Clinton's immensely helpful work on leadership emergence identified a common occurrence in the life of leader he termed 'isolation'.[37] This is when God pulls a leader out of doing what they are gifted to do in order to stimulate some inner-life processing. And that's usually about the leader needing to do what they do to maintain their self-esteem and identity. Some of us have been-there-and-done-that, and most of us didn't like it—but we're better for it.

We should be mindful about becoming the best we can be according to the calling God has placed on us, but sometimes we need to be humble enough just to do what it takes to get stuff done. I'm not sure Jesus would have scored all that well on the 'gift' of foot-washing, but there was a time and a place to do it.

Gift assessment and discovery

Coming off the back of the charismatic movement, the idea of ministering according to gifting gained a fair bit of interest through the '80s and '90s. Assessment instruments were developed (don't look too closely at the theology implied in some of these) which in turn led to discovery processes like SHAPE (developed by a team at Saddleback Church).[38]

SHAPE looks at Spiritual Gifts, Heart, Abilities, Personality and Experience, and has a fairly simple assessment inventory for each aspect. People have adapted different inventories into the framework (for example, using the Myer-Briggs Type Indicator or DiSC to assess personality or temperament) to suit their preferences or contexts, but the general idea is the same.

Similarly, the crew at Willow Creek have come up with the Network course built around examining style, passions and gifts.[39] Over recent years a number of equivalent courses, assessment tools and discovery processes have popped up. Talking to leaders who have used them, they all have their particular strengths and benefits. It seems that it's largely a case of finding

---

[37] Clinton, J. Robert. *The Making of a Leader: Recognizing the Lessons and Stages of Leadership Development* (NavPress, Colorado Springs, 1993).
[38] http://saddleback.com/connect/ministry/shapeguides
[39] https://willowcreek.org.au/product/network-revised/

the process, tool or course that best suits your theological framework, your ecclesial style and your receptor culture.

Am I saying that using one of these is the only or even the best way to help people move toward serving in ministry? Not exactly. But there are loads of churches that have used them to good effect. And there are some that have found them not terribly helpful, which is usually less about the resource they've used and much more about the process of implementation.

The rule in gift assessment and discovery is follow-up, follow-up, follow-up. The church that did this better than any other I've seen was one of about 150 people. The vicar (it's an Anglican church) brought in a facilitator to run a full-day course for the whole congregation. About eighty people turned up. Over the following few weeks, the vicar (with a little help) interviewed each participant individually, coaching them through what using their particular gift-mix might look like. Each person went away with a clear plan on where, how and with whom they could begin to contribute to the service of Jesus and his mission, either in the church or in some other context.

If you use church database software (and if your church is more that about one hundred people, you should), there's usually a field where you can record a person's gifting as they perceive it. Provided you have a clear and frequent process to make use of that data to connect people with a context where they can serve, this can be useful too.

The key is to plan a process in advance to ensure people go from discovering how God may have shaped them for service to trying out their gifts in a safe environment as soon as is reasonably possible. It's best if the follow-up is personal and ongoing. More on the deployment phase in a minute.

Perhaps the idea of assessment inventories and discovery tools leaves you a little cold. The other option is based on trial and error.

Before you knock trial and error as a method for doing anything, most of what we learn about ourselves happens this way. Further, my experience with instruments for determining aspects of temperament or aptitude is that they depend almost entirely on good self-awareness and some degree of prior experience. A person with an inaccurate self-understanding can be steered entirely up the garden path. And if a person has never had exposure to a certain activity, their potential in that area may not show up in a giftedness instrument. This is especially true with younger people (I simply won't use some temperament instruments with people under eighteen: I've had too many confused kids).

Gift discovery by trial and error

The trial and error method begins with a person with some responsibility for a ministry area—it can be anything from serving coffee after church to helping refugees learn English—recognises the need to develop some more human capacity in their area (that's technical language for 'we need a bit of help here').

That person might wonder and pray about whom to ask, but note they don't immediately put a little ad in the church newssheet or schedule an 'advertisement segment' in the church notices. This is, like just about every other step in the pathway, about personal invitation.

Now for the part where it normally goes to custard. The low-yield approach is to ask the person, 'Would you be willing to be on the roster for … ?' Even as you're reading this your reflexive response is 'Err, no thanks.' Slightly better is 'Would you like to be on the team for … ?' But what if the person says yes and then they prove to be unsuitable? Then you have to 'fire' them.

Instead of asking for a commitment, think dating. That's right, think of recruiting volunteers as going on a date. It begins with a question like 'Could you please give me a hand next week with … ?' Note the differences. You're not asking for them to take responsibility, just to help. You're not asking them for a long-term commitment, just a one-off. And you're inviting them to help you—it's relational more than it is functional.

If they say 'yes', all you need to do is give them the most basic of expectations. Something like: 'Great! Can we meet here fifteen minutes before the service next Sunday?' If you're cluey, you'll get their cell phone number and send them a reminder text message the following Saturday.

Once you're there together, you only need to give them the most basic of instructions to get them moving in helping you. The odd word of encouragement and appreciation while you're working doesn't go astray either.

Once the job's done, take a minute to review with them. 'How did you go? Did you enjoy yourself?' If you think they showed potential to take this on more regularly, you could ask, 'Would you like to help again some time?' If 'yes', repeat the process.

If you're familiar with the cell church writers or the earlier small groups movement, you'll be familiar with the idea of getting different group members to take responsibility for different aspects of the group meeting. This allows natural leaders to emerge. This process is a similar idea and applies to just about any context in the church community.

The whole idea of the trial and error method, along with the just-help-once approach, to getting people started is built on the premise that people discover their gifts by trying different things and sticking with the things that seem to suit them. This has certainly worked for me. I knew that teaching was my primary gift long before I had ever heard of the Wagner-Modified Houts Spiritual Gifts Inventory. I knew because I gravitated to teaching opportunities and got fairly consistent feedback that what I offered was helpful.

Keeping the investment and the commitment low means people can have a go without any pressure. If they resonate with the task and seem to show a bit of promise, more investment and commitment can come.

At this juncture let's go over a couple of sticking points. The first is, 'How soon?' This question comes up all the time in workshops. There is a prevailing notion that you shouldn't ask people to help until they're settled-in (anything from three months to two years). There's a counter-notion that involving people helps them to settle in.

I once coached a church planter who had a simple rubric: first time you come, you're a guest; second time, you're a regular; third time, we ask you to help. As it turned out, there were a lot of people willing to help. Asking people to become involved (gently) sends a powerful message of being liked, valued and accepted into the group.

The second is, 'What about risk management?' This one is a little tricky, especially when it comes to working with kids. As I write a royal commission into institutional child abuse is in progress, and let's just say that the church has been shown to have handled this issue very poorly. We now live in a society that's rather suspicious and extremely vigilant when it comes to adults dealing with kids.

Each denomination will have its own risk management policy in this area, and I'm not suggesting you break it. Many denominations have a policy that allows volunteers without a Working-With-Children-Check to help under direct supervision. If so, the just-help-once invitation will still be okay, as long as you provide supervision. If the policy is different, you'll need to adapt. Some churches are now asking people to obtain a Working-With-Children-Check as part of their membership process.

With regard to other risks (for example, health and safety precautions), it's important that you cover these in your basic instructions when a person first agrees to help out. If significant safety training is required before a person can 'just help out', you might want to think about a different point of entry into the ministry area, or you may need to provide very close supervision early in the piece.

Involve, Orient, Equip, Review
Having been over the just-help-once concept, let me go over the process that underpins it.

It begins with involvement: that is, ask someone to become involved by helping. Then comes orientation: give them the most basic parameters. Next comes equipping: either right before or as they are doing the task, provide the minimal instruction and supervision they need just to do what you ask of them. Finally, review: ask the person how they like serving in this way and ask yourself, 'Did they show a bit of promise?'

You'll note a couple of things. Involvement comes before training. This may seem counter-intuitive, but in practice it seems to be more effective and less labour intensive than putting a person through training before you deploy them. Most people struggle to translate learning across contexts, and learning in context in real time means no translation is necessary.

You'll also note that the training is minimal and delivered right at the point where it's needed. In the commercial world this approach has its own acronym: JIT. Just In Time training is built on the idea that people retain the learning they put into practice immediately (and forget just about everything else). JIT training keeps to what the person needs to know and be able to do in the immediate. This equates to lots and lots of little bits of training, rather than huge slabs.

Of course, JIT training means people providing little bits of training all the time, so it means just about everyone in your team will need to be competent in the basics of instruction and supervision (you can train them just as they're about train someone else).

I was told once that the McDonalds Corporation never teaches anyone to do anything—they always teach people how to teach someone else, be it flipping burgers or asking, 'Do ya want fries with that?' I'm not sure if that was or still is true, but it's kind of genius.

Of course you can't be forever asking everyone to help just once without recruiting some people to teams and empowering them to ask others to help just once. Let's step through the process of development in four stages, and each stage has its own rhythm of involve, orient, equip, review.

Helper, Team Member, Helping Leader, Leader
At the lowest level of commitment is what I call the *helper*. These are the people who are being asked to help with simple tasks to see if they might want to help more regularly.

If they show some promise, interest and aptitude, you might invite them to a higher commitment: to become a regular *team member* ('involve'). If they agree, you give them the basic parameters: for example, the simple expectations of when, where and how often and what training they might need ('orient'). Depending on the complexity of the tasks and the risk management requirements, they may need to participate in a formal training process—but as far as possible, train on the job for each little part of the task ('equip'). After their first day serving on the team, and fairly frequently afterward, review their involvement and make sure they're happy and meeting your expectations ('review').

Once they've settled into serving on the team, you might invite them to *help* with a *leadership* task—just once (see where I'm going here?) And you walk them through involve, orient, equip, review for that task. If they show promise, you might give them another go at it, or at something else.

Once they've shown some promise across a range of leadership tasks, you might ask them to take on the *leadership* role while you go on annual leave (annual leave: the best delegation device ever!). Of course, you'll take them through involve, orient, equip and—when you return from leave—review.

A quick comment about large-group ministry preparation training. A number of churches with which I've worked have implemented large-group, rather generic ministry training programs. These are usually classroom-oriented and heavy on content (it's really hard to train for competency in big groups). From my observation and experience, this type of learning generally has fairly poor outcomes in terms of integration (that is, the content delivered has little lasting influence on the convictions and behaviours of the participants). Most people find it hard to translate theory into practice. Without further supervision and accountability, the content of large-group, classroom-style learning generally goes unimplemented.

The effectiveness of large-group learning can be improved markedly by individual coaching to follow up the content delivery. To make this work, you'll need to develop the coaching system and set up the coaching relationships in advance, so that coaching-for-learning-integration will occur fairly soon after the large-group session.

Large-group learning still misses out on the benefit to the person doing the training. If I deliver a session to a hundred people, I benefit from the preparation and delivery experience, and they might gain something from the content I deliver. But if a hundred people deliver JIT training 1:1 to a hundred others, two hundred people benefit, and the training generally has greater impact, because it's delivered right when it's required.

Somewhere in the middle of all this is small group learning, which is probably a workable compromise of efficiency and effectiveness. We'll talk more about that in the next chapter.

A word on leadership and authority

I'm conscious that much of this chapter seems much more geared for larger and more traditionally organised churches, and to a certain degree it is. I've already explored how in a smaller church (or any smaller organisation) there is less scope to concentrate solely on specialisation. It's also apparent that in more organically structured churches (which in general are fairly small so there is less need to systematise) there seems to be less need for formalised roles of responsibility and, dare I say it, leadership.

I will explore the idea and essence of leadership more in the next chapter, but the idea of deploying and supervising people presumes some kind of positional authority. In some circles, the ideas of position, authority and power trigger a kind of immune reaction—and not without good reason. I've taken some time to unpack this in Appendix 4. If words like 'position', 'authority' and 'power' make you antsy, you might want to detour to the appendix before going on.

Getting expectations clear

I'm sounding (unsurprisingly) like an old HR manager here. The number one reason people fail in newly delegated tasks is the failure of the person delegating to make their expectations clear. The number two reason is the failure of said delegator to give the new person appropriate feedback as to whether they're meeting expectations.

Those who have staff, either in a church role or in some other field of work, will recognise these two tasks as the basics of supervision. The first task of supervision is to get clear in your own mind what you expect of the person you're supervising. It sounds obvious, but it's amazing how many people try to hand off a task to someone without really understanding for themselves what it is they want the other person to do. I have lost count of the number of coaching conversations I've had with leaders about the poor performance of their staff. When I step them through the basics of supervision, more often than not they realise that their poorly performing staffer has only a vague idea of what is expected of them.

It's important enough for me to say it again. The first step of supervision (and therefore of delegation) is to be clear about what you expect of the person you're supervising. Skip this step and most well-meaning people will just try to do what they imagine you want. You would be amazed to discover just how creative some people's imaginations can be.

Once you're clear on your expectations, you can communicate them. A little tip here: it takes three times as long for people to get it as it does for you to explain it, so you had better be patient and find multiple ways of communicating. A general explanation followed by a quick demonstration followed by a step-by-step, slow-motion demonstration with explanation is usually what's required (this, of course, varies depending on the complexity of the task).

The task isn't delegated (that is, the person is not effectively trained and deployed) until you have at minimum observed them perform the task or discharge the responsibility successfully, and given them feedback to affirm that they've done as expected.

I haven't seen any studies to this effect, but I suspect that a proportion of workplace stress comes from people not knowing whether they're doing well or poorly (I'm guessing most people who get stressed at work worry that their boss is unhappy with them). The last thing volunteers at church need is more stress, so do them a favour and be clear.

Systems versus superstars

In his 1988 classic *The E Myth*, Michael Gerber argues for organisations to work by systems rather than relying on the talent and judgment of individuals.[40] While a church is not a business, there are some practical applications for E-myth thinking in churches, even small ones.

The central idea of systems in organisations is creating a standard way of doing things. You could argue that the Prayer Book is an attempt to guarantee the quality of church liturgy by standardisation (perhaps Cranmer was way ahead of his time).

On a more practical and localised level, creating standard ways of doing things enables people with fairly basic skills, even fairly basic literacy (you can create procedures and instructions with pictures), both to learn and to teach others the techniques and processes to perform most simple (and many not-so-simple) tasks to a fairly high standard.

While it may seem a little like creating a new book of rules, simple procedures help people feel confident that they're 'doing it right'. These procedures can be written instructions, a set of pictures or even a short video. It takes a bit of preparation, but it actually makes serving in ministry more accessible and helps people tackle new tasks with confidence.

Of course, you can't standardise everything, but you'd be amazed how roles and responsibilities in church life can be made easier to delegate by taking the time to create some instructions.

---

[40] Gerber, Michael E. *The E Myth: Why Most Businesses Don't Work and What to Do About It* (Harper Collins, New York, 1995).

Responsibility, authority, autonomy and ownership

While simple, repeated and routine tasks can be standardised with instructions (or 'E-mythed', as I like to say), there are limitations to standardisation. The limit has to do with adaptiveness. The more a role consists of a set of responsibilities as opposed to a set of tasks, the more it will require judgment: adaptive thinking tailored to the situation.

Ronald Heifetz writes around the idea of 'adaptive challenges' in contrast to what he terms 'technical problems'.[41] In simple terms, technical leadership is about applying a known solution to a defined problem—for example, if your car has a flat tyre, there's a well-known, commonly understood solution. (Some of you are thinking about chocks, jacks, spare wheels etc. and some are thinking 'Call roadside assistance'. Both are technical solutions.)

Adaptive leadership requires applying knowledge and skill where there is no well-worn path, or at least no certainty of outcome to any particular approach. There's a degree of uncertainty, ambiguity and unpredictability about it. It could be as simple a challenge as helping to resolve a conflict. While conflicts have some degree of pattern and process to them, each has its quirks, and application of a technique is no guarantee that the conflict will end. There's always more than meets the eye, always some 'seeking to understand', and it usually won't end until there's a change in the attitude and posture of the stakeholders. Adaptive leadership requires learning, collaboration and good judgment.

You can't E-myth your way through adaptive challenges. That means people with responsibilities that include adaptive challenges need sufficient authority and autonomy to learn, adapt and exercise judgment.

The limitation of standardisation has to do with human motivation. While standardisation makes training easier and increases the predictability of outcome, it works to some extent against the instincts that naturally motivate us: curiosity, autonomy and pursuing personal goals. Some management writers sum this up as 'ownership'.

---

[41] Heifetz, Ronald, Grashow, Alexander & Linsky, Marty. *The Practice of Adaptive Leadership: Tools and Tactics for Changing Your Organization and the World* (Harvard, Boston, 2009).

Ownership has become something of a holy grail in contemporary leadership and management theory. Organisational systems and learning guru Peter Senge uses the terms 'enrolment' and 'commitment' to describe the idea of people wanting the vision of the organisation to come to pass and being willing to do whatever is required to bring it to reality.[42] Another way of thinking about it is 'internalisation': the vision of the organisation making the transition from an externally applied idea that needs constant reinforcement to an internally held conviction that's 'owned' personally. Once a person owns the vision, all they need is resourcing and guidance.

Ownership is generally not achieved by standardisation. Standardisation will reliably get you compliance (all other things being equal). But ownership comes from being invited to bring much more of oneself than following directions. And here's where it gets tricky.

I've watched different churches opting for different priorities depending on their values. Some will prioritise standardisation—or at least predictability, usually framing it as 'excellence'. This translates into expecting high standards of performance and making high demands in terms of attendance at meetings. And it generally translates into a high degree of command and control.

The upside of this option is that stuff gets done, and it gets done well. Small groups will be well led, worship services will run like clockwork and finish on time, parents will feel confident leaving their kids in the crèche because good systems and good training ensure children are safe and happy. There really is a lot to like about this approach.

But some of you, as you read this, will be recalling experiences—lived or recounted—of the downside. The clue is in my use of the word 'demand'. The constant sense of high expectation often wears thin (it generally takes about a year and a half) and the willing workers start to feel a little exploited; they may begin to experience a little resentment, and it all goes downhill from there. In short, the standardisation/excellence model has a reputation for churning through workers. That's not true of everyone—some people will endure massive and relentless demand for years—and it's not true of every

---

[42] Senge, Peter M. *The Fifth Discipline: The Art and Practice of the Learning Organization*, rev. edn (Currency, New York, 2006).

church that values excellence. But there's enough evidence of it being a widespread risk that we need to be careful.

If you're in a church or movement of churches that's opted, by choice or default, for this approach, I'm not calling for its discontinuation. But I do encourage you to be careful of the degree of demand you make, and to look at how you can balance the demand with a high degree of support.

I do, however, want to flag that merely meeting the expectations of a supervisor (whether you're a volunteer or staff) will not, for most people, maintain motivation or build a sense of internalised vision. To achieve that, there needs to be scope for people to bring their own initiative, creativity and agency to their role. This generally means they'll need some scope to innovate, experiment and make their own judgment calls, which in turn requires a little less control and a little more scope for the predictability of 'excellence' to be eroded.

The flip side is to give creativity and agency more prominence, allowing people to shape things as their hopes and passions (or biases, traditions and preferences) lead them. You don't need to be the prophet Daniel to foresee the potential for problems here—and if you've been around churches for a while you're probably recalling the war stories even as you're reading.

The two big issues in this kind of culture are these: vision atomisation and conflict. It's generally necessary for people to have scope to shape their role according to their own values and strengths in order for them to genuinely *enrol* in the vision of the church. However, no one actually enrols in a concrete definition of the vision of the church or its leadership. Their enrolment will actually be in their *interpretation* of the vision as it's articulated. It's not too hard to imagine how, if sufficient scope is allowed, there will be a proliferation of interpretations, and over time a considerable divergence of understanding as to what realising the church's vision might actually look like. Leaders end up feeling like they're herding cats.

When the vision gets atomised, the differences in understanding begin to collide, which brings people into conflict. In the church planting scene, there's a kind of urban myth about 'the year-two fight'. Most of the plants I've coached have experienced some kind of conflict in their second or third year. The conflict is generally around interpretation of the vision or values originally articulated, even if they're not couched in those terms. The conversation generally goes something like this:

'We agreed that the church would ... '

'I never agreed to that.'

'But the vision statement in the original planting proposal says ... '

'Sure, but I though it meant ... '

And so it goes. Vision, mission, values and other statements setting out what Senge calls 'governing ideas' are helpful in that they set out where we're headed, what we're trying to achieve and the 'rules of engagement' in making the journey. But to be helpful, they need to be clear enough to guide decision-making and behaviour, and broad enough to allow people of different backgrounds and temperaments to find a place on the team where their personal values and priorities mesh with the church's governing ideas.

Neither a mindless herd nor herding cats
What's all this got to do with pathways and the 'serving in ministry' step? Plenty. To put it in context, let's summarise the past few pages.

- People will serve for longer and more effectively and will feel more satisfied if they serve according to 'giftedness'—the overlap of their skills, abilities, temperament and passion or however your theology defines it.
- Training is important to help people succeed in service. Training that is personal, specific, on the job and delivered in small bites tends to work best.
- Good supervision is essential to good performance. Making your expectations clear and giving clear feedback as to whether they've been met are the two basic processes of supervision.
- Standardising routine tasks makes them more easily learnt and transferred, but standardisation has limits and limitations.
- Giving people autonomy and scope to make their own decisions and exercise their own judgments gives them a greater sense of ownership, but too much freedom can lead to things going pear-shaped.

So we want training and standards so that people know what to do and what's expected (which actually reduces their stress) along with ownership without people going rogue: some degree of control, some degree of autonomy. We don't want a mindless herd, but neither do we want to be herding cats.

Where's the balance? Well, that (I say, stroking my beard sagely) is an adaptive challenge, not a technical problem. I can't give you procedure, but here are a few thoughts you may consider in contemplating the challenge.

Perhaps a metaphor would be a helpful start. Do you want to give people a line to walk or a field to play on? Some tasks need defined procedures and clearly delineated standards of performance—that is, you need to draw a line for people to walk. There are not that many jobs like this in a church community, and they're either elementary (for example, 'Here's how to operate the dishwasher') or to do with risk management (for example, every leader in playgroup must go through the Kidsafe program and get a Working With Children Check). Very few volunteers will last if their whole volunteering experience is doing exactly what a procedure demands and there is no scope to bring their own initiative.

Some tasks and responsibilities have a reasonably clear goal, but no mandated method to achieve it. It's like a game of football—kick the ball through the goal to succeed, and provided you play by the rules, the path you take is up to your own creativity and initiative. There may be skills, tools and techniques to learn, but everybody will bring them together uniquely. Quite a few of the roles and responsibilities around a church community are like this.

In these cases, accountability is more helpful than control. In other words, the aim is for people to take responsibility for the outcomes of their service, not just obey orders. The question becomes 'Do you think you achieved what we agreed to?' rather than 'Did you do as I told you?'

And that leads me to talk about relationship. Just doing a job as a volunteer tends to get old after a while. Too often, once a person has taken on a role we adopt a 'set and forget' posture and expect them to just keep on keeping on *ad infinitum.* Unless we're in regular thoughtful dialogue with volunteers, we're in danger of ignorance on two key fronts.

First, we may not know whether the person is fulfilling the task appropriately—that is, meeting expectations and staying within the 'fences' of policy and propriety. Eugene Peterson recalls how, when he suspected that his ministry reports were not being read by his superiors, he decided to spice them up a little. When there was still no feedback his 'reported' behaviour became increasingly outrageous. (Hopefully that's made you curious enough to read Eugene's wonderful book *The Contemplative Pastor*.[43])

For the sake of the health of the church and the safety of its participants, we need to maintain close enough relationships with people who serve in the church community to be able to vouch for the quality of their work.

Second, and perhaps more important, we need to keep in close enough touch to be cognisant of the state of their soul. Often a person's resignation, breakdown or spectacular failure seems to come as a complete surprise to those who are supposed to be watching over their welfare. It's all too common for people to throw themselves into ministry tasks and forget to cultivate their own spiritual life. This of course is doubly unhelpful. It means that the person's own soul begins to suffer, and their ministry will increasingly be based on skills, knowledge and duty, rather than being the outflow of God's action in their inner life. And that often leads to decreasing fruitfulness.

A close supervisory/mentoring relationship gives the leader opportunity to inquire as to the state of a person's soul and to ensure they are maintaining a sustainable balance of service and refreshment.

It's been said by psychologists that a person can endure a great deal of hardship if they can describe their experience to just one other interested person. While I'm not sure service in the church should be hardship per se, sometimes it is just plain hard. As leader or supervisor, I really do have a vested interest in the people for whom I am responsible. They're more likely to endure the tough times and grow in their maturity if they're confident that I understand and care about what it's like for them—both in the service for the kingdom and in their lives more generally.

---

[43] Peterson Eugene H. *The Contemplative Pastor: Returning to the Art of Spiritual Direction* (Eerdmans, Grand Rapids, 1989).

Further, as a leader I recognise that what's in my heart leaks out and effects those who follow me—in the words of Maxwell Smart—'for niceness or for evil'. If I have a heart of thankfulness and count it a privilege to serve, it's more likely that those serving on my watch will feel encouraged, supported and appreciated: and they'll likely share that with those they lead. What's in my heart will serve to foster an environment where everyone feels more positive and energised. Conversely, if I become disenchanted or cynical, the leaders in my area are likely to pick that up too. They may become discontented and de-motivated, or begin to feel unappreciated. They might just share that around, too, and in no time I've got a whole bunch of people offside.

Some leaders attempt mass encouragement with lots of 'stage energy' and 'good news' stories. This approach is okay as far as it goes, but in my part of the world (Aussies are famed for their slightly ironic cynicism), this can backfire if it's not matched with personal, sincere and thoughtful contact. It may be a little different in other parts of the world, but I suspect only a little (except in New Zealand, where they're even more suspicious than Aussies!).

Let me put it this way—and I'm going to take off my coach's cap and be blunt here: if you don't have time to be in fairly regular personal touch (minimum monthly) with the people who are directly responsible to you, be they staff or volunteers, your diary and probably your priorities need an overhaul. As leader it's your job to know what's going on with the people who are your direct 'reports', and to know what's going on you need to be in personal touch.

Another consideration as we think about the balance between control and initiative is to regularly (it will feel like constantly) articulate the God-given mission of the church, and the commonly understood process of ministry that your particular church embraces to fulfil that mission. The mission of every local church should be more or less the same: to continue the mission of Jesus in the world, which is to show compassion and make disciples. This is the reason the church does what it does—the answer to the 'why?' question. While this should be unforgettable, every community needs more or less constant reminders.

The ministry process of each local church is somewhat unique. Thom Rainer and Eric Geiger have done a great job spelling out the idea of ministry process in *Simple Church*. It's the answer to the question: how does this church show compassion and make disciples in this context at this time? Ministry process is usually formed by the tradition of the church, the formational experiences of the leaders and the characteristics of the context.

In one church the process of ministry might be built around inhabiting what Ray Oldenberg calls 'third places'.[44] This might mean a small team making a coffee house their lounge room, forming relationships with the staff and regulars, and seeking to live out the kingdom under their noses. Another church might have a ministry process built around enriching programs, offering a series of groups and classes to address people's needs and interests. Done well and in the appropriate context, both of these and dozens of other approaches can be effective. It's the answer to the 'how?' question.

However, effectiveness depends on a general agreement that this is the process the church will pursue, so the church as a community pulls in the same direction and various parts and activities integrate. Ministry process also needs constant reinforcement and explanation so that people can align their energy and initiative with the collective mission effort.

One of the best ways to do this, and in the meantime encourage everyone, is to tell stories. A church plant I'm coaching at the time of writing just celebrated a young woman making her first faith commitment. The church is loosely following the 3DM approach, so the planter could show how the ministry philosophy of the church was effective in providing a pathway for this woman to become a disciple. This kind of storytelling not only reinforces the ministry philosophy in people's minds, it gives them confidence that it's effective.

Let's pull these thoughts together.

People are more likely to be effective and stay engaged in serving the mission of Jesus if they serve according to their giftedness, with a clear understanding of their role and what's expected.

People are more likely to stay motivated and demonstrate ownership if they have sufficient autonomy to bring their own initiative and creativity to the role, and are guided through a supportive relationship.

---

[44] Oldenburg, Ray. *The Great Good Place* (Marlowe & Company, New York, 1991).

People are more likely to stay focused if they remain clear about the mission of the church—that is, 'why' we're doing this—and the ministry philosophy of the church—the 'how' we do this.

The dark side of ownership

Before I leave this section, let me take a few paragraphs to explore the dark side of ownership. If you've been around churches for a while, especially small churches, you've already seen this.

One little church with which I worked had a treasurer who would never seem to quite get a full and accurate set of accounts prepared. He would always be 'taking care of things' unofficially and 'just sorting out some details'. When the vicar finally called 'enough' and got someone else elected treasurer, the previous guy would not hand over the books. Being treasurer had gone from being a job, to a responsibility, to a source of identity and status.

Another church I served had a 'chief steward'. He had been 'chief steward' apparently since some time shortly after the First Fleet arrived. It was his job (among other things) to greet people at the door and say the offertory prayer (using exactly the same words every time). He was there every week and for every service and would insist on being accorded the right to greet and pray, even at youth services where everyone else present was his junior by more than five decades. A job had become a responsibility and gone on to become a right and privilege.

When roles become sources of identity and status, or a matter of rights and privileges, developing a culture of giving oneself in the service of Jesus becomes increasingly difficult.

Part of the leader's role is helping people remain clear that the service rendered in the Christian community (and hopefully everywhere else) is service to Jesus—an act of worship. Service is undertaken for his kingdom and his glory. Peter Senge said, 'In the absence of a great dream, pettiness prevails.' It takes ongoing effort to keep this thinking at the forefront so that people are more likely to pursue the great dream of the Kingdom of God and not get too attached to any particular role within it.

If a new believer has matured into a devoted follower of Jesus, serving in ministry for the sake of his kingdom, they're really only an invitation away from entering the sphere of leadership. This takes us to our final stage in the Pathways philosophy.

Chapter 10
Leading Ministry

The idea I want to explore in this chapter is the deployment, development and multiplication of leaders. Those words and their order are important. Important also is the absence of the words 'elect', 'educate' and 'employ'. I'll get to why in a minute.

John Maxwell believes everything rises and falls on leadership.[45] You might want to stop and ponder that for a second. Is it true? Even if it is only more or less true, the implications reach a long way. Assuming he's more right than wrong, leadership development has probably the second highest leverage factor of any activity in the leader's life.

In case you're wondering, the highest leverage activity is prayer—so says Bill Hybels in *Too Busy Not to Pray*.[46] Further, the leader you should be most committed to developing is you. While it's your own life for which you must primarily give account, I think there's an even more compelling reason to go to work on yourself. That reason is that the primary quality of leadership is character.

It's about character
In his multi-gazillion bestseller *The Seven Habits of Highly Effective People*, Stephen Covey laments that somewhere in the early 20th century the focus in leadership literature switched from character to technique.[47] He would be pleased, I think, with the apparent rediscovery of the importance of character for leadership in the wake on Enron, the Lehman Brothers and— unfolding as I write—the Volkswagen emission test defeat scandals.

In an increasingly shallow, cynical and corrupt world, people are looking for leaders they can trust, respect and perhaps even aspire to emulate. Before we begin to talk about process and content for developing leaders, it begins with you and me. We need to be leaders worth following.

---

[45] Maxwell, John C. *The 21 Indispensable Qualities of a Leader* (Thomas Nelson, Nashville, 1999).
[46] Hybels, Bill. *Too Busy Not to Pray* (IVP, Downers Grove, 1988).
[47] Covey, Stephen. *The Seven Habits of Highly Effective People* (The Business Library Melbourne. 1997).

And here's the catch if you're reading this as a young leader in seminary or early in your career, hoping to get the good oil on how to be an effective missional leader: character takes time. If Robert Clinton's research in *The Making of a Leader* is right, you'll still be wrestling with your character long after you've gained most of the knowledge, skills and techniques required for effective ministry. I'm nearly fifty. I can assure you, God's agenda in my life at the moment is almost entirely about character.

Knowledge and skills are so much quicker to master and integrate, yet capacity for influence without the character to direct that influence toward godliness can be courting disaster.

Having made the point that our first priority in leadership development is paying attention to our own development, the next point to make is about the kind of culture that is fostered by your own leadership.

Leadership versus pastoral culture

Whole denominations in Australia are suffering such a profound shortage of leadership that they're importing clergy from other countries. At the same time, attendance in the worship services of those denominations is generally in a fairly steep decline. Meanwhile, movements like the Pentecostals seem to produce an abundance of leaders and are growing at several times the population rate.

Let's take a second to get inside this. The difference can probably be most clearly seen in the priority of the respective church cultures. Declining churches tend to be characterised by what may be termed 'pastoral culture'. This is evidenced by words like 'together', 'family' and 'unity'. These churches tend to be very sensitive to the feelings of individual members and careful to avoid upsetting people. A good degree of energy goes into honouring the past. People are appointed to positions of influence (for example, church council) generally based on their years of attendance.

Ministry attention tends to be on avoiding complaints and ministering to the person who presents with the highest need. To get close to the minister, you need to have some kind of acute need. Some of you are reading this and beginning to feel defensive. Some are flipping to John 21:15ff. Stay with me for a second.

Churches in the faster-growing denominations can be characterised by what may be termed a 'leadership culture'. This is evidenced by words like 'vision', 'mission' and 'passion'. These churches put a lot of emphasis into getting things moving, creating a positive environment and often measuring results. A good degree of energy goes into creating a preferred future.

Ministry attention in these churches tends to be on executing plans and investing in the people with the highest potential. To get close to the minister you need to be willing to serve and to learn. I acknowledge that these same churches tend to be the ones we looked at earlier when we discussed possible downsides of an emphasis on excellence and getting demand out of balance with support. Being mindful of the risk of being overly demanding, I believe churches with a leadership culture have something to teach the rest of the Body of Christ.

As you read you may be wanting to remind me that Jesus was noted for his compassion, and that he came not to call the respectable 'high-potential' people, but outcasts. Well, yes and no. Let's take a closer look.

It's a little paradoxical that Jesus built his team of apostles from among those who were not quite from the mission focus group we examined earlier (disadvantaged Galilean Jews). Sure, they were Jewish and most of them were from Galilee. However, the majority were not outcasts, but like Jesus himself were middle class, or from the class comprised of merchants, artisans and those with some means of production. At least four of them were fisherman of sufficient means to own boats and have hired employees.

Sure, Jesus met plenty of need—but when it came to his leadership team, he seemed to go for potential. Further, these twelve men got the very best of his time.

When I teach this in colleges, I take the class on a little geographical study through the middle of Mark's gospel, from chapter 6:30 to chapter 8:30. I gave you a summary of this in chapter 2 when we were discussing ministry focus groups. Now I want to go over it in a little more detail (as my Dad used to say, the three keys to learning are repetition, repetition and repetition). If you have the time, pull out the passage and a map and trace it through with me. Watch for the patterns.

We begin with Jesus and his disciples tired from a big mission season and Jesus grieving the loss of his relative, John the Baptiser. Jesus and the twelve get into a boat and head off for a little R&R. The crowd sees them leave and runs around the lake to meet them. Jesus teaches, heals and feeds them, then dispatches the twelve in the boat in full view of the crowd before sending the crowd home.

Once they've gone and Jesus has a little downtime with the Father, he walks on the water to catch up with the twelve. Perhaps the walking-on-water miracle was not just a sign of his mastery over natural law, but an elaborate effort to give the endlessly needy crowd the slip. Certainly John's description of the crowd's relentless pursuit of Jesus fits this theory (John 6:22-24).

Alas, to no avail. A crowd forms at Gennesaret, and Jesus goes through the teaching and healing routine again (no miracle feeding this time, much to the chagrin of the people [John 6:25-42]). After dealing with yet another theological argument with the religious professionals, Jesus makes himself scarce, heading right out of the country to Tyre on the Phoenician coast.

He tries to remain incognito, but a desperate woman recognises him, and after some debate he heals her daughter. His cover blown, he immediately leaves before a crowd can form. Heading even further away, he stops in Sidon before making an about-turn and heading back to Galilee, straight over the lake and down into the region of the Decapolis—again, outside his home country, in a place away from his mission focus group.

In the Decapolis he's recognised again and people bring a deaf and mute man to him. Jesus pulls him aside to avoid creating a spectacle, heals him and tells him and his friends to keep quiet. But again Jesus' efforts to remain anonymous are thwarted. Another crowd forms, and feeling more compassion, Jesus feeds them too. Immediately he leaves to go back to Galilee. The Pharisees recognise him and predictably want to start another dispute. He refuses to play and sails up to Bethsaida.

There the pattern repeats. Jesus is recognised and asked for a miracle. He pulls the blind guy aside and does a kind of two-step miracle (I wonder if this was an attempt to dampen people's enthusiasm?). He tells the man to stay out of town to keep things quiet, and then slips out of the country again, this time all the way north to Caesarea Philippi (definitely not his mission focus group). Once there he finally gets a bit of time alone with the twelve.

It's pretty obvious that Jesus was not out there looking for more needy people. In fact, the evidence in the text points the other way. He was trying to avoid the crowd to get some time with the twelve. At the end of his ministry, the thousands who came to listen and be healed had largely dissipated back to their respective towns. Perhaps they were among those reached by the apostles after the resurrection. But while Jesus was walking the earth as a rabbi, his first priority was the twelve men to whom he would entrust the future of God's redemptive plan for humanity.

I'm not pretending that my ministry or yours is as seminal to the future of humanity as that of Jesus, but as the ambassadors entrusted with the mystery hidden for ages and revealed in Christ, we should probably take our little corner of God's plan just as seriously.

Like Jesus, you may need to go to extraordinary lengths to get away from the incessant needs of the crowd and congregation to make time with your key leaders. In my observation, senior ministers and the planters of growing churches are much more likely to put their best time and effort into their key leaders and those leaders they're seeking to develop. Senior ministers and planters who get swept up in the ocean of need will reach the end of their capacity before they see the end of the need.

I've heard pastors boast that they work 168 hours a week (yep, I've actually heard ministers say that) because they're always on call. I usually cock my head to one side and ask them if they're seeing someone to help them with that. Being the ultimate resource for your congregation creates a culture that inadvertently rewards poor functioning.

Ephesians 4 seems to indicate that the role of vocational ministers (God's gift to the church, apparently: see vv. 9-11) is to prepare others for works of service (v. 12), not just do the work ourselves. Pastor-teachers who run themselves ragged doing the pastoral and teaching work without preparing others are caught in an ultimately self-defeating cycle.

Let me stop here for a second and get a little more serious. Some of you are reading this and saying to yourselves, 'That's all well and good, but you don't know my situation. You don't feel the weight of expectation. You don't know how scarce talent is in my church.' You're right, I don't. But I think we both know—if we're prepared to confront the brutal facts—that maintaining a pastoral culture and trying to meet everyone's needs and expectations is very likely either to burn you out or see your church age and gradually die off, perhaps both. You might buck the trend, but the weight of recent history is against you.

If you feel like it's you that I'm talking to, please get yourself a competent ministry coach who can help you sort this out. Life is too short.

Much of what we learn in seminary is about ministry skills—the skills to be able to do the works of service to build up the body of Christ. It's all well and good, but it's miles short of what is required. As leaders our focus must be on preparing and empowering others.

Further, if our churches are to grow, we will very soon reach the limits of our capacity to prepare others for works of service—and our role will need to move to preparing others to prepare still others for works of service. Tom Peters said, 'Leaders don't make followers—they make more leaders.'

If Maxwell is right and everything really does rise and fall on leadership, we'd better develop a fairly consistent supply of competent and godly leaders or the rising will eventually give way to falling.

If you're serious about missional leadership, you need to be serious about developing leaders. And if you're serious about developing leaders, you'd better become very serious about the development of your own character. Congratulations. You just signed up for the long haul.

And so we come to leaders and leadership. I guess a working definition might be a good place to start.

Leaders: the people other people follow
In the simplest terms, a leader is someone who is followed. I know, that's kind of obvious, but the implications are not. Following, as it turns out, takes some thinking about.

Following is to some extent a giving up. As a follower of Jesus I give up my discretion on a variety of issues and take on my best understanding of his positions. This includes my opinions about morality, priority and ultimately reality. It might mean taking positions for which I can't provide a cause-and-effect rationalisation. As a disciple of Jesus, I willingly give up my 'right' to make my own call on everything and submit myself to him. If I'm not doing that, I'm not really following him.

The benefits of following Jesus are articles of faith. I can't empirically prove that I will be with Jesus for eternity, but I have reason to believe I will. Neither can I prove beyond all doubt that living by Jesus' teaching will result in a better life for me and a better society than if I just live life by my own judgment. But the overwhelming body of evidence points that way.

Following is always a giving up of an individual right or privilege in order to get something perceived as more beneficial—otherwise it's coercion. Jesus invited the fishermen to come with him (the implication being to give up fishing, and the secure income it represented). Apparently being up close with Jesus and learning to fish for their fellow man was better than earning a good living with boats and nets. When the going got tough and Jesus started to say some difficult things, he wondered out loud whether those same fishermen might want to reconsider. Peter still saw the original deal as a good one: 'Lord, to whom shall we go? You have the words of eternal life' (John 6:68).

'Following' in the Christian community can become a little complex. Trace this line of logic with me. The apostle Paul urges the church in Corinth to follow him as he follows Christ (1 Corinthians 11:1). We hold this up as exemplary leadership. It could be that an elder in the church at Corinth urges the Corinthian congregants to 'Follow me as I follow Paul who follows Christ.' Then an up-and-coming leader in the Corinthian congregation could say, 'Follow me as I follow the elder who follows Paul who follows Christ.' It's beginning to sound like the old woman who swallowed the fly.

At the same time each of us is seeking through prayer and study of the scripture to follow Jesus directly. So our leadership is shaped by leaders we follow (and the authors we read) who are following other leaders. Meanwhile, we're all trying to follow Christ.

There are a bunch of authors I've quoted to you whose thinking I've found helpful. I don't 'follow' them to any great extent, other than allowing them to shape my thinking. In so doing I give up only a fraction of my perceived right to original thought.

However, in my invitation to take up leadership in the local church, I could be asking people (directly or indirectly) to give up some fairly important resources in terms of time, effort, money and lifestyle choices. They had better see some benefit.

As we think about following, it involves the same kind of personal change or repentance that we discussed all the way back in the 'Embracing the Gospel' chapter. Let's give that a little more thought.

Maxwell boils leadership down to a simple idea: influence. A leader is a person who influences another. How do we determine influence? Generally by the degree of change evident in another person attributable to their interaction with the leader (or the leader's ideas).

As a leader in both my local church and in a denominational setting, why would people be influenced by me? What is it about their interactions with me (or my ideas) that might lead them to give up aspects of their rights and freedoms, or their time or money, or to change their ideas or priorities or behaviours? When you stop and think about it, there's a fair bit at stake.

Let's think back to 'following-leaders-who-follow-Jesus-while-following-Jesus-ourselves'. Why did people follow Jesus? And by that I mean, what led that 120 to gather in the upper room after the ascension? I can only guess at this, but here is my best shot: Jesus was compelling.

People marvelled at him being very different to the other religious teachers. Sure, he taught with authority (Mark 1:27), but he also had apparently inexhaustible compassion (Mark 6:34). While other religious leaders loaded people up with guilt and obligation (Luke 11:46), Jesus invited them to walk beside him and learn (Matthew 11:28-30).

Jesus was shocking in a way that delighted the crowds—sticking it to the religious elite (Mark 12:37), throwing out the religious racketeers (John 2:13-17) and affording profound dignity and tenderness to a grateful woman while gently rebuking the self-righteous Pharisee (Luke 7:36-56).

Sometimes he was crazy-brave (John 8:58) and other times he showed wise discretion (Matthew 21:27).

And overarching all of this was deep love that told the truth and offered comfort and confronted the worst and brought out the best and persevered and forgave and entrusted and laughed and cried and served. And in the end was tortured and abused and executed.

While thousands were healed by Jesus, and thousands more heard his teaching, those 120 were the ones who had walked with him long enough to experience his love over and over. They followed him because apparently it was worth everything to be his friend.

It's obvious that none of us can hold a candle to Jesus for the sheer compelling nature of his life and presence. But if we're to take Paul's example seriously, the bedrock of what leadership means in the Christian context is to bid others to 'follow me as I follow Christ'. And that goes a long way beyond Bible knowledge, exegetical ability and preaching skills. If a leader is someone who has followers, then to be effective leaders, we need to be worth following.

As we turn our attention to the art and science of developing leaders worth following, we must bear in mind that we first need to have lives that are both compelling and exemplary, for we will reproduce after our own kind.

Leaders: how do you get them?

Getting leaders is a lot like getting food. The least sophisticated and least reliable method is to hunt and gather. This means hoping people with the right character and skills will cross your path (that is, wander into your worship service or one of your other activities) and accept your series of invitations to take on more and more responsibility.

Heaps of churches take this approach. Most are small. Many have leaders at cross purposes with the overall direction of the church. Often churches that just hope good leaders will turn up elect whoever is willing to stand—and so their boards, councils, diaconates, elderships or whatever their leadership group is termed can look more like the cast of the *Vicar of Dibley* than the church at Antioch. And that's why I'm not so big on simply electing leaders.

Hunter-gatherers sometimes figure out that there's better hunting in the territory of an adjoining tribe. So they quietly pop over and see what they can bag. Churches do this too: sometimes in rather underhanded ways.

Of course, you can get your leaders like most of us get our food—rock down to the supermarket (seminary) and purchase pre-packed, sometimes highly processed leaders. This is generally the preserve of wealthy churches, and pre-processed leaders are generally rather expensive. Although they're the ideal solution for a church that wants to increase ministry capacity quickly, simply buying in the labour tends to 'professionalise' ministry.

Most seminary graduates are trained to provide excellent sermons and highly skilled pastoral care. Perhaps that's just what's required for a congregation that expects excellent religious services. However, most seminary training is less likely to train leaders that encourage and empower disciples who make disciples just for the love of Jesus and humanity. That's why I'm a little wary of educating-and-employing as a leadership development strategy.

Which takes us back to the metaphor of farming. Farming leaders means developing the disciples in your church into leaders—that is, growing leaders 'from scratch'. It's not a new idea. At least as far back as the Celtic monks, Christian leaders have sought to grow new leaders from those who come to faith through their mission process. This tradition was replicated among the Wesleyans and in the early days of the Salvation Army, and it continues today in movements of cell churches, simple churches and most of the Pentecostal movements.

Just as farming food has meant reliable food supply for sustaining civilisations, so farming leaders enables a ready supply of leadership to sustain the church and enable growth.

You may be thinking, 'I've heard all this before.' Before you start flicking pages, stay with me for a minute—there's some hitherto unpublished content about to be revealed. Through my study of various churches and movements that have intentionally and consistently produced leaders over years and decades, a consistent pattern has emerged. It can be summarised as 4 Cs: Context, Community, Curriculum and Coaching.

Let's take these one at a time. As we go, you might want to evaluate what you already have in place.

1. Context
The overwhelming majority of effective 'leadership farms' I've observed operate on the basis of apprenticeship. Learning is on the job, so emerging leaders need a job to be on. Paul urged Timothy to test people before appointing them to a role such as deacon (1 Timothy 3:10). Apprenticeship allows for a period of testing and exploration before anointing a person as a leader.

This is pretty much the reverse of the way we've traditionally trained vocational ministers and professional people in general. The inherited thinking has been to learn about the job before you do it.

Here's the catch. Most people find it near-impossible to translate theory into practice (which is why, if you really want to make the most of this book, you would do well to get a coach and a peer learning community—but more on that in a minute).

This is not a ground-breaking insight. You've probably spoken to an old-school, hospital-trained nurse who has lamented that newly minted grads from the nursing degree courses in university know a lot of theory but are not much use on the wards. And it's not just nursing. In my field of HR, the degree is the ticket to ride, but you begin to learn how to actually manage HR as a business discipline once you get into the workforce.

If you want to raise up leaders in your church, be it a corporate-sized mega-church or a cell network, give people some responsibility and opportunity to exercise some influence. If you cast your mind back to the previous chapter, where we talked about the sequence of involve, orient, equip and review, you might consider using the same process here. Ask a person to do a small leadership task just once, orient them to the task, give them the minimum equipping they need to succeed, and review afterwards.

Here's an example of how involve, orient, equip, review might work in practice. Let's imagine a task is to organise a community service event. Remember, this is a leadership assignment, not just 'helping'. You could begin by inviting the person to consider leading the event (it's probably going to be someone who was involved in helping run the previous one). If they accept, you might talk over the basic parameters of the event with them and perhaps send them away for a week to sketch out their best shot at a game plan. If yours is an E-myth kind of church, there may already be a flowchart or a checklist for such assignments.

A little while later you meet to discuss their plan, coaching them through the various aspects and helping them to rethink aspects that may not be appropriate or realistic, and to fill in the missing bits. In the time leading up to the event, you might keep in touch with them to provide encouragement and support.

Once the event has been run you could meet with the leader, debrief, discuss learning and (if they showed some ability and potential) wonder with them whether they might want to take on another leadership role.

What you didn't do was immediately anoint them as community outreach pastor, hand them a file of random ideas and say, 'Go for it'. We've all heard the success stories of this approach, and most of us have seen the disasters.

Apprenticeship as a development model allows for action-reflection learning, and gives space for mistakes to be made before the stakes are too high. It also enables people to explore their gifting and vocation before they've invested too much in one particular field.

As a learning model, apprenticeship throws up a series of learning challenges in the midst of the growing responsibilities assigned to the apprentice. The most effective form of learning is a situation where a person has a strong need or motivation to learn because they require the knowledge and skills immediately. You'll remember we talked earlier about JIT learning. It's effective because there is minimal lag between the cognitive acquisition and behavioural practice. The longer the distance between these two, the less effective the learning (and remember my story about unit circle trigonometry).

2. Coaching

Leaders develop more reliably right across their lifespan when they participate in empowering relationships. I've already described how important coaching has been for me, and how you are reading this book because I got myself a coach to keep me on track to write it.

At its best coaching pulls together a number of powerful dynamics. I spoke earlier about balancing support and demand. We have higher expectation of leaders than we do of helpers and workers. Greater responsibility and greater visibility unavoidably make the task of leadership more demanding. The higher degree of demand must be balanced by a higher degree of support. The upside is that highly demanding, highly supportive environments tend to produce a higher rate of development and lead to high performance.

Think for a minute about an institution like the Australian Institute of Sport (if you're not in Australia. I'm sure your country will have either national or code-specific sporting academies to develop high-end talent). At the AIS there is a lot of demand. If you're in one of their programs, you will turn up at training and you will stick to your diet and you will submit yourself to a whole range of disciplines to help you become your best. At the same time, there is a lot of support: coaches for skills, fitness and tactics; psychologists, masseurs and dieticians. There's a lot of expectation and a lot of help. And the performance is generally pretty high.

Coaching is one of the most effective means of providing a balanced demand–support environment. It's just a case of being clear on how much demand a person is willing and able to sustain, and providing support to match.

Much has been written about the benefits of action-reflection learning. Apprenticeship provides a context for this to take place, and coaching contributes to the process. Good coaches ask thoughtful questions that invite a person to think hard. As a coach I love to see a client draw breath and look skyward. I know the question I've asked has got them working, and hopefully learning: thinking fresh thoughts, making connections and gaining new insights.

Coaching is also a pretty useful process for supervision, which raises the question, 'Can a supervisor be a coach?' It's a question that's hotly debated among my coaching buddies. Here's my take on it. Coaching works as a supervisory method about seventy per cent of the time—in other words, if you're a supervisor, about seventy per cent of the time you spend face-to-face with one of your direct reports you can ask questions informed by a coaching framework, and that will serve your team member or employee very well.

I just know you're going to ask me about the remaining thirty per cent. Here are a few things supervisors need to do that coaches don't. Critically, a supervisor must make the job expectations clear, and give feedback about the worker's performance in meeting those expectations. In the case of paid staff, this may occasionally require banging the table, or even firing them. Also, as a supervisor, sometimes you need to 'go in to bat' for your worker, which may mean advocating for them further up the chain of command or supporting them through crises. A supervisor has broader responsibilities than a coach.

The bottom line? As a supervisor, you can't just assume a coach will take care of all of your responsibilities. You'll still need to provide some degree of oversight.

A coach can and will sometimes double as a mentor. This is especially important with younger leaders. What's the difference? It depends on your framework, but here's mine. A coach's primary mode of influence is to ask questions that invite deep thought and reflection. A mentor's primary mode of influence is to share experiences from which the younger leader can learn. I'm game to coach just about anyone, but I will only mentor people younger than myself.

In developing leaders, there is a necessary place for what may be termed 'wise counsel'. Sometimes you can use questions to help a person steer a straight, and sometimes they just won't get it and you'll need to express your own opinion. If you can tell a story to illustrate and/or refer them to the thinking of one wiser still, all the better. Strictly speaking, offering 'wise counsel' isn't coaching, but it's an important part of helping leaders through their development. Just be careful to ensure you're not doing their work for them or depriving them of learning. A bloody nose is sometimes the best teacher.

A further benefit of coaching is to help the emerging leader gain some insight into their unique giftedness and vocation. This can be a joy, as the reflection process helps the emerging leader gain insight as to how God has made them powerful. And sometimes it's hard yards, where the emerging leader comes to realise the limits of their ability, capacity and perhaps even potential. A coach who's willing to ask the hard questions can sometimes save a young leader from a very painful and costly side-track.

3. Community
Truth be known, I'm a bit of a lone wolf. I do a lot of solitary stuff, from hiking and biking to swimming and running. I can easily slip into the illusion of self-sufficiency (until I try to lose a few pounds or get a book written). I'm regularly reminded and at times surprised at the seemingly inexplicable benefit people derive from learning in community.

Yet the evidence is everywhere. As I write I'm part of a reading group that's working through Roberta Gilbert's *Extraordinary Leadership*.[48] Even though I've read it at least twice before, I'm reading it through part-by-part along with the rest of the group. And though I've read more than a dozen books on family systems theory (on which Roberta's work is based), I'm learning more than before. There is something about the interaction that enhances the learning experience.

Learning communities—or as they've recently been termed, 'communities of practice'—have become increasingly popular in a huge variety of fields. Their origins can be traced back to medieval times and perhaps further, when artisans would form communities around a master. Rather than being a simple master-apprentice arrangement, the master's studio-workshop was somewhat similar to the Greek notion of an *oikos*—a household of extended family and employees.

In their study of apprenticeship as experienced in communities of craftsmen, anthropologists Jean Lave and Etienne Wenger observed that such communities acted as a kind of living curriculum for apprentices. They coined the term 'communities of practice' to describe contexts where practitioners gather to enrich and extend their knowledge, skills and experience.[49]

Communities of practice tend to be resource-rich, where everyone has an opportunity to learn from everyone else, even though experience and training may vary. Rather than a group of students simply being instructed by a single teacher, the journey of inquiry, discovery and mastery is lived out together.

In a larger church setting, this may mean involving interns in some of the functions of the senior leadership team. For this to be effective the team must learn together, not simply 'do business'. In smaller churches or missional communities, it may mean bringing apprentices along to regional networks or huddles where peer learning and accountability take place.

---

[48] Gilbert, Roberta M. *Extraordinary Leadership: Thinking Systems, Making a Difference* (Leading Systems Press, Falls Church, 2006).
[49] http://wenger-trayner.com/introduction-to-communities-of-practice/

Individually focused, maven-like people such as myself can get a little lost, beavering away on our own projects. A learning community for leaders, or 'leadership community', helps me to lift my head, see that I'm part of something much bigger and notice that I'm almost certainly missing some stuff. Annoying as it may be for me, it's common for group interactions to remind me of the things I already know but have forgotten to incorporate. Just yesterday I felt a pang of dismay as a gracious bishop put the case to 'interrogate reality' as a balance to my plan to 'begin with the end in mind'. Both are important, and I had forgotten one of them. It took being part of a larger group for me to regain my perspective.

Leadership communities also have an accountability dynamic that is often more implied than explicit. Even if no one is eyeballing me and asking me to give account for my actions and priorities, there's a kind of positive peer pressure to keep pace with the rest of the team. If I sense I'm lagging a little, I'll take some steps to lift my game. This doesn't work for everyone, but anecdotes suggest that if works for most.

I've also watched leadership communities provide a level of pastoral care that far exceeds what might be achieved one-to-one. I confess I'm not pastorally gifted (some would suggest I'm pastorally challenged). I'm more likely to suggest a civil engineering solution (build a bridge and get over it) or perhaps a domestic appliance solution (buy yourself a vacuum cleaner and suck it up) than to sit for too long with a person's complaint. And sometimes I just completely miss what's going on.

Fortunately most of the leadership communities I've led have included pastorally gifted people who are much more attuned to people's emotional state. I've marvelled at their ability to pick up a nuance (to them it's a flashing red light and warning buzzer, but to me it's practically imperceptible) and act to provide what psychologists call a 'holding space' where a person's distress can be expressed and processed without them being 'fixed'.

As leaders we need to recognise our limits. The emerging leaders I mentor need the ministry of other leaders with different gifts to balance my peculiar strengths and deficits. The church needs leaders like Jesus, not just copies of me (or you), and it will take a community of leaders to shape them.

Being part of an authentic community that provides both care and challenge helps leaders at every stage of the development process to keep growing and to overcome the challenges that would otherwise take them out of ministry.

I've trained and coached a large number of church teams through the development of a leadership farm. As you've read, it's not rocket science. But it does take discipline, particularly the discipline of scheduling leadership community and sticking to it (remember in the last chapter the extraordinary lengths Jesus went to to get time with his team?). The number-one-by-a-country-mile reason why leadership development initiatives in local churches fail is that more urgent, more anxiety-laden stuff gets in the way.

For leadership community to be effective it needs to be monthly at minimum, and it needs to be sacrosanct (that is, it simply never gets cancelled). If Jesus was prepared to traipse all over to get away from the urgent for the sake of the important—putting his crew's development before the crowd's needs—then, I would humbly suggest, so should you.

4. Curriculum

Most leadership development programs begin with curriculum and learning materials. Rock down to your local Christian bookshop and they'll likely have a whole shelf of leadership development materials, from books by John Maxwell to multimedia kits from mega-churches. Just for fun I googled 'christian leadership development resources' and in a third of a second I got more than five million results.

If curriculum alone was going to deliver us all the leaders we need to fulfil the mission of the church, then surely we'd have got the job done by now, Jesus would have returned and we'd all be in heaven blowin' horns (this may not fit your eschatology or taste in music, but you get the idea). However, provided you're willing to provide context, coaching and community, some consideration of curriculum can be helpful. Helpful, but nowhere near as critical as you might think.

One of the exemplar churches I studied in developing the material in this chapter did a superb job with context, coaching and community, even asking people to give up a day a week to serve and participate in peer learning. They produced dozens of highly competent leaders every year, and some of those leaders are now in senior roles at the denominational level.

Their curriculum? Four books: just four, read over two years. And in case you're wondering, they were these: *The 21 Irrefutable Laws of Leadership* by John Maxwell, *Courageous Leadership* by Bill Hybels, *Spiritual Leadership* by J. Oswald Sanders and *The Making of a Leader* by J. Robert Clinton. You'll note that these four books are primarily concerned with character, not skill, strategy or technique.

Did that provide all the information and wisdom they'll ever need? Nope. Or form all the skills necessary for a lifetime of ministry? Not remotely. But it didn't need to. People have a surprisingly finite capacity to integrate new learning, so there's no point inundating their minds with more information than they can put to use.

Taking it slow and reading in community socialises participants into the habit of reading to understand and to integrate, not just reading to get useful quotes for an essay. Developing the habit of how to read for impact is possibly more important than the actual content you set.

It's important to keep in mind that the formal curriculum is only a small part of the leadership development process. Remember how Lave and Wenger found that communities of practice provided a living curriculum for apprentices? The mission and ministry context in which the apprentice leader is serving should throw up a steady stream of learning challenges that can be addressed in coaching and leadership community. Sooner or later a leader needs to be a self-motivated learner. Trying to create a comprehensive curriculum is probably over-functioning.

That said, you may want to consider some basic leadership skills as part of the curriculum. These could be anything from leading a group meeting to time management. You may also want to consider some knowledge and understanding, but I counsel you to keep this to a minimum. People are much more likely to retain knowledge if it's associated with an immediate challenge or opportunity. Your chances of perfectly timing the content to meet their challenges and opportunities are pretty slim.

You may also want to think about the habits and disciplines that would be helpful to foster in the life of your leadership community. The exemplar church I mentioned before had their people learn a memory verse every couple of weeks. Although it's a discipline that's dropped out of favour (and would definitely earn the label 'daggy' in an Aussie youth church), it's a powerful means for renewing of the mind.

I know I spent a while talking about personal devotional habits in the 'Following Jesus' chapter, but it's really common for people to allow these to lapse. Reinforcing personal spiritual disciples at the leadership level is a helpful thing to do. If in doubt, ask yourself whether you really want people leading significant chunks of your church who don't engage the thoughts of God and pray most days.

And while we're talking personal disciplines, now's a good time to reprise the high-support/high-demand paradigm. For leadership community to be effective, a higher degree of accountability is required than you might expect of your average disciple. At the 'Following Jesus' stage of development, you can encourage and ask tough questions, but the support-demand level is reasonably low. You're not going to give up on a person who fails to develop a daily devotional habit (well, not straight away).

However, when we're developing leaders—to revisit the athletic metaphor—we're wanting to think more 'athlete' and less 'social player'. That means some basic standards of conduct and personal discipline will be required to stay a part of the leadership or emerging leadership group.

It's up to you the exact standards you set, but I would encourage you to link them to some extent to your curriculum. If you're learning about some idea (say, time management) you should expect the participants to be implementing their learning, and the community should expect that there is clear behavioural evidence (for example, 'Show me your model week—where does your devotional life and reading fit in? How effectively are you implementing the plan?').

If an emerging leader is fairly consistently failing to implement their learning, it may be time for what Susan Scott calls a 'fierce conversation'.[50] As a leader you will get what you tolerate—and if you tolerate leaders essentially 'hearing but not practising', as Jesus discussed in Matthew 7:24-27, well, that's what you'll get. Read the simile in Matthew's gospel and it's a scarily accurate prediction of where you might end up.

---

[50] Scott, Susan. *Fierce Conversations: Achieving Success at Work and in Life Once Conversation at a Time* (Berkley, Ney York 2004)

To sum up the last few paragraphs: make sure your accountabilities match your curriculum or you'll be merely educating people about leadership, not forming leaders.

While we're thinking about curriculum, let's take a minute to think about delivery. First, let's think about the form of the content.

While those four books worked for the church I introduced earlier, George Patterson, working with barely literate farmers in Honduras, used what amounted to cartoons to train an army of disciple-making leaders. At every stage, think about your mission context, and tailor every aspect of your pathway to the people you're reaching and subsequently developing as leaders.

This means your curriculum may include everything from books to multimedia to seminars to whatever else works for your group. And while we're thinking about 'whatever works for your group', let's have a think about experiences.

Jesus' ministry with the twelve was a kind of extended road trip, stretching over a couple of years, perhaps a little more. While it included sitting in on a fair bit of teaching, there was plenty of 'road time' talking to Jesus and some short-term assignments: 'Out you go, two by two with no money or resources, and let me know how it turns out.' As it happens, it turned out surprisingly well.

Such short-term challenges stretch faith and teach young leaders to rely on God. This is not a justification for throwing underprepared emerging leader to the wolves, but it is an encouragement to give leaders an opportunity to go some way beyond their own comfort and into a space where they may 'get to the end of themselves'. Just make sure it's short-term, and there is plenty of space to pull out if it gets too difficult. It's also prudent to schedule in some recovery time afterward to debrief.

Taking emerging leaders with you into all kinds of circumstances is useful for their development—from basic pastoral visitation (if that's what you do) to getting them to carry your bags when you teach a class or lead a workshop.

You may also consider 'liminal experiences' like short-term ministry trips. These can be deeply formative if they're conducted thoughtfully. While I'm not a fan of what I've heard termed 'whitebait' mission, exposure to a different culture or circumstance for the purpose of learning, reflection and formation have been pivotal events in the lives of a number of leaders I know.

Ongoing development

While the early stages of leadership development can be quite intensive, it's important to think about ongoing development of leaders at every level and development stage in your sphere of influence. A leader never really outgrows the need for the 4 Cs.

In this respect, the 'leading ministry' step could be broken into any number of steps that address leadership development, from a leader of a small group with limited responsibilities, to a leader with multiple strata of leadership within their responsibilities.

For the sake of simplicity, the Pathways model doesn't set out to provide a map for leadership development over the lifespan. There are plenty of others who have done excellent research on this area. I recommend that every leader read and understand Robert Clinton's theory of leadership emergence set out in *The Making of a Leader*. It's perhaps most helpful if read by those over thirty-five.

The foregoing notwithstanding, leaders who are not developing are stagnating, and leadership stagnation tends to be a somewhat contagious malaise. The most common indicator of stagnation is a leader's choice of conversational topic. When the conversation becomes less about the leader's own learning, hopes, challenges, goals and questions and more about the shortcomings, failures and ineptitude of others (particularly those in authority, and even more particularly those in denominational roles like bishops and superintendents), there's a good chance the leader is experiencing some kind of 'stuckness'. You can do some research on projection phenomena in dispersed hierarchies once you're through reading this book.

A further indication of plateau is distraction—the leader who either has their fingers in a number of different pies or who is constantly looking for pies into which to insert their fingers.

Leaders of leaders do well to keep an eye out for these indicators, and treat them as an opportunity to introduce some challenge in the life of the stagnating leader, preferably in the area of their core responsibilities. (Some of the 'professional development' I've observed, which amounts to deepening knowledge of finely grained and rather peripheral theology seems to entrench stagnation rather than challenge it.)

One of the most important responsibilities of a leader, and even more so for leaders of leaders, is to *personally* be continually growing in wisdom and developing in capacity, and to ensure that the leaders you're developing and leading are also continually growing in wisdom and developing in capacity.

God will provide you with no shortage of opportunities for development. The difficulty lies in seeing challenges—be they shaped as possibilities or problems—as opportunities to become more mature, more competent and more like Jesus. A culture that encourages and intentionalises ongoing development is far less vulnerable to the corrosive effects of stagnation.

Leadership fatigue and disenchantment

Before I finish this chapter, let me address for a few minutes the issues around fatigue and disenchantment. You'll note my intentional avoidance of the over-used and highly emotive term 'burnout'.

Some in leadership roles are particularly vulnerable to saying 'yes' to every opportunity and invitation. As a leader it's important to be mindful of my own tendency to be attracted to the new and shiny opportunity. It's also important to be aware of this tendency in those I lead, and to gently hold them accountable to limiting their commitments to that which is sustainable.

Too many responsibilities, or even too much delegated responsibility, is not the only cause of leaders feeling fatigued, overwhelmed and wanting to quit. While it's common for leaders to experience these impulses just in the normal ebb and flow of life (because the challenges that bring growth tend to also bring discomfort), it also common for leaders to feel overwhelmed because they're taking responsibility for things they should leave in the hearts, hands and heads of others.

Proponents of family systems theory call this 'over-functioning' and several volumes could be written dealing with this phenomenon and providing guidance in dealing with it. The good news is that such volumes have already been written. Just as I believe every leader would do well to read Clinton, so I recommend every leader should learn to 'read' their organisation as an emotional field (some people may say 'minefield', but that's another issue).

If you're exclusively in the ministry space, a great place to begin with family systems is Roberta Gilbert's *Extraordinary Leadership.* If you're leading laypeople who might operate more in the business world, Jeff Miller's *The Anxious Organization: Why Smart Companies Do Dumb Things* is a good place to begin.[51]

In my experience, it's not workload or stagnation per se that causes people to feel overwhelmed and drop out—it's anxiety. Family systems theory is the best approach I have seen to help leaders make sense of inevitable anxieties they will both observe and experience.

To pull the main ideas of this chapter together, let's remind ourselves that developing leaders should be one of our highest priorities, because it expands the capacity of the church. Jesus went to enormous lengths to make time with his team a priority.

While we can hunt and gather leaders, or try to buy them off the shelf, Jesus' example and the example of effective movements throughout history is that leaders are best 'farmed'. Effective leadership farms include emerging leaders being in a leadership context, being coached, participating in a leadership community and learning a basic curriculum.

---

[51] Miller, Jeffrey. *The Anxious Organization: Why Smart Companies Do Dumb Things* (Facts On Demand Press, Tempe, 2002).

Part 3
Implementation

Chapter 11
Leading the Learning

So we come to the question of making all this work on the ground. I've written this section assuming that you, the reader, will have a significant role in the implementation process. As you read, if you get the impression that I'm talking to church leaders and church planters who'll be putting these ideas to work in their congregations, you're right—I am. If you don't fit that description (for example, if you're a seminary student), please accept my apologies. I respectfully request that you make the effort to translate.

To begin, take a deep breath and remind yourself of Ronald Heifetz's adaptive leadership concept.[52] For our purposes, Pathways theory might be *technical* but implementation is *adaptive*. What I mean is this: treat your implementation as a series of experiments or pilot projects. Whether you get the results you expected or not, treat your efforts as learning opportunities. This not only takes the pressure off, it gives you the space to make a series of attempts and observe the outcomes rather than staking your reputation (and mine!) on your ability to arrive at an effective intervention first time.

I can't prescribe for you a sure-fire solution to every challenge. Your church is unique with a unique culture and a unique history. Treat it with a bit of holy respect.

Implementation goes through a series of stages. Typically, churches in my programs sign up to a two- or three-year process built around Pathways and including a number of other discovery and learning exercises. It's beyond the scope of this book to take you through the whole shebang, but let me encourage you, at minimum, to do some thinking, praying and observing around the idea of your mission focus group.

Usually I will have had a number of conversations with the senior minister and perhaps even conducted some discovery work with the church leadership team before I schedule a Pathways workshop. Some of the work I typically do around mission focus groups is set out in the Appendix 1. In

---

[52] See chapter 9.

general, the church will benefit more from the Pathways discovery process if they've done some work to get clear on the mission focus group or groups.

A Pathways workshop generally takes six hours and is divided into two parts. The first is built around educating people in the theory; the second is the initial discovery process examining the status of the church in Pathways terms. Think of it like this: first I give the church leaders a lens to look through (the theory) and then I guide them in a process of looking through the lens at their church to see what they can see.

I do the education and examination on the same day because learning that is not immediately applied tends to quickly get lost. The whole process is built using an adult learning framework developed by Bernice McCarthy called 4MAT,[53] which is in turn built on David Kolb's work. You'll remember Kolb from our earlier conversations about discipleship as learning.

Visit www.pathways4mission.com for resources listed throughout the next section. The site is designed to be a companion to this book and to provide you with simple tools to implement your learning.

In the education section of a workshop we undertake a series of orientation exercises, and then work through the seven steps as set out in the schematic at Figure 1 (p. 176-177). Because I use an adult learning approach, I work hard to connect with peoples' previous experiences and to draw from them what they already know. Jesus counselled us to do to others what we would like them to do to us. I don't want to be lectured, so I don't do it to workshop participants.

Some leaders—impatient, action-oriented types—will be tempted to skip the educative part and jump straight to discovery. Others might have already figured out where the blockages and opportunities for change might be and are tempted to push ahead, skipping the discovery process altogether. Please don't do either. The 'why?' is just as important as the 'what?', and if you exercise a little patience and follow the process now, you might just save yourself some resistance and even conflict later.

By now you've read about sixty thousand words of this book and have done a lot of thinking (well, I hope you have anyway). It's worth the wait to give

---

[53] http://www.aboutlearning.com/

your people a little time to catch up. People are less likely to resist change that is based on their own discoveries and ideas. If you can take them on a journey of discovery, they might just catch the vision for change themselves, saving you the effort to convince them that your ideas will work.

By whatever means you think is best (I'm tempted to recommend that you purchase copies of this book for everyone in your church and encourage them to read it, but that would be a little disingenuous of me), help your people gain a basic understanding of the Pathways concepts.

The fundamentals that are most important to understand are:

Get clear on your mission focus group—Some people will latch onto the idea that you can't reach everyone all at once in a flash. Others will confuse mission focus with ideas of exclusion. Still others will take a while to realise that something they find familiar and nourishing as a fifty-year churchgoer may be a little less appealing to an unchurched stranger.

Think process—Some people take a while to give up on the idea of silver-bullet evangelism. They may not immediately grasp the idea that it generally takes time, and a number of relationships and interactions in several environments before a person makes a faith commitment.

Think relationships—Conversion is at least as much socialisation as it is education. Some people will take a bit of convincing that simply communicating your take on the gospel as a news bulletin, devoid of relational context, is generally ineffective as a disciple-making strategy.

Get clear on the stages—In my experience, people take a while to gain a clear understanding of the characteristics and purpose of each of the Pathways stages. These characteristics are all important to understand if the Pathways concept is going to be applied effectively in your church. For example, you need to be clear on:

- whether an activity is designed for believers or people yet to believe
- how many Christians an unchurched person might be able to meet if they participate in a particular activity
- what kind of spiritual content might be appropriate at a particular step.

In the workshop I use a card-sorting exercise to get people thinking about it (you can download the card master from the www.pathways4mission.com). It's helpful, but I will usually ask clarifying questions throughout the learning process to help people correct their assumptions.

Think growth transitions—Those with a mind for manufacturing may understand Pathways as a kind of disciple-factory process map, where people are pushed like widgets from one value-adding step to the next (these people are usually more task oriented than relationship oriented). It sometimes takes a while for people to recognise that people progress from one step to the next through invitations and relationships. Conversely, relationship-oriented people sometimes react to the idea that people are being 'processed like sausages'. It may take them a while to become comfortable with the idea that the intention of the process does not override the underlying motive of genuine care in the context of friendship. It may take a few hearings before the idea sticks that people adopt the faith of their friends, not their 'project manager'.

An inside look at a Pathways workshop

Most people who are currently in church have experienced some aspects of mission pathways as they've made their faith journey, even if they haven't thought about it in those terms. Hopefully you related a little to the four stories at the beginning of the book, and found links to your own story. Likewise the workshop begins by asking each participant to share their story of becoming a fully committed disciple (since they've given up a big chunk of their weekend to be at the workshop, I'm assuming they're committed disciples).

Even people who've grown up in the church can see how they progressed in their faith through various activities and relationships, and how different challenges and environments further developed their faith. A little bit of reflection on their own story helps people realise, 'I already know something about this.' This helps to orient them toward new thinking and ideas, and helps to reduce the resistance to some concepts that may grate on them as the workshop unfolds.

Before I jump into the detail of the various Pathways concepts, I spend a little time with Jesus' parable of the man sowing seeds in Mark 4:26-29. This usually means getting small groups to draw the lifecycle of wheat. It's an engaging way of introducing both the idea of development through stages and the metaphor of the farm. It provides a kind of anchoring concept for the content, which in turn enhances the retention of content.

Next comes some teaching about the seven steps that lie at the heart of the Pathways paradigm. This teaching is summarised in the schematic at Figure 1. You can download the summary of this content in the PDF booklet at www.pathways4mission.com. A word of caution here: reading the booklet for content is not the same as learning for integration. Don't assume that once people have read the booklet they'll get the whole paradigm and you can jump straight to the discovery process.

Some kind of intentional integration exercise will help to cement the learning, even if it's a discussion group and a couple of 'test your learning' activities like the one with activity cards I mentioned earlier. After working through the content, I always do the card exercise—it's amazing how often people don't grasp ideas until they are required to work with them.

Once you're confident that your people have a basic grounding in the paradigm, I recommend you take them through the analysis process in the next chapter as promptly as you can (ideally on the same day).

Stage	Potential Contact	In Touch	Belonging	Embracing the Gospel
Description of people at this stage and what they need	People we don't know and who know no one in the church. Need to make contact.	People who know at least one person in the church. Need an attractive group in which to belong.	Know several people and are a regular part of a church group. Need an opportunity to find out more about Christian faith and a reason to consider commitment.	Interested in knowing about Jesus. Need to hear the gospel and establish a relationship with God.
Aim of activity at this stage	Let people know we have something to offer. Encourage people to make an initial contact with us.	Encourage people we know to become regular participants in a program or group.	Cultivate relationships between believers and people who participate in a program or group. Share spiritual life.	Create an environment where people can explore the gospel in a meaningful way. Ensure there are opportunities for people to make a response to the claims of Jesus.
Example activities	• Website • Sign • Fete/fair • Finding opportunities to connect with people we bump into: neighbours, wait staff etc.	• Reception • Responding to inquiries • Funeral ministry • Cultivating relationships with people in our work, school, social spheres	• Playgroups • Kids' clubs • Sporting clubs • Interest groups • Book clubs • Regular social gatherings	• Alpha • Christianity Explained • Catechumenate courses • Evangelistic Bible studies

Figure 1: Pathways schematic

Following Jesus	Serving in Ministry	Leading Ministry	Stage
In a process of learning, obeying and growing in faith. Need teaching, encouragement and accountability to support Christian life.	Have identified gifts, skills and ministry and are serving others in Jesus' name. Need opportunities and training to develop gifts.	Take up a leadership role.	*Description of people at this stage and what they need*
Teach, encourage and share accountability with people as they shape their life to be followers of Jesus.	Encourage and equip all people to exercise their gifts and talents.	Train and encourage people to be leaders in the church.	*Aim of activity at this stage*
• Life groups • Cell groups • Life Transformation groups • Sunday school	• SHAPE course • Training sessions • Apprenticing arrangements • Program team meetings	• Church council • Leadership community	*Example activities*

Figure 1: continued

Chapter 12
Analysing Your Own Church

If you're planting ...
This chapter deals with analysing an existing church. I have used this process with several church plants less than a year old with a high degree of success. That said, you need to have something to analyse. If your plant is up and running—that is, you have a team of people meeting regularly (not necessarily in public worship) and you have good engagement with your mission focus group—the following process will probably serve you well enough to help you sharpen your mission activity.

If you're still forming a team, still developing a plan or are yet to make any significant inroads into forming relationships with the people you're hoping to reach, it's probably a little early for this process.

I've set out some specific thoughts about applying Pathways thinking to church planting in Appendix 5. I encourage you to read that over, then perhaps come back here and read for insight rather than taking your team through the process.

Mapping your pathway
This is where the humble post-it note comes into its own. (A hint: use the genuine 3M Post-it Notes®, with the trademark and all the details, not the cheaper knock-offs—the genuine post-its stick better.) I begin by throwing a stack of yellow post-its onto the table and get the group to brainstorm all the activities and initiatives run in or by the church. This includes everything from the sign out front and the website to the worship services and church council. The rules I state up front are:

- Write one idea per post-it.
- Write with a marker, not a pen or a pencil (this prevents people writing too much or too small to read).
- Anything that is either done or used once a year or more (and is likely to be done more than once) can be written on a post-it if people choose.
- If an item involves the same group of people in the same place at the same time it only gets one post-it. (For example, don't break a

worship service up into segments—people experience it as a single activity from car park to coffee, so it just gets one post-it. But separate services can each get a separate post-it.)

Here's a list of some of what we might typically find in a medium-sized Australian suburban church:

- Church council
- Worship service: 8.00 am
- Worship service: 10.00 am
- Wednesday night prayer meeting
- Youth social night
- Youth Bible study
- Youth cell group
- Cell group leader training
- Christianity Explained course
- Playgroup
- Conversational English group
- Leadership training nights
- SHAPE course
- Sunday school
- Kids' after-school club
- Conversational English ministry team
- Website
- Signboard
- Letterbox leaflets
- Fete/church fair
- Tennis club
- Adult Bible study
- Cell Group
- Worship services team meeting
- Band rehearsal
- Weddings for unchurched people
- Funerals for unchurched people
- Financial counselling service

Each of these will be written on a separate post-it and dropped at random on the table.

Then I give the group a large sheet of card (usually A1 size, and if they have a lot of post-its, two A1 cards taped together). The task for the group is to divide the board into seven columns (one for each step of the pathway from 'potential contact' to 'leading ministry') and then put each of the post-its they've written into the appropriate column.

At this stage some of you will be wondering why I didn't just begin with the board and ask the group to allocate activities to the appropriate column as they were written—surely it's much more efficient.

Undeniably it's more efficient, but in my experience, less effective. Brainstorming tends to be more imaginative and expansive, given to including possibilities and making associations. It's what people might describe as 'right-brained' (I know the neurobiology is not that neat, but the concept is helpful). Categorising tends to be analytical and reductive, given to excluding possibilities and making distinctions—or, in the parlance, 'left-brained'. When you try to do both together, there's a risk that the group will get side-tracked in debate about categories and get away from calling to mind all the 'stuff' that happens around the church.

No matter how well you think you've taught people about the characteristics of each step, inevitably workshop participants will miscategorise things. At the risk of giving you all the 'right' answers, set out in Figure 2 is how the list above should be categorised.

It's likely that you'll want to dispute some of my categorisations. And this happens in workshops when I question people's placement of their post-it notes. Let's work though some of the helpful 'check' questions.

Who is the activity 'for'?
This question is not as simple as it seems. First, people get confused as to whether the purpose of the activity is to give people an opportunity to serve or whether it is for the people being served. The answer is *always* the people being served (or the primary, overtly stated beneficiary). The activity being an opportunity to express gifts of teaching, hospitality or whatever is not the key question.

A Bible study group's primary beneficiary is a person who wants to learn about the Bible—not the leader who's looking to express their teaching gift.

Potential Contact	In Touch	Belonging	Embrace the Gospel
• Website • Signboard • Letterbox leaflets • Fete/church fair	• Weddings for unchurched people • Funerals for unchurched people • Financial counselling service	• Youth social night • Playgroup • Conversational English group • Kids' after-school club • Tennis club	• Christianity Explained course

Figure 2: A typical church pathways board, categorised into seven steps

A playgroup's primary beneficiary is generally the parents and grandparents who want social interaction while helping their kids to learn to socialise.

A website's primary beneficiary should be the person you don't know yet but who is looking for something you offer.

Anything in the first four categories is primarily for the benefit of people who *do not* yet call themselves followers of Jesus. The implication is that any activity that has been placed in any of the first four categories but primarily serves Christians is either in the wrong column or is failing in its purpose. I encourage you to read this paragraph again and check your categorisations carefully.

What's the place of public worship services?

This conversation brings me to the questions about worship services. I would be moderately wealthy (well, I'd have enough for a nice dinner out anyway) if I had a dollar for every time I've had someone protest, 'Our worship services are for believers *and* seekers.' It's a debate I believe is important but one I get the feeling nearly always leaves people with their doubts. Let me have a go at explaining my position.

Unless your service is either intentionally designed for seekers and *not* for believers (the old 'seeker service' that harks back to the church growth movement) or is an old-time 'gospel service' replete with altar call or an equivalent, your service is probably geared to believers.

Following Jesus	Serving in Ministry	Leading Ministry
• Worship service: 8.00 am • Worship service: 10.00 am • Youth Bible study • Youth cell group • Sunday school • Adult Bible study • Cell Group	• Wednesday night prayer meeting • SHAPE course • Worship services team meeting • Band rehearsal • Conversational English ministry team	• Church council • Cell group leader training • Leadership training nights

Figure 2: continued

Here are some questions that may help to nail it down for you. First, a theological one: should an unbeliever (or yet-to-be-believer) participate in communion? Read 1 Corinthians 11:27-29 and think it over before you answer. (If you want to be really scholarly, research the practices of the early church around the Lord's Supper as well.) Most people, after a bit of thought, will answer, 'No, communion is for believers.' You've got to ask who the service is for if it includes a ceremony that's only for those who recognise the death of Christ as the means of salvation for humanity.

A second question is about language. Does your service include language that's unfamiliar to outsiders? As a non-Anglican coming into the Anglican Church, I was bewildered by the vast lexicon of peculiar terms used to describe the various items and processes of ritual and tradition. Every time I heard one, I was reminded that I am an outsider. When a 'cradle Anglican' hears them, somewhere deep inside there's a warm reassurance that they're an insider. You can't say a service is 'for' unchurched people if it's laden with terms they don't understand.

A further question relates to the content of the sermon. Just who is the imagined audience of this weekly piece of public oratory? Unless the preacher very intentionally writes with the unbeliever or seeker in mind, the inevitable drift is toward the believer—and probably the long-time believer at that.

None this is criticism so much as observation. Let's just be honest about the target audience of our public worship services and categorise them accordingly.

That still doesn't answer the question as to whether the service can span multiple categories. Rather than argue the point too much, let me just offer this counsel: you'll be better off if you assume it can't. I've worked with and even been a congregation member of a number of churches that have tried to make the service 'work' both for believers and those who are yet to believe, and it's generally been vaguely unsatisfying to one or both types of people. Most churches would be far better off confining the purpose of their worship to a single stage in the pathway, and be intentional about what goes before and after.

There are a few exceptions to this principle. In my observation and experience, those exceptions always revolve around a profoundly gifted orator. For the 99.9 per cent of us who are not modern-day Spurgeons (you may think you are but it's safer to assume you're not), the very best we can aim for is for our services to be edifying for those who believe and *accessible* to those who don't.

Let me unpack that for a minute. Being accessible means keeping in mind that people who don't believe the Christian gospel will likely wander into your worship services for time to time, and for a bunch of different reasons. Being careful not to use jargon when a common word will do, explaining concepts and rituals that may be unfamiliar to the unchurched, and having an intentional approach to welcoming people at the door are all behaviours that are considerate of those who are likely to find a church service and it's various components unfamiliar. For example, I definitely appreciate those usher-types who play traffic cop in traditions where people leave their seats to receive the Eucharist at an altar rail at the front of the church. I usually fail to discern the implied traffic pattern and collide with people going the other way.

Just because a church service is not designed specifically for the unchurched doesn't mean it won't be meaningful for them. It's okay for church to be a little mysterious and for people not to understand everything that's going on—provided they can feel reassured they're not going to commit some faux pas that will bring them embarrassment and humiliation. Even little things like instructions in the liturgy as to when to stand or sit can be helpful.

Just about every church with which I've worked has had unchurched people randomly come along to a service, decide to keep coming and become part of the congregation. This does not mean the church service was designed for them. And while it's not uncommon, in general it's not so common as to be a viable mission strategy in and of itself. And importantly, without a specific 'embracing the gospel' environment, they could come along to church every week for years and never make a profession of faith—and we've already been over the drawbacks of that.

So unless you have a really good reason to think otherwise, your public worship services will belong in the 'following Jesus' category, and that's just fine.

How many people who fit the category does it serve?
It's not uncommon to see people put activities they might describe as 'outreach' in the 'Potential Contact' or 'In Touch' columns, without thinking too much about the criteria for those categories. Sometimes I see things like 'homework club' in the first or second column.

I'll usually ask, 'Who comes to the homework club?' The answer usually goes something like, 'Well, kids who struggle with homework.'

'Do you know their names?'

'Err, yes.'

'Does anyone else know their names?' (By this time they're looking at me with a mixture of suspicion and incredulity.)

'Yes, of course. All the helpers and leaders know the kids' names.'

'So a kid coming to homework club has opportunity to form a relationship with a number of people from church every week. Yes?'

'Sure, but ... '

'And how many people from church does a person at the "potential contact" stage know?'

(Flicking through the workshop manual to find the answer) 'Wait a second ... they know ... oooooh! I get it. So this activity should go in the "Belonging" column.'

'Right.'

Sometimes I'll see activities like 'men's breakfast' slapped into the 'Belonging' column. This always makes me curious. In one church, the monthly men's breakfast attracted more people than Sunday morning worship, and more than half the men present would only attend a church service if it was their dear mother's funeral. In this case, the activity is correctly categorised. But that kind of men's breakfast is, in my experience, much less common than the kind where the men of the church get together on a Saturday morning to consume enough saturated fat to kill a brown dog and listen to a speaker talk about something vaguely Christian or offer a devotion. The total count of unchurched people is usually closer to zero.

If the activity is in practice held for the benefit of those who already come to church, it can't really be categorised as a 'belonging' activity, since 'belonging' activities are designed to provide a context where unchurched people can build relationships with Christians who will share with them the love of God.

The same could be said for some church outings, activity-based groups or anything with the word 'fellowship' in the title. Which leads me to my next, and somewhat provocative, question: 'Is this activity designed just for fellowship?'

Too often the answer is, 'What's wrong with that?'

Well, in my view, plenty. As I explained earlier, longstanding activities comprised of the same people tend to calcify and become difficult for newcomers to 'crack into'.

How do you categorise 'fellowship' activities? Truthfully, I really don't know, other than to observe that a church that puts effort into fellowship for its own sake is in danger of becoming more of a social club than a disciple-making community. I usually encourage people to stick such activities in the 'Following Jesus' column because they're only attended by Christians, and such activities usually have more potential to be transformed into contexts for genuine growth than to be useful as environments into which unchurched people can be invited.

We'll talk a little later about what you might want to do with those activities that have no purpose other than fellowship.

What about fundraising activities?
Possibly the stickiest issue to come up at this stage of a Pathways workshop is the question of fundraising activities. In which column do you put these?

All sorts of arguments can be made about the potential of fundraising activities for mission: fetes and fairs can be categorised under 'potential contact', as can sausage sizzles and car boot sales and the like. In the Anglican diocese I currently serve, many churches run opportunity shops ('thrift stores' for those in the US). These can roughly fit the criteria for 'belonging' activities when you think about them from the perspective of the volunteers who serve (most op shops have a large volunteer workforce, and there's usually a reasonable proportion who don't attend church).

But here's the real question: are these fundraising activities undertaken for the purpose of mission or for money? Or put another way: if these were deemed an ineffective means for mission, would you stop doing them?

The churches in which I grew up and in which I have served as a leader have all paid their bills out of tithes and offerings. The dependence of some local churches on fundraising to meet their day-to-day expenses has recently been somewhat of a revelation me. I've added as Appendix 6 an article I wrote about this a few years ago. If you're curious, read it to discover why I use the phrase 'sausage-sizzling yourself to death'.

The uncomfortable reality for many small parishes is that they've placed themselves in a situation where, at least in the short-to-medium term, they are forced to fundraise or face being unable to pay their clergy. If a church is resigned to continuing its fundraising activities as they are, those activities should probably be categorised as 'serving in ministry' if church members actually serve in them, or 'potential contact' if it's mostly strangers coming and going from the church campus.

How many Christians will they know?
Another clarifying question for classifying activities asks, 'How many Christians will people know?' To be a little more precise, how many Christians will know someone's name through their engagement or participation?

Remember, if we're applying the question to any of the first four categories, we're asking from the perspective of the person who doesn't call themselves a believer or a member of your church. For example, it's possible—perhaps even probable—that a person will attend a church fete or fair and never have a person representing the church community learn their name or get their contact details. If this is the case, it's likely the purpose of the fete is simply to make people aware of the church and its contribution to the community. In order be categorised as anything else, the fete team would need to go to considerable effort to get to know people and make enough connection to be able to get in touch with them again. It's not a problem to assign the fete to the 'potential contact' category—provided you can figure out how to help a person make a connection from there.

Another example might be a family that contacts the minister to arrange a funeral. It's possible that the only believer they will meet who actually learns their name will be the minister—so 'funerals ministry' generally fits into the 'in touch' category. Given that people aren't going to regularly turn up at funerals even if a family meets more people than just the minister, it would be unlikely that 'funeral ministry' would be in 'belonging'.

How often?
'Belonging' activities need to provide good opportunity to be known by several Christians, so they also need to be reasonably regular—ideally weekly, and no less than monthly. The one-off or once-a-year event might allow someone to meet a bunch of church people, but it won't really build a sense of belonging if the unchurched person won't be back any time soon.

Most other questions about categorisation can be settled by looking at the criteria set out in the matrix at Figure 1 (you really should fold over the corner on page 176 so you can find it easily).

By this stage you should have a pathways board of post-it notes in seven columns, each representing a Pathways step. Each post-it represents an activity or initiative of the church, and the column in which it is placed is determined by the purpose and function of the activity. No activity or initiative should span more than one category. You've used the criteria in Figure 1 and the descriptions I've given to check your categorisations and you're confident each post-it is in the correct column.

All good? Now for the next challenge.

Sorting for mission focus groups

Once things are in their categories, you can begin to sort them into mission focus groups. It's not simply a matter of having some kind of activity or item in each column. You need something in each column that will serve each mission focus group you're reaching.

Set out at Figure 3 is the pathways board we saw earlier, but with the first four or five steps sorted into activities geared for two specific mission focus groups (and the remaining activities otherwise uncategorised for mission focus groups).

You'll note that the further to the right you look, the more general the activities become in terms of their tailoring to a specific mission focus group. You may or may not have a specific public worship service targeted for a particular mission focus group. You almost certainly won't have a specific church council for each mission focus group—although you would hope that the church council considers the needs and interests of all the mission focus groups equally.

Hopefully you've begun to appreciate why we do all this on post-it notes. Just writing directly onto butcher's paper leads to way too many scribble-outs and the end product becomes unreadable.

You could break this pathways board down futher, perhaps looking to identify a youth pathway and a pathway for parents with toddlers (making use of playgroup). But for the purposes of learning how the process works, let's just work with two.

If you look at the 'Potential Contact' column, you'll notice that the signboard is a primary means for people to become aware of the conversational English group. For this to be valid, the conversational English class would need to be prominently featured on the signboard, or have a prominent signboard of its own. The second means of making people aware is the website. For this to be valid, the website would need a prominent panel promoting the conversational English group (preferably a promo panel that has a click-through link to its own into page—and bonus points if information is presented in a few of the common language groups in your area).

MFG	Potential Contact	In Touch	Belonging	Embrace the Gospel
People from non-English speaking background	• Signboard • Website		• Conversational English group	• Christianity Explained course
Young couples	• Website	• Weddings for unchurched people		• Christianity Explained course
Others/not categorised for MFG	• Letterbox leaflets • Fete/church fair	• Funerals for unchurched people • Financial counselling service	• Youth social night • Playgroup • Kids' after-school club • Tennis club	

Figure 3: A typical church pathways board, categorised into steps and mission focus groups

You'll also notice that the website serves as the 'front door' for young couples looking to get married at the church. For this to be valid, a similar panel and page should provide information to assist and encourage engaged couples to get in touch.

The website is duplicated in both rows because on the website there will be clearly delineated panels and pages for each mission focus group.

If you look further to the right, you see that Christianity Explained is also duplicated in both rows. In this case it's because separate Christianity Explained groups would probably operate for each mission focus group. The group for those coming through conversational English might meet during or right after the conversational English class. For engaged or newlywed couples, Christianity Explained may be conducted on a couple-by-couple basis rather than in a group.

Following Jesus	Serving in Ministry	Leading Ministry	MFG
• Worship service: 10.00 am • Adult Bible study • Cell group	• Conversational English ministry team • Wednesday night prayer meeting • SHAPE course • Worship services team meeting • Band rehearsal	• Church council • Cell group leader training • Leadership training nights	*People from non-English speaking background*
			Young couples
• Worship service: 8.00 am • Youth Bible study • Youth cell group • Sunday school			*Others/not categorised for MFG*

Figure 3: continued

In the next column, you'll notice that the rows merge into one. In this example, the Sunday worship service and adult Bible study are geared to serve the needs of both mission focus groups. The further to the right on the pathways board you go, the more likely you can merge the rows.

Analysis

Once you're happy with the categorisation both in terms of steps (columns) and mission focus groups (rows), it's time to ask some questions. Ideally you would question every step and transition for every mission focus group. Practically that's quite laborious and your energy will probably give out before you've completed an exhaustive analysis.

Years of experience have given me a sense of where the biggest challenges and the best opportunities are likely to be found. That's the advantage of a professional consultant. However, the advantage of people working on their own church is that they know their church, its programs and its culture and will instinctively zero in on the challenges and opportunities unique to them.

As a consultant, I usually wait until the church team has got to the end of their best thinking and insight before I begin to ask them questions. It's not uncommon for the team to find all the necessary 'gold' themselves without any help from me.

In the pages that follow I've used lots of example questions that I would ask if the church team was struggling. If you're a consultant reading this book, you probably already know it's best to let people make their own discoveries. Even if you're a senior minister, I would encourage you to be patient and let people wrestle a little before coming in with the killer question.

Marking your insights
As you work through the issues and questions below, you'll undoubtedly see opportunities where you could make some changes to your church's activity or programming to improve your mission effectiveness. I encourage workshop participants to write down their lightbulb moments as they occur, and I provide regular breaks in the workshop process for people to record their big ideas. Sometimes people won't actually identify their specific learning until you ask them to write down an idea or two that came to them as they asked questions about their board.

Sometimes I hand out different coloured post-it notes for people to capture their ideas. And a quick tip for consultants: don't put the new colour on the table until it's needed, otherwise people use them to record existing activities and the benefit of the colour difference is lost.

Where are the gaps?
If you take a look at the pathways board for the example church, you'll notice there's nothing in the 'In Touch' column for the first mission focus group. On the face of it, there's a gap. A gap is your invitation to dig in and find out if it's causing a problem. The first step is to ask some questions about the activities in the columns on either side.

I would usually ask, 'How many people who want to improve their English come along to the conversational English group?' If the answer is 'Heaps!' or 'The group is nearly full', I might follow up with 'Are those people forming relationships?' If the answer is affirmative, the perceived 'gap' is not really causing a problem. Things seem to be working well enough, even though there's technically a gap on the pathways board.

If I'm still curious, I might ask, 'The people who do come, how did they first come to know about the group?' The answer might be 'They saw the sign and just turned up!' Or they might say, 'Most people hear about the group through friends who already come—it was only the first two or three brave ones that came because of the sign.' In this case there is something in the 'in touch' space: that is, friendships outside church. It's just that this is more 'organic' than 'programmatic' and no one saw it clearly enough to write a post-it note. Either way, if plenty of people are making it to the 'belonging' stage, you could choose just to leave things as they are until things stop working or you're looking to expand to more groups.

The lessons here are these:

1. Purity to the model is less important than mission effectiveness. The purpose of the model is to make mission initiatives more effective. If something is working well but doesn't quite fit the model, don't feel the need to 'fix' it so it complies with an abstract theory. The name of the game is making disciples.
2. Pathways will often combine organic, personal actions that aren't necessarily visible on a church calendar filled with more obvious programs and initiatives. If you cast your mind back to the original stories in chapter 1, you'll remember that the 'in touch' context for Frank, Therese and their family was a chance meeting with Dora at the primary school gate. In the story of Mike, the 'in touch' context was the treatment table in his own physiotherapy practice (no pun intended). The Christians in both these stories were being very intentional, even though they weren't using a formal program.

Let's assume that when we examine the 'Belonging' activity on the right side of the gap, we find there are very few people of the mission focus group coming to the program. In this case, the gap represents a problem in the effectiveness of the pathway, and a conversation as to how to bridge the gap would ensue.

Turning to the second mission focus group in our example church, young couples, you'll notice there's a gap in the 'Belonging' category. I might ask, 'How many newlyweds do Christianity Explained?' but I reckon I can guess the answer. Perhaps the minister might persuade a couple to consider their spiritual growth and development during marriage preparation, but it's likely that all the excitement and planning pressure associated with the wedding would be filling their minds.

The conversation about this gap would be around the needs and interests of engaged and newlywed couples in the surrounding community, and what kind of ministry might appeal to them leading into and upon return from the honeymoon. In the story of Andrew and Jackie in chapter 1, some thoughtful 'in touch' work on the part of the minister after the wedding led to an invitation into a 'belonging' activity, where Andrew and Jackie joined a bunch of other young couples who were interested in getting their marriages off to a good start.

This is not a prescription so much as an illustration of the kind of ministry that might be fit for service. A less programmatic possibility might be inviting the couple to a barbecue or dinner, along with one or two other couples, who could in turn extend further invitations. Remember, the key to effective 'belonging' environments is unchurched people forming sincere friendships with disciples.

Blockages

Blockages are a little harder to spot on the pathways board, and usually turn up as a result of some thoughtful questioning. Most of the churches I've taken through the workshop either have a gap in the 'Embrace the Gospel' column, or a blockage between their 'Belonging' activity and their 'Embrace the Gospel' activity. Armed with this knowledge, I usually zero in on this part of the pathway.

With the first mission focus group above, my opening question in this regard might be, 'How many people from the conversational English group have completed Christianity Explained?' If the answer is something like 'about three or four people each year' or 'one or two every time we offer the course', I would likely congratulate them on an effective transition point (unless of course it was a mega-church with dozens of people in conversational English classes each year).

More common is the response, 'Well, we run Christianity Explained, but people from the conversational English class just aren't interested.' A response like that is a sure indicator of a blockage, and that's where I become annoyingly curious.

'Wow!' I respond. 'What are your thoughts about why you don't get any takers?' The conversation will then work through issues such as, 'When and where do you schedule Christianity Explained to run?' This question is designed to test whether the time and place suit the mission focus group. If the participants in the conversational English class are women with kids, for example, an early evening course is likely to be unsuitable.

Other questions might address issues such as venue suitability, transport, parking and childcare. If the participants are diverse in their age and cultural background, it might be that there is no universally suitable time, setting and format, and a series of one-to-one meetings would be more suitable.

Given that the mission focus group are those whose English is limited, an 'embracing the gospel' process in their heart language may be more appealing.

Obvious and inviting transitions
When I ask questions about the pathways board, I sometimes find there is no apparent reason why people aren't making the transition from one stage to the next. Let's assume that our example church has worked hard to ensure that Christianity Explained is at a time and place and is supported by services that make it perfect for the majority of people in the conversational English class, but is still not seeing many or any take it up.

My question might turn to 'How do people become aware of Christianity Explained?' If the answer is 'it's in the church bulletin' or 'it's on the website'—or worse, 'we announce it in church'—the reason for so few transitions is easy to spot. The 'next step' for unchurched people is just not obvious to them: it's unlikely they will see the promotional piece, and even if they do, it's unlikely they will immediately think to themselves, 'Hey, that's just what I want!'

If the response is 'we hand out a flier' or 'there's a poster on the noticeboard', the opportunity may be a little more obvious, but it's certainly not inviting.

You'll remember earlier we talked about people adopting the faith of their friends, and discussed how we invite people to come with us through the transitions and don't send them off to the next thing like a widget on an assembly line. So fliers and posters, unaccompanied by warm invitations from liked and trusted friends, are likely to be just more advertising noise.

Sometimes the blockage is a symptom of the ineffectiveness of the activity in the previous column. The most successful transitions are made when a person expresses interest or curiosity. I'm focusing on the transition from the 'belonging' step to the 'embracing the gospel' step because it seems to be the toughest transition, and it's the one where interest and curiosity seem to play the most crucial role. That said, the principles we're discussing here apply right across the pathway.

You might want to go back over the section in chapter 6 where I develop the idea of witness. If the lives and conversations of the believers that inhabit the conversational English group are an eloquent advertisement for Christian faith, the unchurched participants will be more likely to be curious and interested. They will, in all likelihood, begin to ask questions. At this juncture, an invitation to Christianity Explained is both natural and a caring response to the unchurched person's need (and nothing like the hard-sell of a used car salesman). Conversely, if the Christians in the group are silent about their faith and don't take the initiative to build relationships with the unchurched people, there will likely be few transitions to Christianity Explained.

We need to be clear on the need

Sometimes the questions around blockages—where an activity that involves a lot of people is seeing very few transitions to the next step—lead to a conversation around people's needs. You'll remember back in chapter 2 we looked at the important difference between felt needs and discipleship needs.

It may be useful to think about what's happening in the environment where the people are banking up. Let's imagine that in our example church there's healthy attendance at the worship service and adult Bible study, but few people seem to be willing to step up and take significant responsibility. Most people will, even if a little grudgingly, agree to serve on the various rosters around the place, but it's very common for churches to struggle for people to take on roles involving responsibility and commitment.

The most obvious place to begin questioning would be the activities in the column in which the people are accumulating. In this example, there are plenty of people at the 'Following Jesus' step, but they don't seem to be moving forward to 'Serving in Ministry'.

We could begin by asking some questions about the SHAPE course. How many have done it? When is it run? How is it promoted? Are people invited personally? Are their felt needs and life-stage constraints considered? These are the obvious questions you would ask of just about any activity. If the answers reveal some clues about the blockage, you can begin to do something to remedy the situation.

But because it's specifically a giftedness-discovery program, I might have some more pointed questions.

'Could you step me through how you use SHAPE?' would be one. Here I'm looking for the overall process. I've seen programs like SHAPE and Network used to good effect, and I've seen them fail miserably. The determining factor is nearly always that of follow-up after completing the inventory. I might ask further questions: What follow-up is provided after completing the assessment? How does the 'ministry matching' work? Is there appropriate introduction, induction, supervision and review?

Where giftedness-discovery programs work well, there is nearly always a personal one-to-one follow-up interview, and each person who completes an inventory ends up with a personalised game plan for exploring and developing the gifts they have discerned through the process. This knowledge comes simply from the experience of working with a wide variety of churches.

I share this to illustrate the benefit of using either a specifically trained consultant or a highly experienced minister or denominational leader. You may not need them to facilitate the whole process, but they can be extremely useful in helping you figure out the gaps and blockages in your pathway.

Playing out the imagined scenario with our example church, let's imagine we find that the SHAPE course has shifted to the backburner because it wasn't all that effective, mainly due to the lack of follow-up interviews. Armed with this knowledge, the church can make some plans to change things.

Doing a little research
Before we leave our example church, I might be tempted to ask some questions about the conversational English ministry team.

My questions might begin with, 'How many people have joined the team in the past year or so?' If the answer indicates a healthy number I might follow up with 'Did they stay?' and 'How many people have left the team?' You might be thinking, 'Wow, this guy really gets in your face!' and perhaps I do (we Aussies are known for being direct). In practice, it's usually fairly gentle, accompanied by appropriate encouragement.

The truth is, we're involved in a serious enterprise here—the gospel of Jesus Christ is the hope of the world, and the church has sole agency. The task is sufficiently important for us to ask hard questions in order to achieve optimal results.

Let's imagine that we find the conversational English team struggles to retain people. People are coming to faith through the ministry and logically want to serve in the area that was most helpful to them. They offer to help and come along to a few team meetings, but then they find reasons not to keep serving.

Any leader worth their salt would have a bevy of questions to ask around this scenario. I would have questions around issues like training, clarity of expectations, and the time and place of the team meeting. I might even encourage some interviews with people who have joined the team only to leave soon after. Frequently an issue that begins with an observation in a Pathways workshop follows a trail of breadcrumbs to the skill and style of the leader. You might not be able to discuss or even clearly identify the cause of a blockage during the workshop, but the discovery of a blockage should begin a process of careful and sensitive inquiry on the part of the church leadership.

Now let's step back for a minute and look again at the pathways board for our example church. We imagined earlier a situation where the adult Bible study and worship service ('Following Jesus' activities) attracted healthy numbers, but the number of people stepping up to ministry responsibility in the 'Serving in Ministry' space was rather sparse. So far we've looked at the SHAPE course and the conversational English ministry team for explanations.

A lot of people may not indicate effectiveness
Let's go back to the previous stage to ask some questions about the worship service and Bible study. If these are not serving to prepare, challenge and encourage people to take up ministry, it might go some way to explain why

people aren't moving on. It's common for churches to have a disproportionate number of people wanting to be taught and cared for, but with no real interest in putting their shoulders to the wheel. This, of course, is a discipleship issue.

I might begin by asking some questions around the purpose and content of sermons, or the purpose, process and content of the Bible study. Discipleship effectiveness is proportionate to the ratio of leader/mentor to disciples (a ratio of 1:1 has optimum effectiveness, and a ratio of 1:3 is more effective than 1:12). I might also ask some questions about the level of accountability and the discipleship relationships between the group leaders and whoever oversees their ministry. This is driven by the philosophy that in order for the followers to be growing toward Christlikeness, the leader must be growing toward Christlikeness. If I'm feeling really cheeky I might even ask the person or persons overseeing the small group leaders, 'What is God seeking to change in your life right now?' Any Christian who is growing should be able to answer that question in fairly short order.

If it turns out that the purpose of the sermons and Bible study is to educate rather than to provoke repentance and obedience to Jesus, it might be time for some changes. Remember our earlier discussion about Ephesians 4: growth is measured in developing maturity, or in progress toward attaining to the full measure of Christ, not in knowing the answers to theological questions.

All work, no prayer
I know I shouldn't have to remind Christians that prayer fuels everything that's worth doing, but it's helpful sometimes to ask questions such as 'How often do the conversational English team pray specifically for the unchurched people in the group?' That doesn't necessarily mean pray *with* them, but it certainly means praying *for* them.

I might also ask, 'Do the Bible study group leaders pray personally and specifically for the people in their group?' In the whole enterprise of making disciples, if you're not regularly praying for people, well, you haven't got a prayer.

Other observations

Standing back and looking at your pathways board, you'll hopefully make some other observations. You might notice, for instance, that there are a lot of post-it notes in one or two columns and very few in others.

One small church that did a Pathways workshop filled their board with post-it notes—so many that they formed long tendrils of notes stuck one to another, running off the bottom of the board. I stared at masses of yellow notes, each one representing an activity that consumed the time and energy of the church members. Somewhat flabbergasted, I wondered out loud, 'Are you guys tired?' There was an audible collective sigh among the participants: 'We are *so* tired.'

I mentioned earlier the dangers of putting too much time and effort into activities that don't serve to make disciples, specifically those designed purely for 'sweet fellowship' and to raise funds.

You may also notice that there are a number of activities in one column all serving the same purpose with the same mission focus group. Earlier I observed that churches and movements that are effective at forming people in the ways of Jesus tend to use two or three mechanisms based on different sized groups (for example, Wesley's societies, classes and bands). The evidence suggests that this kind of overlap is helpful, particularly in the 'Following Jesus' category.

Less helpful is the situation where competing programs exist that duplicate one another. One US church bravely decided against an adult Sunday school because they already had adult home groups, which were of similar size and served the same purpose with the same demographic.

One reason certain columns fill up and overflow is a simple quirk of description. Imagine a row on a pathways board for 'High-school aged kids'. In the 'Belonging' column there are a couple of dozen post-it notes for activities like 'Laser tag', 'LAN games', 'Water fight', 'Asian banquet' and a host of other social activities. A few questions reveal that these activities each happen perhaps once or twice a year but fall in a regular fortnightly timeslot for youth group social activities. You could stack them all up under a collective heading of 'Youth social activities'. Hopefully your board will look a little more manageable.

Having a bunch of different one-off activities that run in succession over a year is far less of an issue than having a bunch of activities that run concurrently and compete for participants and resources.

Before you go making plans to slash programs (we'll talk a little about this in the next section), remember that at this stage we're observing and seeking to understand. In this case, it's a matter of getting a clear understanding of the meaning of each item on the board, rather than taking the axe to activities because a certain category appears to be too busy.

Summary of analysis

Analysing your pathways board is a process of noticing, wondering and asking questions. Sometimes the questions are obvious; sometimes they come out of intuition and experience. Just because there is some activity in every column doesn't mean the various activities are working in unison to form an effective mission pathway. Conversely, what might appear to be an incomplete pathway may be surprisingly effective, simply because there are unidentified or 'organic' processes occurring that are not represented by a post-it note on the board.

Analysis is a matter of finding the gaps and blockages. Gaps exist where there is no clear and obvious next step into which you can invite people at any given stage. Blockages exist where there is a possible or even intended next step but for some reason people are just not making the transition. The blockage could be caused by problems in the program that has plenty of participants who are not taking the next step. It could be caused by poor promotion and invitation. Or it could be that the program that people are not stepping into is missing the mark in some way.

The analysis stage may also yield other observations such as an overemphasis on 'fellowship', a dependence on fundraising or duplication of programs that could be competing for participants and resources.

At the end of the 'analysis' step, most churches will be feeling a little overwhelmed. It's normal for an average-sized church (about seventy people on a Sunday) to identify between six and ten opportunities to make some changes to the way they operate in order to improve their missional effectiveness.

Now let's take some time to think about turning our learning into action.

Chapter 13
Starting Work

Most workshops and seminars you will attend over your lifetime end where the real work begins. For reasons lost in the sands of time and in the blinding glare of the Enlightenment, we teacher-consultant types tend to think we can give a person some new ideas and they will, as a matter of course, go and implement them faithfully because it makes no sense not to.

Humans, for the most part, don't make a lot of sense. This is why I'm not an economic rationalist.

This is also why I try to help teams develop a tangible and achievable game plan before they leave the workshop, and why I have developed the policy of refusing to conduct a workshop with a team whose leader will not sign up for monthly coaching as part of the deal.

Understanding change
Change is difficult, and most of us will avoid it without a concrete plan and a coach who is both supportive and challenging. You're reading this because I had to admit to myself that I needed a coach in order to help me to change (that is, quit procrastinating and write the book).

I know I've already banged on about getting a coach, but just to be consistent (my kids call it 'predictable'), let me encourage you one more time to get a coach to work with you through the implementation process.

A resource-hungry environment
Most people and most churches attempt *more* than they can achieve but achieve *less* than their potential. At the end of the analysis process, churches will almost certainly be confronted with more opportunities than they have resources to pursue. In fact, almost all of the churches with which I've worked were already operating well beyond their optimal workload before their team walked into the workshop.

Let me unpack that for a minute.

In the first edition of *The Fifth Discipline*,[54] Peter Senge included a case study of a start-up airline (it's not included in later editions, I don't know why). From the case study I learned the difference between *optimum* and *optimal*. As the Senge tells it, the airline had a great business model with a well-differentiated value proposition, and in a flurry of early success they expanded as fast as they could—that is, at the *optimum* rate. This was a trap because in doing so they eroded their value proposition and ended up in trouble. Analysing the history, Senge points out how they could have used pricing to slow down the expansion to the rate that they could sustain while preserving their value proposition—that is, grow at the *optimal* rate.

While this example uses a lot of business jargon, there's some learning that goes beyond prfit-driven enterprises. So let's find the common element. Churches, businesses and all kinds of other human organisations are constructed of the same essential material: people. In the case study, the airline tried to do too much too quickly without developing the people required to fulfil their mission. Sure, they had people doing all the jobs required, but *how* they did those jobs missed the mark. They fell short of the mission. The vision was thwarted. (Beginning to sound familiar?)

Now away from airlines and back to the church. Most churches are already doing more than is optimal and operating close to optimum—that is, they're running at pretty close to the limits of their immediately available capacity, usually just to keep their existing programs and routines going. That means they're operating beyond their capacity to do things to the quality required for their activity to be effective.

Here's a simple example. In Australia, one of the most common and effective 'belonging' activities is to run a playgroup. To keep a basic playgroup going requires a coordinator and one or two other volunteers to set up, pack up, do the promotion and admin and so on. A playgroup serving fifteen families can be sustained by three committed volunteers.

But effectiveness as a 'belonging' activity requires friendships to be formed and cultivated: unchurched people to be cared for, play-dates set up, coffee arranged afterwards, invitations to social gatherings extended. To do the missional work as well as the administrative and program work requires at

---

[54] Senge, Peter M. *The Fifth Discipline: The Art and Science of the Learning Organization* (Random, New York, 1990).

least twice as many people. (It's almost impossible for individuals to do a good job of the program and admin stuff *and* the people stuff as well.)

Imagine a church with a playgroup that is just being sustained as a program. That church completes a Pathways workshop and realises that, in order to reach the young families they hope to reach, they're going to need to make playgroup a genuine 'belonging' environment, with all that entails. That church now needs to find a bunch of people who are willing, available and suitably formed to fulfil the relational and spiritual aspects of making a playgroup an effective belonging environment (you could go back to chapter 6 to remind yourself of the essential elements for a 'belonging' environment).

How many churches do you know who have these kinds of people just hanging about ready to deploy? I don't know of any either.

It's one thing to see the need for change. It's quite another to have the necessary resources.

The bad news is this: that's not the only inherent challenge in putting your insights from Pathways into practice.

Change equals pain and effort

Change requires energy. If you don't believe me, brush your teeth with your non-preferred hand and see how much more effort is required. You need more mental energy to do things differently—even the most basic tasks.

I vividly remember the first lesson in my second-year drawing class at art school. I had spent the previous year producing highly realistic drawings, trying to perfect the technical skills of perspective, proportion and chiaroscuro (that is, the stuff of the Renaissance). The work I and my fellow first-year students created was 'tight', using highly controllable media such as graphite pencil. I produced some creditable work. I thought I could draw.

On the first day in second-year drawing class, we were instructed to put away the pencils and pick up broad felt-tip markers. Holding these in our non-preferred hands, we began to unlearn our 'tight' techniques and learn the genuine 'art' of drawing.

On the exterior I wore a wry grin (art students are supposed to be cool), but on the inside I was screaming in protest. The sense of awkwardness, the feeling of being exposed as incompetent, the fact that the image on the easel in front of me was crude, out of proportion, childish and bore almost no resemblance to the still life arranged in the centre of the studio—all this produced in me a nearly unbearable anxiety. And worst of all, I couldn't change the marks I'd made. It was like a bad dream. I desperately wanted things to return to normal, where I could control the image, erase things that were 'incorrect' and regain my feeling of mastery.

Change involves loss—loss of feeling competent, loss of position, loss of the comfort of the familiar. Loss is unpleasant, evoking feelings of unfamiliarity, anxiety, awkwardness and even grief. At the prospect of change being foisted upon them, most people will experience a cocktail of unpleasant emotions and do what they can to protect the status quo.

Let's go back to our example of the playgroup run by those three faithful people and serving some fifteen families. From the pathways workshop the church leaders attend, they realise there is a blockage between playgroup and the next step, which, for argument's sake, we'll presume is Alpha. Imagine that, in the five-year history of the playgroup, no one from the group has ever signed up for Alpha. Unchurched families join the group, stay until their kids begin preschool and then move on.

The playgroup team are tight-knit, hard-working and do a great job with the program and administration of the group. They are friendly and caring, but don't form much more than acquaintance-level relationships with the participants. No one on the playgroup team has done Alpha. They see the playgroup as a success. Their program is full. People enjoy themselves. The team receive nice little gifts from the parents at the end of the year. From the team's perspective, it's all good and, by implication, doesn't need changing.

However, for the playgroup to be an effective context from which to invite people into Alpha, things are going to need to change a little. The church leadership can see it—but how do they help the playgroup team to see it? To embrace it? To take ownership of making playgroup a caring community where people experience the love of Jesus and share a little of the lives of his followers (which is more than just providing a good community service in a friendly environment)?

Simply telling the playgroup leaders they need to change has almost no possibility of success. Getting them to read this book may help, but most people won't read something just because they're told to. Push on the playgroup system and you can expect the playgroup system will push back. Pushing too hard runs the risk of conflict, which could spread into the wider church community. This is going to take some prayer and time and care and thought.

Ultimately, changing the culture in the playgroup will mean a change of mindset for its leadership, and that usually involves a journey. Such journeys take time, requiring regular and caring contact with mentoring figures. It's going to take some personal attention from already busy people.

Imagine putting that level of care, attention and diplomacy into all the good ideas that come out of a Pathways workshop. Ideas are not that hard to generate. Effective implementation is another story.

Sorting out the ideas

Now that I've made it all sound too hard (remember Paul's counsel to think of ourselves with sober judgment in Roman's 12:3? It's also good counsel for organisations, especially churches), let's get back to the process.

I encourage participants in the workshop to pool their ideas and observations, and to seek to prioritise them. There is no scientific way for figuring out which idea should be given first priority for implementation, but here are some thoughts.

The low-hanging fruit

Occasionally there will be a clear and obvious 'win' staring the group in the face. Like a ripe peach within easy reach, it just needs to be seen and picked. These are the opportunities where a clear and simple step will likely yield significant and fairly quick results. More often than not, these are represented by a yawning gap after a well-established 'belonging' activity.

For example, a couple of churches that completed the Pathways workshop had been running meals programs. These were not the 'Here's your soup, mate. Next!' type of soup kitchens you sometimes find in the inner city (there's nothing wrong with such activities per se—they're just not all that effective as 'belonging' environments). Rather, these were environments where regular church attenders and 'guests' sat down together to eat and form friendships. Sure, the people receiving a free meal were undoubtedly poor, but in each case there was genuine dignity and reciprocity in the conversations that took place over the meal.

Both of these programs had been operating for a number of years and a sense of community had formed. After doing Pathways, both churches saw the opportunity to run an 'embracing the gospel' activity and invite people from the meals program. One church chose Youth Alpha, the other Christianity Explained. The new programs were promoted in up-front announcements, and then personal invitations were extended. In both cases, more than a dozen people immediately signed up, and a string of faith commitments followed.

Another common type of low-hanging fruit lies in the online space. Some churches quickly improve participation in their 'belonging' activities and even the visitor traffic in their worship services simply by improving their online presence.

One church with which I worked had identified families with toddlers as their mission focus group and decided to begin a playgroup. They got banners made up and did some newspaper advertising. A smattering of people attended. After a while, the leader realised that the local government website had a listing of the playgroups in the area. She applied to have their playgroup included on the list. Within a month the group was full with a waiting list.

The big opportunity
Sometimes a Pathways workshop will see an opportunity that has significant mission potential but will require considerable effort and resources. This may simply be a matter of recognising that a church is either in touch with, or at least in easy reach of, a large number of people all with a common characteristic or interest. Here are a couple of examples.

One church was already running a legendary kids' program—this program was amazing! It attracted over a hundred kids to their school holiday program and perhaps half that many to a weekly kids' club during school term (in a church with average weekly attendance of a little under two hundred). In the wash-up of the Pathways workshop, they realised the potential to build a pathway for the dozens of parents that came to the church premises to drop their kids off and returned to collect them.

Seeing the enormity of the potential, the church restructured their staff to give dedicated resources to reaching the parents of primary school kids. Relationships were formed, and a 'belonging' activity was created around parenting skills and resources. Alpha was scheduled, new friends were invited. Within a year people began to make faith commitments.

In another example, a church with no missional activity and no intentional contact with unchurched people began by looking around for God's invitation to mission. Across the street (literally, directly opposite) was a primary school. The church wondered how they could possibly begin to reach the school community.

By thinking pathways, they realised that their first step was to see how they could begin to get in touch with people in the school community. The opportunity became obvious—at the end of the school day, parents would wait for their kids on the front lawn of the church in the shade of the church building. On a warm day, offering cool drinks and striking up conversations seemed like an easy way to begin to get to know people. It was only the beginning of a pathway, but over a year this church went from no mission focus group and no mission activity to having a clearly identified group and a number of budding friendships formed with parents. Their next challenge will be to see what kind of 'belonging' activity might serve a felt need among the parents.

Capacity-building
Sometimes a church will participate in a Pathways workshop and come to the realisation that they have very little capacity to introduce new initiatives to address the gaps and blockages they've identified using the pathways board.

One way of addressing this challenge is to intentionally begin a capacity-building initiative, or, in Pathways terms, to put the initial effort into the 'serving in ministry' and 'leading ministry' categories. This will not yield quick growth results in terms of filling the pews. It may, however, shift the church's culture in terms of disciples serving the cause of Jesus.

One church completed the Pathways workshop and recognised that, while they were doing good work, they were well and truly operating closer to optimum than optimal. There were opportunities to eliminate gaps and clear blockages in their pathways, but all of them were going to take significant resources, and most of the leaders in the church were already doing several jobs. In family systems terms, a small group of leaders were over-functioning while a large portion of the congregation were under-functioning.

The church decided to work through a training module called 'Developing Leaders', which is basically chapter 10 of this book in the form of a workshop. The senior minister changed his understanding of his role. Less emphasis was placed on 'doing the job of running programs' and more on 'leading and developing the people to run the programs'.

The first person to commit to change was the senior minister, who put aside some of his other tasks to focus on creating a leadership community where emerging leaders could be formed while they served in various ministries of the church.

Start by doing less
Remember the exhausted church whose pathways board grew long tendrils of post-it notes? For them, the idea of adding another commitment to their already overflowing list of activities and programs seemed beyond the realms of sanity. For them the place to begin was to decide what they could cut.

As they talked, it became clear there was a rather large 'elephant in the room'. Its name was 'The Fete'. Every year this small church put on a fete of epic proportions. So elaborate was the fete that it took about six months to prepare. People complained about the workload, the inconvenience and the stress, but they were in general agreement that to discontinue the fete would be sacrilegious, financial suicide and earn the ire of the surrounding community.

The senior minister (a patient and very determined fellow) worked through the issues one by one. As it turned out, the fete cost about $4500 to put on (by the time all the input costs by various church members were accounted-for) and brought in about $6000. If the thirty or so people who busted their chops each year to put it on could each kick in an extra $50, they could each gain days or even weeks of free time.

The minister also asked how many people had become members of the church or had joined any other program in the church through the fete. A little research established the answer was zero.

Finally the minister proposed, 'How about we cancel the fete for one year and see what reaction and result we get? If we get negative feedback or we suffer financially, we can reconsider.'

That did it. There was never another fete. Some of the released energy went into another community event that the church had also been running annually. Other energy went into the programs designed for their specific mission focus group. The finances were never troubled.

Sometimes doing less can be achieved by simply not 're-starting' an activity after a holiday recess. Annual events can sometimes be deleted from the calendar without the epic battle of slaying a sacred cow. However, when choosing which activities to cut, it's always better to cut a program that is not part of a pathway or has little potential for mission, rather than simply choosing the one that will trigger the least resistance.

Ceasing to be all things to everyone
By now you'll realise that I'm pretty committed to the idea of a church identifying one or more mission focus groups. Most churches, on completing their pathways board, will have a bunch of yellow post-it notes that don't really fit in the pathway of any mission focus group.

If things haven't become a little tense yet, they sometimes do so now. This is because it's at this stage of the process that conversations arise about the validity or otherwise of 'fellowship' activities. I've been promising to deal with them for a couple of chapters, so now is as good a juncture as any.

One option I've observed is to play double-or-nothing. By this I mean the leadership of the church simply makes an executive decision to discontinue any program that has no practical potential for mission. It's really only possible with a great deal of goodwill and credibility 'banked' with the congregation. Without it, the keepers of the ill-fated program may simply leave in protest—it's not unheard-of for all the participants in the program to leave over a short space of time and reconvene under the auspices of a neighbouring church.

Alternatively, those disenfranchised by the decision might decide to dig in and fight. Now you've got yourself a holy war. You would be amazed how focused, motivated, organised and downright ruthless those apparently sleepy parishioners can become when they feel threatened. I'm all for decisive leadership, but tread carefully. Protracted conflicts will keep you from mission as much as ineffective programs – perhaps more so.

Another approach is to take a leaf from the parable of the barren fig tree in Luke 13:6–9 (not to be confused with the story of the cursing of the fig tree in Matthew 21:19—that would take things in an altogether different direction). Fellowship programs are a bit like trees without fruit: they have a certain ornamental appeal but don't really produce anything. Perhaps giving the program a season of fertilising might enable some change toward fruitfulness. By this I mean spending ongoing time discipling the leaders, helping them to grasp the importance of mission, helping them to think through how the program could yield more than just fellowship. If they begin to get on board and try a few things, all the better. If not, you might end up considering the first option.

Or you could try a third option, which is a little more subtle and possibly less likely to generate resistance. Basically it's the opposite of the second option: rather than pouring more resources in, it seeks to curtail the fellowship program's drain on resources. Or more accurately, where this fellowship program competes for resources with more fruitful activities, the more fruitful activities are given priority. This is best done by formalising a 'Mission gets priority' policy by the church council then applying it consistently. If your church council doesn't have the gumption to make such a policy, I would venture that you have more fundamental issues to resolve than a stubborn fellowship activity.

Disputes over the tangible resources of money and floor space are not uncommon in church life. Simple unwavering adherence to a mission-first policy should get things settled. There will be grumbling, but seldom outright hostility. But it will take the council being resolute and clear-headed.

The real clincher is to divert people away from fellowship for its own sake and into mission, where deeper and more satisfying fellowship occurs as a by-product. That means getting beside the high-potential people who attend the fellowship program and investing in them, giving them opportunities to grow and develop, and offering them ministry opportunities that make the most of their gifts and interests. The key to this strategy being successful is giving those high-potential people the frequent and direct attention of prominent leaders who take a personal interest in their development. I know this should go entirely without saying, but I've watched too many leaders promote people into roles for which they're not prepared and in which they're not supported only to see them pull out eighteen months later.

If a high-potential person begins to feel a little time-pressured, it's likely they'll ditch the fellowship activity before they pull out of their new ministry opportunity because the new activity is more life-giving.

The blessing of not knowing

It's not unusual for churches to look over their pathways board, see a range of challenges and then draw a blank on what to do. For example, in the all-too-common instance of a gap in the 'embracing the gospel' space, many churches see the need but have no real idea of what sort of ministry would be appropriate. This has been especially evident in my current setting, where the more traditional and Anglo-Catholic parishes don't resonate with many of the off-the-shelf catechesis processes like Alpha or Christianity Explained, but also believe that the traditional catechism would be unpalatable to their mission focus group.

I'll often suggest their first action should be one of research—go find out what is out there. Ask some ministers in growing Anglo-Catholic parishes what they're doing.

Another common 'unknowing' happens in churches that have identified a mission focus group but have no existing service-offer to them. Typically churches in this situation will take a guess, based on what might have worked for a church in a similar setting. Sometime this results in an effective program being initiated, sometimes not.

Others will research churches effectively reaching people similar to their chosen mission focus group. Still others will begin by engaging their mission focus group directly, not with a service-offer, but with questions. For a church seeking to reach a school community, a meeting with the principal might be a good place to begin, followed by conversations with the welfare coordinator, or even the remedial learning coordinator (if they school has one). Most school staff are delighted when a church approaches them saying, 'We would like to be a resource for you—what can we do to be of benefit?'

Too often our anxiety drives us to take a guess at what might be good news for our community, when some careful and patient research could save us from a lot of wasted effort, false starts and tainted goodwill. Remember, Pathways is not a quick fix but a long-term discipline. Taking a few months to understand before you act is often a delay worth enduring.

The problem trap

What are we going to do with (insert perennial problem program here _____)? Frequently in Pathways workshops, church teams get all of their activity mapped out on their pathways board and then get drawn into an often hackneyed conversation about some longstanding problem.

Effective organisations—be they families, community groups, corporations or churches—tend to commit their best resources to their biggest opportunities. Less effective organisations are more likely to commit their best resources to their biggest problems.

Unfortunately, denominational leaders too often model the actions of the less effective organisations. In my conversations with bishops, superintendents, denominational consultants and presbytery ministers I frequently ask about the proportion of their time they spend with churches in crisis or conflict. The answer is nearly always well over half. If I push further, it frequently turns out that the problem churches that are consuming denominational time and resources today are generally the same ones that were consuming those resources three years earlier—same churches, different 'issues'.

Paul Borden makes some rather forthright observations in this regard in his classic *Hit the Bullseye*.[55] If this is an issue for you, reading Borden, and then some family systems material (begin with Roberta Gilbert, Peter Steinke or Ron Richardson), will do you the world of good. If you're a denominational leader or executive, you really, *really* should read Borden.

Let me be clear on this: don't ignore problems, and don't throw all of your resources at them either. Instead step back, take a deep breath and ask some questions.

Often intervening in 'problem' situations with your own effort and resources in order to 'solve' the problem really amounts to little more than rewarding bad behaviour. If you do 'solve' the problem, you'll probably find yourself back in the same context twelve to eighteen months later, saving the day

---

[55] Borden, Paul D. *Hit the Bullseye: How Denominations Can Aim Congregations at the Mission Field* (Abingdon, Nashville, 2003).

with a new problem that's arisen among the same people. It's like Groundhog Day.

Asking yourself questions like 'What is my responsibility here?' can save your sanity. (Here's a clue: 'Ensuring we all get along nicely' or 'Making sure no one has hurt feelings' are always incorrect answers.) Another useful question is, 'What is the reasonably predictable outcome if the problem continues?' It may be that you only need to pay the issue sufficient attention to keep it contained, which might simply be keeping in thoughtful contact with the key players, and asking them about their responsibilities and what they plan to do to discharge those responsibilities.

Put another way, a useful general rule is to give problems sufficient attention to keep them from getting out of hand, and no more. If a 'problem' ministry dies for lack of attention, it's probably for the best.

Avoid deconstructing

There's a whole genre of local church mission literature that sets out to deconstruct the Western-world church. Sometimes church teams look at their pathways board and, feeling a little overwhelmed, begin to enter into a despairing conversation about the parlous state of their church (which inevitably widens to the church in general). This is especially likely if your team contains a few Gen-Xers.

In my twenty-odd years of vocational ministry, I've learned that God seems to be okay working with somewhat dysfunctional and conflicted systems. We don't need to get everything sorted out in order to begin serving the community with compassion and making disciples. In fact, the very act of pursuing the mission of Jesus seems to have the effect to sorting things out over the long term.

There will always be people doing the right stuff for the wrong reasons and vice versa. There will always by people protecting turf and misunderstanding and sabotaging. The structures will only ever work in a 'more-or-less' sense. But the problems, barriers and sub-optimal attitudes that appear to be insurmountable very rarely are.

Even after years of diligent work, your pathways will have plenty of room for improvement. Attempting to get everything structured and organised perfectly before you begin will only pull you out of the game.

Unless confronted with something that is totally unworkable, I encourage church leaders to avoid getting caught up in deconstructing. Unless the system is toxic and has virtually no goodwill, leaders are better off accepting the imperfections and seeking to get some observable progress with whatever they have. It's kind of like renovating a house while you're still living in it.

Ordering the priorities
There's no rubric I can offer that will help to prioritise a church's actions. If there is a low-hanging-fruit opportunity, and the church has the resources to pursue it, there's a lot to be said for a simple initiative that could deliver some encouraging results fairly quickly.

If there's a big opportunity that has potential to deliver significant results, it may be prudent to make this a high priority—but consideration will need to be given to the church's capacity to put in the effort and resources to pull it off.

Capacity-building may be worth pursuing, especially if the church already struggles for leaders and workers. This could be done in concert with cutting back some activities. Perhaps some people could be diverted from 'fellowship' activities into a capacity-building initiative.

Even if there's a clear opportunity emerging, it may be worth doing a little research before you commit to a specific plan of action.

Sometimes it will be clear that one initiative may be required before another has opportunity to succeed—that is, there will be a logical sequence in which to implement various actions. For example, you may want to work on the quality of relationships and witness in a 'belonging' environment before you launch an 'embracing the gospel' activity.

I encourage church teams to talk over the options, weighing their various advantages and drawbacks. Most groups will fairly quickly settle on an order of priority.

Creating a plan
This is the stage where things can become unnecessarily complex, simply because we overestimate a church's capacity to undertake significant and sustained change and because we try to define too much too early.

The universe already contains more than enough books, manuals, software packages and post-graduate qualifications in project management to cover the process of creating a plan in response to your Pathways discoveries. You can read, purchase, work through, download, install and enrol as you feel the need. And in the meantime, here's a collection of pointers to get you started.

One thing at a time—maybe two
Organisational change is like driving a car at high speed. Unless you're an absolute expert, it's very hard to find the upper limit of its capacity without exceeding it and courting disaster. Drive with a safety margin and you're less likely to crash, even if you have to make some adjustments for unforeseen obstacles. Drive the car on the limit and even the slightest miscalculation or disturbance could find it in the repair shop and you in hospital.

Going a little slower is unlikely to harm your church. The same can't be said for trying for too much too fast. People need time to digest ideas and to adapt. I've watched leaders wrestle in their own heads with an idea for years, then hatch a plan to implement it, expecting their congregation to understand and embrace the idea almost instantly. Even if the people are cooperative, if they don't understand the change sufficiently to implement it properly, you'll end up with a half-baked change initiative.

A similar principle applies with resourcing. We tend to underestimate the overall draw on resources that is generated by change. Consulting, planning, dealing with questions, more planning, piloting, evaluating, more planning, monitoring, adjusting, correcting, more planning—it all takes up a lot of people's time.

Then there are the issues of grief, resistance and push-back I described earlier.

For all the reasons set out above, I counsel churches to aim to change one thing at a time (or in a large church, for each ministry department to change one thing in their pathway at a time). That doesn't mean having only one point of action in a plan, but it does mean staggering or even sequencing the actions so that the change is sustainable in terms of people's learning, the resources the change consumes, and the degree of emotional disturbance that might be aroused at any one time.

Think long haul in big pictures
If your plans require a big change in people's understanding, a big change in practice or a big change as to who has power and kudos, you'll do well to think of it as a consistent and determined campaign rather than a lightning victory.

Sometimes you really do need root and branch change—but it's far less often than most people think.

Sketch out the changes you need to make in order or priority, outline-planning perhaps three and probably no more than five initiatives (depending on size, scope and complexity) over a period of six months or so. If yours is a very large church that can set multiple teams to work on multiple pathways simultaneously, you might want to think about three 'live' initiatives per team over six months.

If you're a large church pastor I can pretty much guarantee you're thinking, 'We can handle more than that.' There is a huge difference between getting stuff checked off on your to-do list and creating sustainable, effective, lasting change. I have watched far too many large churches waste their change efforts because the need for speed has robbed an initiative of impact.

It will take much longer to transform your processes and culture so that everything is consistent with Pathways thinking, but a good start with some clear wins early will give you as leader the credibility, and your team the confidence, to create the momentum to accelerate the pace (a little) in the next round of planning.

As you begin to put together your plan, you might want to look at the template we've provided at www.pathways4mission.com

Based on the example church we've been using throughout this section, on pages 222-223 there's a Pathways plan for their Mission Focus Group 'People from non-English speaking background'.

Things to note about the plan
You'll note this plan covers only one pathway. I generally encourage smaller churches to pay attention to just one pathway at a time. Most don't listen and attempt two, but usually only make real progress with one.

You'll also note the plan is not 'church-wide'—it just deals with the programs and activities that pertain to the primary mission focus group. As a church you don't need to be working on changing and improving everything all the time. Doing so risks spreading the resources for change too thinly and in the end making little if any progress anywhere. It's okay to keep most things ticking over while you work on your best opportunity.

In a larger church this plan could be run just by the conversational English ministry team provided there was not too much change going on elsewhere in the church. Meantime, another team reaching another mission focus group could work on a similar plan.

Keep the details to a short timeframe
While this hypothetical team have identified twelve initiatives to improve, they've only put tangible action plans to three of them. There's no point putting effort into further actions too far ahead of time, because the effects of implementing the earlier initiatives, and the learning derived from the exercise, will shape the plans for subsequent initiatives.

Back a few decades, when the church growth movement was in full swing and everybody was embracing rational-comprehensive planning methodologies, churches tended to attempt to plan everything before doing anything. I remember coaching a planting team that had structured out their church for a congregation of about three hundred. They had plans for half a dozen staff and various departments.

Their team at that stage was about six. Not six staff—six people in the whole enterprise. They didn't need detail about a program-sized structure that far out. They needed a plan to build their team and begin to engage their receptor culture. At that stage they could have validly operated with a planning horizon of no more than six months, and the detailed planning only needed to take in about twelve weeks.

Mission Focus Group: People from non-English speaking background

Pathway Step	Current Activities	Initiatives to Improve
Potential Contact	Signboard Website	Refresh Signboard for new group Update website for new group Create Facebook page for conversational English
In Touch		Invite-a-friend campaign
Belonging	Conversational English group	Increase invitation to social interaction outside class and to Christianity Explained Launch a second conversational English class
Embracing the Gospel	Christianity Explained course	Run the course at two more suitable times in appropriate languages with childcare if needed
Following Jesus	Worship service: 10.00 am Adult Bible study	Launch a Mandarin Bible Study group Launch a Portuguese Bible Study group
Serving in Ministry	Conversational English ministry team	Introduce prayer and accountability triplets Run refresher training in 'testimony soundbites'
Leading Ministry	Cell group leader training	Prepare leaders for LOTE Bible study group

Continued...

Action for Implementation
Priority 7 Priority 9 Priority 10
Priority 8
Priority 1 **Who**—Judy **What**—Introduce an 'invitation prompt' segment in team huddle before conversational English. **When**—From first class in 2016 (i.e. Feb. 1) Priority 6
Priority 3 **Who**—Gail **What**—Research suitable times, languages, venues and supports needed for new Christianity Explained groups to be most convenient to conversational English participants **When**—by April 1, 2016 **Who**—Tommy **What**—Coordinate launch of two new Christianity Explained groups **When**—First group by June 1, 2016; second group by Aug. 1, 2016
Priority 5 Priority 12
Priority 2 **Who**—Judy **What**—Research, design and pilot accountability triplets that includes accountability for: • Praying for three Friends in the conversational English class • Sharing relevant 'testimony soundbites' • Inviting friends to social interactions and Christianity Explained **When**—Launch first triplet before March 1, 2016 - Launch three triplets by May 1, 2016 Priority 11
Priority 4

Remember to think of your planned changes as a series of experiments. As the implementation proceeds, the unforeseen will inevitably arise and you'll need to adapt. Your plan may fail, sending you back to the drawing board.

I'm not saying you shouldn't think further ahead—you'll note there are twelve initiatives included in the plan, which may take up to two years to implement. I *am* saying that much of the detailed long-range planning over which churches labour for days and weeks never comes to fruition and only saps energy. Plan with enough detail to keep things moving and to give a general sense of the direction ahead.

Unless you're building a new auditorium or something of that scale, it's probably better to plan in detail on a relatively short timeline, while keeping in mind the longer-term plan in outline form.

In the traditional 'plan everything before doing anything' schema, plans could take up to a year to formulate and would remain essentially unchanged for up to five years while hapless teams laboured to implement them.

Using the lighter, simpler and more dynamic approach advocated here, the plan takes a couple of hours to develop sufficiently for implementation to begin. Teams should treat the plan as a dynamic document, adding detail to initiatives, changing priorities and adapting as the plan unfolds. Typically such a plan would be updated every two or three months. More recently, writers such as Will Mancini have pushed into the idea of an 'eye on the horizon' while focusing on the next ninety days.[56]

Responsibilities with individuals, not groups

You'll note from the example that responsibilities for change initiatives are always assigned to an individual rather than a group. There's a very important reason for this, and it's encapsulated in this maxim: *A shared responsibility is a shirked responsibility*. I can feel some of you rankling even as you read it. Let me unpack it with a couple of stories.

Back in the dim dark past of my early human resources management career, I worked primarily in occupational health and safety. There's a common-slogan pasted up in manufacturing plants that proclaims, 'Safety is everyone's responsibility.' And that—hopefully—is true. Kind of.

---

[56] Mancini, Will & Bird, Warren. *God Dreams: 12 Vision Templates for Finding and Focusing Your Church's Future* (B&H, Nashville, 2015).

If you read the legislation under which an employer is liable to be prosecuted if a worker is injured, it becomes abundantly clear that individuals — manufacturers of plant, suppliers of chemicals, occupiers of premises, employers, employees and contractors — all have very specific responsibilities. It would have been more accurate to paste up a sign saying, 'Every individual has specific responsibilities to ensure this workplace is safe and without risks.' But this takes more words and is nowhere near as catchy.

Everyone has some degree of responsibility for safety, but those responsibilities differ significantly. The way to make a workplace safe is for each individual to have a clear understanding of their specific responsibilities and to be diligent in discharging them. And my personal responsibility was largely to make sure that each person did and was.

Committees and teams tend not to nail things down to the responsibilities of individuals. Instead, it becomes 'the team job'.

The ineffectiveness of this was demonstrated to the point of farce in an investigation into procurement problems in the Australian armed forces. This was the umpteenth review that had been carried out in the now-defunct Defence Materiel Organisation. Each previous review had discovered there was insufficient scrutiny of specifications, product compliance to specifications and supplier capabilities to consistently deliver product to specification. And each review recommended another layer of accountability to review decisions. All told, there were up to twelve layers of decision-making. Each layer was not an individual, but a board or committee.

In the defence force, people get moved around and so an individual may only occupy a position or a seat on a committee for eighteen months or so.

Let's imagine that a proposal for a tank landing barge has come before a review committee. Three layers below have given it the green light, and a further two more senior bodies will review this committee's decision subsequent to their approval. The fine officers on this committee are probably thinking, 'Well, surely those guys have reviewed this thoroughly and ensured that the barge is fit for purpose and offered at a competitive price — and if not, surely the brass above will pick it up.' And they're likely also thinking, 'We've got a lot to get through, and I don't want to be the guy who holds everything up with inane questions.'

As you're already suspecting, this mindset could be replicated throughout the process. Meanwhile, no one was stopping to ask how the procurement process for the new tanks was coming along.

Now let's imagine further that the tank procurement process is going swimmingly, and the tank corps is eagerly awaiting the arrival of their new tanks, which are not only faster, stronger and more capable, but also larger and heavier than those used previously. By the time it becomes apparent that the new barges will not carry the new tanks, six committees involving perhaps thirty people in total have all given their approval. Who is held responsible? Multiple committees all depended on each other to cover all the bases. And by the time a review is launched, the individuals who served on most of those committees have moved onward and upward.

Hopefully this only partially apocryphal story has illustrated the logic of my recommendation that every action be assigned to an individual who has the responsibility and the commensurate authority to carry it through.

That doesn't mean the church becomes a loose coalition of mavericks all doing their own thing. Nor am I ignoring Paul's body ministry argument in 1 Corinthians 12. Paul is arguing that everybody has a part to play. It is in no way counter to Paul's argument to hold that individuals should be accountable for playing that part with diligence.

Working as a team means making use of the multiple capacities resident in the group. An individual can call on the capacities of others without handing off their personal responsibility for completion of a task. Let's not confuse teamwork with groupthink.

What and when
You'll also note that the sample plan includes some very specific statements about the tasks to be done. This is essentially good old SMART goal setting (Specific, Measurable, Achievable, Relevant and Time-framed). I know the idea of SMART goals has become a bit clichéd, yet so many teams, boards and church councils spend valuable meeting time thrashing out action plans that are so fluffy it's impossible to determine where to begin and whether any progress has been made.

Be as concrete as you can in defining what is to be done by when, even if you have to break the goals in your plan down into smaller tasks to be recorded in your team minutes. Don't be afraid to set small, short-term goals if that's all that can be achieved in the time between team meetings. Something as simple as 'Bruce will investigate and evaluate Alpha, Christianity Explained and Pilgrim as possible "embracing the gospel" activities and bring a recommendation to the next meeting' is far more useful than 'Playgroup team to launch Alpha in 2017', which may not get any attention until June or July 2017.

Summary
Let's sum up this chapter.

- When developing a Pathways plan in response to your discovery process, it's generally better to be a little pessimistic about how much you can achieve.
- Develop a simple plan that has a long-term outline with only the relatively short-term details filled in.
- Treat your plan as a working document, not a master blueprint—amend and update it regularly as implementation unfolds.
- Set goals that give personal responsibility to individuals. Be specific about the task and the timeframe.

Chapter 14
Managing and Evaluating

It begins with you
The journey to becoming a church that organises all its activity by Pathways principles is a long one. Many churches don't make it because, quite frankly, their leadership lacks the discipline and patience to relentlessly make decisions using questions that arise from Pathways thinking.

Some of you will be recoiling as you read, shocked at the apparent arrogance of the previous paragraph. You might be asking yourself, 'Who does this guy think he is?' A valid question. Before you take to social media to give me a pasting, though, carefully read the paragraph again, this time substituting 'mission' for 'Pathways'. Pathways is not the silver bullet or the golden key. It's one of a number of paradigms designed to help local churches accomplish the mission of Jesus in the world.

If you're attracted to an alternative paradigm (Christian Schwarz's 'Natural Church Development',[57] for example, or maybe Alan Hirsch's 'Forgotten Ways'),[58] and if you believe it will serve your church more effectively than Pathways, I encourage you to finish reading this section and then work with your leadership team to relentlessly pursue your chosen paradigm, with as much discipline and consistency as you can muster, for at least a decade.

Most organisational change initiatives fail to achieve their goals. The vast majority of change initiatives in churches fail. According to John Kotter, they fail for a variety of reasons, all of which trace back eventually to a lack of leadership discipline, focus and sustained effort.[59] I encourage you to find the footnoted article and read it through.

One factor I see repeatedly in companies and churches is described by Kotter as 'Not Anchoring Changes in the Corporation's Culture'. Sometimes this happens because a new challenge arises that consumes all the oxygen in the leadership team (for example, a church conflict or a building program).

---

[57] http://www.ncd-international.org/public/
[58] https://www.theforgottenways.org/alan-hirsch.aspx
[59] Kotter, John P. 'Leading Change: Why transformation efforts fail', *Harvard Business Review*, January 2007, pp. 92–107.

Sometimes it happens because the organisation's leadership suffers from a kind of corporate Attention Deficit Hyperactivity Disorder and is constantly grabbing onto the latest shiny new idea that drifts into their peripheral vision.

However, even more pervasive than these is what Ed Friedman calls 'homeostasis'—the inexorable force that causes organisations to settle back to the way they've always been.[60] Peter Drucker is quoted as remarking, 'Culture eats strategy for breakfast.' Unless the leadership of your church is willing to be relentless and consistent in applying missional thinking to every decision and in every allocation of resources over months and years, your Pathways odyssey will peter out, gradually subsumed by the invisible power of 'the way we do things around here'.

As I write this chapter I am studying Robert Quinn's classic *Deep Change*.[61] The uncomfortable truth with which Quinn confronts me is that change initiatives fail because the leader themselves fails to change. To bring Kotter a little closer to home, change fails because the leader fails to anchor changes in their personal thinking, values and decision-making—that is, their own intrapersonal culture. To use Friedman's language, the first place to deal with homeostasis is within yourself.

Let's be frank. While to this point I've written close to eighty thousand words attempting to explain it, Pathways is not that hard to understand. I doubt you've read a single paragraph where you've crinkled up your eyes and rubbed your face exclaiming, 'Ugh! This so hard to get my brain around.'

By far the most significant factors in the success or failure of a Pathways initiative is the willingness of the leader to change their own habits of thought, decision-making and behaviour, and the discipline to see it through all the way until it *is* 'the way we do things around here'.

If you're a church leader and you're contemplating using Pathways to organise mission in your church—or you want to lead *any* initiative to improve the missional effectiveness of your church— there are two fairly fundamental questions you'll need to address.

---

[60] Friedman, Edwin H. *Generation to Generation: Family Process in Synagogue and Church* (Guilford, New York, 1985).
[61] Quinn, Robert E. *Deep Change: Discovering the Leader Within* (Jossey Bass, San Francisco, 1996).

First, are you prepared to do the painful work of personal change as you discover how your own *modus operandi* is hampering the mission of the church? (And before you glibly answer, remember that you're probably yet to discern it.)

And second, are you prepared to chip away at this year in and year out, to deal with the resistance and the rolled eyes and the muttered 'I'm so sick of this Pathways stuff!'?

If you thoughtfully answered 'yes' to these questions, and you're still yet to sign up with a coach, put this book down and make an appointment with yourself in your diary to do what it takes to get a coach. There are some helpful beginning places at www.pathways4mission.com.

Getting in the rhythm

If you've completed the workshop with the post-it notes and developed an implementation plan, it's best to begin a rhythm of planning and review. To do that, you'll need to answer some basic questions.

First, who is the keeper and custodian of the plan? This could be the leader or pastor of the overall pathway (more on that in the next chapter). It could be the leader of the most prominent program in the plan—some churches refer to the pathways by the 'belonging' activity within it, for example, the 'Playgroup Pathway' or the 'Basketball Pathway'. They do this because the pathways tend to merge to some degree around whatever stage contains the public worship service. In a small church, the keeper of the plan is probably going to be the minister.

Second, who will hold this person accountable? If you're a solo pastor, this might be your coach, or a peer—say, an elder in the church. If the keeper of the plan is not the senior or solo minister, the keeper's direct supervisor is usually the best person.

If you don't have clear supervisory relationships in your church, you've got some serious work to do that's beyond the scope of this book.

Systemic approaches like making the progress of each pathway a standing item on the church council agenda is another way to lock in some discipline and accountability. The aim is not to be some kind of oppressive overlord, but to serve people by ensuring the main thing stays the main thing and doesn't get lost or consumed by the urgent. Just make sure that the council respects the line between governance and operations, and doesn't go tinkering with the detail of operational decisions.

Third, which team or forum will implement and develop the plan? This should be pretty self-evident, based on the team or forum in which the keeper of the plan serves.

Fourth, when you've got the people stuff sorted, you'll need a regular habit of reviewing progress, planning next steps and updating the Pathways plan. In my experience, a monthly rhythm works best. If it's any less frequent than three-monthly, you'll probably lose momentum and focus.

Asking the right questions
In your pathways plan, you'll target gaps and blockages you've identified as part of your post-it notes exercise, where you created a pathways board. Where you've identified gaps you'll probably begin a new program, activity or initiative to fill the gap. The goals you'll set will probably follow a sequence of research, plan and implement. Once that's done, you'll need to review effectiveness, which I address in the section below.

When dealing with blockages, you might be working on several steps in succession, since each pathway is a system and each element has some effect on the others. Whether you're dealing with gap or blockages, once you're well into the implementation, you'll need to start asking questions about effectiveness—first the effectiveness of the changes you've made and then the overall effectiveness of the pathway.

Programs in a pathway
As each step in the pathway is designed to achieve different things, you'll need to assess activities at different steps by different criteria. That said, there are two general questions you can ask for every step.

First question: how many people are participating in this step? If an activity is struggling to engage and retain people, you have a *participation* problem. This may be caused by a failure at a previous step, or it may be a symptom of failing to meet or consider *felt needs*. Either it's not scratching where people are itching or there are logistical, cultural or educational barriers.

Second question: how many people have progressed from this step to the next? If there are plenty of people coming along but little movement to the next step, you have a *progression* problem. This might be because the step in question is not meeting *discipleship needs*, so people are just not ready to take the next step. (To determine this, have a look back at Figure 1 and try to figure out if the discipleship need is being adequately addressed.)

Progression problems may also be caused by a poor transition strategy—failing to promote and invite. A further reason may be that the activity at the next step is suffering from the participation problems I described above.

Asking these two basic questions will generally be sufficient to enable you to see where the pathway is working and where it is struggling. Once you've established where the pathway needs some tweaking, it will be helpful to think about the specific activity that seems to be struggling, identifying its place in the pathway then reading over the chapter in Part 2 that deals with the relevant step. For example, you might have a pathway that uses the Pilgrim series at the 'embrace the gospel' step. Asking the two questions may reveal that plenty of people are attending the program, but very few are making faith commitments and progressing into the 'Following Jesus' step. In this case, reading back over chapter 7 ('Embracing the Gospel') could help you identify the blockage.

Sometimes it's useful to measure more specific indicators than attendance and transitions. Studying the relevant chapter and understanding some of the specific behaviours and conditions that correlate to effectiveness can help target specific discipleship issues. Once these are clarified, the team may consider programming, training or accountability options.

For example, you might have a meals program (a 'belonging' environment) that serves fifty people a week, and yet almost no one progresses to the next step, which for arguments' sake might be Christianity Explained (an 'embracing the gospel' program). A close look at the program reveals that, while plenty of people receive food (felt need), very few form meaningful friendships with Christians (a discipleship need at the 'belonging' stage). Each of your team may decide to commit to forming friendships with three people in the meals program, look for opportunities to bear witness to the goodness of Jesus and personally invite them to the next Christianity Explained program. The team agrees to meet in triplets before the team meeting to pray and hold each other accountable.

I realise this can make some people a little squeamish or seem a little contrived and intrusive. I also acknowledge that there are limits as to how much 'push' people will tolerate. But up to a point, churches that are more willing to intentionally strategise around these issues tend to see more people progress through their pathways.

Programs with no identified pathway

Remember all those activities on your pathways board that didn't serve any particular pathway? As you work on your Pathways plan, it's a good idea to keep reviewing these based on three questions.

First, is this activity achieving results that are worth the investment of the resources it consumes? The activity may not achieve much but may not take up much in terms of time, money and floor space. It might not be worth the heartache to end it. Or it might be resource-hungry for no lasting benefit, and you could take the tough decision to put it out of your misery.

It's amazing what kind of stuff churches get into the habit of doing. One church with which I briefly worked put thousands of dollars and hundreds of hours into running a 'festival of lights' each Christmas. When they asked themselves the cold, hard questions, no one could point out a tangible benefit that justified the cost and effort. They had 'always' done it. It was a kind of community tradition. People liked it. There was no better argument for it than that. No one ever became a disciple because of it. So they stopped. After a brief period of discontent, everyone was relieved. And the December electricity bill was reduced by about eighty per cent.

Second, is the activity doing good for people who would otherwise be in need? This is especially relevant for activities that serve those outside the church, and even more important if those people are poor and marginalised.

I am wary of churches simply becoming welfare agencies and I would always argue that it's preferable to have a pathway by which you might lead these people to faith in Jesus. However, sometimes it's enough to take care of orphans and widows in their distress simply because it's good to do. This in itself proclaims the kingdom of God.

If the activity is demonstrably worth the effort and being a benefit to people in need, the third question to ask is: can we build a pathway through this activity? This will throw up questions about next steps and resources, but it's a worthwhile discussion.

Shiny new ideas

Churches are prolific generators of ideas weird and wonderful. In the face of this reality, Thom Rainer and Eric Geiger in *Simple Church* counsel leaders to 'say "no" to almost everything'. Pathways gives you a simple framework by which to sort the gold from the mullock. Try some of these questions:

- Which mission focus group is this designed to serve?
- Is there an existing pathway to reach this group?
- If there's not, is God calling us to create one?
- If there is an existing pathway to reach this group, does this idea fill an identified gap?
- If not, is it a better bet than the program already serving this purpose?

Most shiny new ideas don't survive this set of questions. The ones that do are generally good ideas that should be considered.

Summary

Pathways is not a 'set and forget' intervention. It's a way of thinking and requires persistence and discipline to be effective. Part of the discipline is regular review, asking tough questions of your activities and programs to evaluate their fitness for purpose.

When gaps, blockages or even less-than-expected outcomes are identified, it takes the discipline of careful thought and examination to review the pathway or its parts in light of the theory, and to make adjustments.

Don't underestimate the value of re-reading the theory, particularly the chapters that pertain to the step you're seeking to improve. As Roberta Gilbert often says, 'If you know the theory you can use it. If you don't you can't.' You probably paid good money for this book. It would be a shame not to get the maximum benefit from it.

Chapter 15
Expand the Possibilities

Complimentary pathways
One effective pathway deserves another, to torture a well-worn phrase. Let me illustrate. Imagine your church has done a great job of reaching women with pre-schoolers through a playgroup. Imagine that over time a couple of dozen have come to faith and are now in active discipling relationships. What further possibilities could present themselves?

For starters, those pre-schoolers are probably by now beginning school, and your young Christian mums are about to form a whole new circle of friendships as their kids begin school. This presents an opportunity for a new pathway for mums with junior primary kids. You might want to think about encouraging invitations for coffee after-school drop-off, or maybe a reading group around parenting, or any other kind of 'belonging activity' that cements the new-found friendships into a sense of being welcome and appreciated. These could be formal and programmed or informal and organic.

Another possibility is a pathway that serves the needs of junior primary kids. This could spring from a 'belonging' activity like an after-school club, or a junior gym program using all that under-utilised space in your church building.

Of course, those mums probably got to be mums because they have a husband or partner. Strong relationships with the mums gives entrée into relationships with dads, and the possibility for a complementary pathway.

I like to encourage complementary pathways because they tend to work through naturally expanding relational networks. In observing the characteristics of Christian movements, Steve Addison pointed out that the gospel tends to spread through relational networks, and that the interconnected nature of relationships means that each new believer spreads the influence of the gospel into new social circles.[62]

Complementary pathways seek to build on the patterns present in relational networks, which means new pathways begin with a ready pool of people already at the 'in touch' stage. Because people tend to connect with others with whom they hold something in common (socioeconomic status, proximity, life stage, familial ties, a school), activities that already exist further along the pathway are likely to be more suited to participants in a new pathway.

Conversely, beginning a new pathway from scratch with an unrelated mission focus group may mean creating a whole chain of activities or environments, perhaps even a unique worship service. This isn't bad or wrong; it's just more work and more risk.

Using Pathways as a staffing tool

In the introduction I stated that this is not a book about structure. However, at this stage it's probably appropriate to have a little fireside talk about pathways and structure.

In the denominational system I currently serve, we have a legislated structure of a parish council and wardens. (I always picture wardens as hulking prison officers wearing dark uniforms and surly faces, carrying truncheons and chips on their shoulders—like something out of the *Shawshank Redemption*. Just can't shake the picture. Anyway ...) Those kind of structures are primarily bodies for governance—and the larger the church the more focused on governance they must be. I want to focus more on staff or key volunteer ministry leaders.

There's a bunch of literature around about the leadership and accountability structure of ministry functions in churches. Some of it is helpful. Some of it is, well...

There are churches that will grab pathways with both hands (a good start) and then decide to organise around the seven stages. They'll appoint a leader for communications and a leader for community connection, and then a leader for belonging, and then one for evangelism, and one for discipleship,

---

[62] Addison, Steve. *Movements That Change the World: Five Keys to Spreading the Gospel* (IVP, Downers Grove, 2011).

and one for ministry training, and usually the senior minister takes on leadership development. Hopefully you can see all seven stages represented here.

This is a helpful structure for a manufacturing plant, where you might have departments for purchasing, inward goods, casting, pressing, painting, assembly, packaging, finished goods and dispatch. In the church, it's not so helpful. Widgets in a factory have no choice. They're simply pushed from one stage to the next. In the church, there are no forklifts to shuttle people from one department to the next. Those transitions are made relationally, by invitation and freely chosen acceptance. When you structure according to developmental steps, people are shuttled from a ministry under the care of one leader and on to the next, under the care of a different leader. The oversight relationships run at right angles (that is, vertically down the columns of the pathways board) to the direction of discipleship, which flows horizontally from left to right.

This kind of structure interferes with relationship continuity because people get 'handed off' into a new set of relationships in a new department. Alternatively (especially in very large churches) it tends to press people into cohorts that are pushed through the process according to the calendar rather than by their progress toward Christlikeness.

And it gets worse. Because a leader of a column like 'Belonging' will have responsibility for a range of programs, there will be a tendency to make them similar so they're easier to understand and manage. However, the various activities in a certain column should serve various mission focus groups, each with unique felt needs and practical constraints. While consistency within a column makes life easier for the leader overseeing that column, it's of no real value to the people for whom the activities in that column exist.

Far more important is consistency across the row—that is, across all the activities in a particular pathway that serves a particular mission focus group. All of those activities should involve the same community of people, be mindful of the same needs and constraints, and logically report to the same leader who oversees the ministries within that pathway.

I realise I'm doing serious violence to some models of ministry while totally validating others. If you're doing 3DM or a similar missional community model, the argument of the previous few paragraphs will probably seem obvious to you – each missional community creates a tailored pathway for a particular mission focus group. Conversely, if you've embarked on an exercise to structure your church according to the five-fold ministry gifts, you may have already thrown the book into the rubbish bin. If you haven't (yet), you've probably got some reservations, to say the least.

Indulge me in a small diversion because this is important. Let's do a little rough-cut exegesis in Ephesians 4.

Paul ends chapter 3 with a benediction concluding with 'Amen'. It's fair to say he's beginning a new 'chapter' on a new-but-related topic. The new line of argument is about unity (v. 3) through Christlikeness: humble, gentle, patient, forbearing and loving (v. 2). The rest of the chapter expands this. He begins with the rationale for unity (one body, one Spirit, one Lord, one faith, one baptism, vv. 4–6). Then he goes on to how this comes about.

It's easiest if we trace the causes and effects backward from outcome to source—that way we keep the end purpose in mind. The endgame is set out in verse 13: 'we all reach unity in the faith and in the knowledge of the Son of God and become mature, attaining to the whole measure of the fullness of Christ.' There it is: unity through Christlikeness.

That outcome is the result of the body of Christ being built up (v. 12b). This comes about by God's people doing works of service (v. 12a), which in turn is made possible by them being prepared. This preparation is the function of apostles, prophets, evangelists, pastors and teachers (v. 11). Those people are gifts from Jesus, which he gave like a victorious king showering his people with the spoils of victory (v. 8). If, like Paul, you can self-identify as an apostle, the good news is that you can rightly claim to be God's gift to his people—because that's what those ascension, or 'victory procession', gifts are. They're gift-people. And the role of those gift-people is to prepare all God's people to attain unity by attaining maturity.

Some see these verses as a prescription for a particular structure or argue this is a definition of particular roles or positions. But this is simply torturing the text. Paul's argument is for unity; the means for that is becoming Christlike; and God has given us all these people who help us to help each another get there.

There is no ideal or optimal church structure set out in scripture. There are references to various roles, mostly with very little definition. The mission of the church, however, is reasonably clear, and it's my contention that we're charged with the responsibility of organising ourselves to achieve it. Structures result from adaptive challenges, and each situation will require its own solution.

If you staff by pathways instead of staffing by functions, you will appoint leaders in roles with titles that reflect the church's mission focus groups. You might have a 'pastor for ministry to children and families', a 'youth minister' and a 'coordinator for ministry to migrants'. Each of these will carry responsibility for the end-to-end ministry to these mission focus groups— from community awareness through to leadership development.

Of course it will get sticky somewhere around public worship services, because this tends to be the point where pathways begin to converge. The service or services will usually seek to cater for a broader variety of people than a single mission focus group.

Some churches have multiple Sunday services, each with a kind of default mission focus group. It's not uncommon for pastoral-sized (about one hundred people) Anglican churches in Melbourne to have an 8.00 am service that serves mostly retired people, a 10.00 am service for families and a 6.00 pm service for youth and young adults. In this case you could be daring and put each worship service under the care of the leader who oversees ministry to that mission focus group. It's not a perfect model, but there's a lot to recommend it in terms of consistency of relationships and catering to specific needs.

In churches that work along conventional lines—be they small neighbourhood chapels or mega-churches—Sunday at the church campus is like game day at the sports stadium. Because the instinct is to make the worship service the feature piece of church life, most churches will throw a disproportionate amount of resource at the service, including a good chunk of their staffing dollars. That plays out in the appointment of ministers with responsibility for worship or music, which tends to focus on the 'following Jesus' stage (that is, it follows the staff-to-function approach rather than staffing according to mission focus group).

My counsel in this situation goes something like this: 'Whatever you feed is most likely to grow.' If you feed resources into your public worship service, it will probably grow—but initially the growth will be mostly transfers of people looking for a better Sunday experience. If you feed mission, the initial growth will be in the early stages of the pathway, and will in time bring growth to the worship service, even if you end up planting a new one. You'll need some patience.

If your church can engage staff for two or three pathways and staff for the Sunday service as well, all the better. But if you have to choose, my counsel is to choose for mission.

In the case of large churches (corporate-sized churches over 450 people) there is probably scope for staffing both to mission focus groups and to functions. In fact, most large churches run a kind of hybrid model, with staff for children, youth, young adults, families and seniors; and perhaps one or two ethnicity-specific staff, as well as a worship pastor, perhaps a music director and even pastors for evangelism and discipleship.

This has potential to get complex when function and mission focus groups collide. For example, who has responsibility for evangelism among the Chinese-speakers—the 'evangelism pastor' or the Chinese pastor? If asked for advice, I would counsel that it is preferable to give the line of authority (and the budgetary authority) to the mission focus group pastor. That person must lead the community of people that that reaches Chinese-speakers who don't yet know Jesus.

What then is the evangelism pastor's role? I would argue to be a resource person: to provide coaching and training to 'prepare God's people for this work of service'—but not to exercise authority over the community that is actually doing the work of mission.

If we move our thinking further along the pathway, the same would go for a 'discipleship pastor'. Coach, train, encourage, resource—but leave the leadership of the team doing the work of ministry to the person overseeing end-to-end mission to the particular mission focus group.

Summary
Effective pathways are the ideal seedbed for new pathways. People who have embraced the good news of Jesus and begun following him as disciples give

entrée to new social circles. Since the gospel tends to spread through relationship networks, it's easier to build new pathways to reach people in those social networks—partners, siblings, parents, friends and neighbours.

While Pathways is not a structural model, structuring the church according to mission process and mission focus groups makes good organisational sense. It's an approach with several significant advantages over structuring according to functions like 'evangelism', 'worship' or 'discipleship'.

A final word

The website www.pathways4mission.com is designed to be a resource companion to this book. Initially the bare-bones tools will be there. As more resources become available, they'll go up on the site. It's worth checking in from time to time.

I devote much of my time and energy to leaders as they endeavour to lead churches into fruitfulness. Some are church planters—local missionaries on the frontlines. Some are denominational leaders who are kept awake at night by stuff that seems far removed from the mission of Jesus, yet they long to see his kingdom come through the churches they serve and oversee. Some belong to emergent tribes and hope to make dozens of disciples and never begin a public worship service. Others live with the pressure of creating a worship service each week and hope to make disciples around and through it. Some lead large and complex churches, others small churches with a different set of complexities.

This is my prayer for them, and for you as a leader in the church seeking to continue the mission Jesus Christ in the world.

I pray that you will have the clarity to focus on making disciples among the people to whom God has called you, and not let the clamour of everything else keep you from the main game.

I pray that you will live by the conviction that programs and activities are only useful as 'containers' and contexts for the transforming relationships that are the essential medium by which the kingdom comes.

I pray that you will only serve, fuel and resource that which fulfils the purpose for which your church is consecrated, and have the wisdom to see the clutter that must be cleared.

I pray that you will have the persistence to persevere, because this is a long road and there is much to discourage and distract.

I pray that you will have the courage to patiently but firmly deal with the inevitable push-back from those who are threatened, annoyed or simply don't get it.

And I pray that you will remain in Christ, bearing abundant and enduring fruit.

Appendix 1: Identifying a Mission Focus Group

Rationale

Churches that effectively introduce people to faith tend to reach a small number of fairly narrowly defined people groups. They might be defined by a particular life stage (for example, people with a toddler) or a particular need (for example, to improve their English) or by particular association (for example, students, parents of students, and staff of a local school).

To be effective in making disciples among those who have little or no church background (in Australia that's about three-quarters of the population), it's usually best to be clear on where you're going to begin. To put it another way, if you try to reach a smaller section of your community that shares a common interest, need or experience, you can tailor your efforts and concentrate your resources. As you make new disciples, new relationship networks will open up and your capacity to diversify your activities will grow.

Conversely, research by George Barna and more recently by Thom Rainer and Eric Geiger indicates that churches trying to reach everybody all at once often struggle to reach anyone at all.

This is not about being exclusive. Effective churches tend to welcome everyone, and take the care they can for whoever comes their way. And they recognise the unavoidable reality that every decision they make will inevitably suit some people more than others. So they make decisions about resources, strategies, schedules and style with a particular group in mind, in order to reach and make disciples among them.

Before your team attends a Pathways workshop, it's helpful to be reasonably clear about your mission focus group—that is, the slice of your community you are best positioned to reach, or the group you feel most strongly called to reach first.

If yours is a small church (less than fifty average weekend service attendance), you would do well to begin with a single mission focus group. If yours is a medium- or pastoral-sized church, perhaps you could begin with two. Larger, program- or corporate-sized churches can usually look at reaching a much broader slice of the community, and may have complete pathways for various age groups through the range of the human lifecycle (that is, from families with babies right through to the frail elderly). Even for larger churches, doing some careful missiological examination of your community can help you match your tone, style, vocabulary, priorities and budget to the particular socioeconomic and perhaps cultural strata you're called to reach first.

There is no foolproof formula to identify a mission focus group, but there are four clusters of questions I've found helpful for churches to consider.

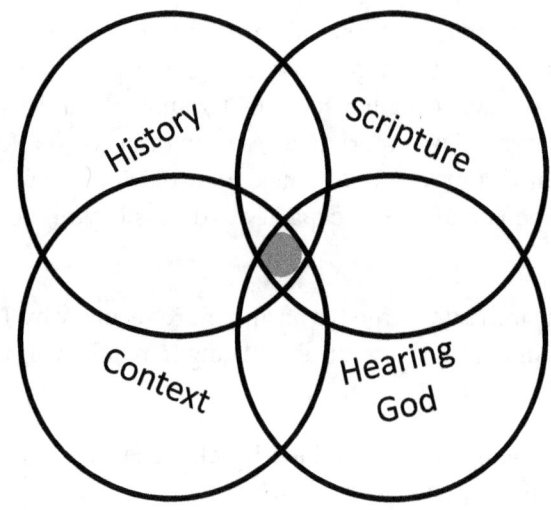

Set out below are some questions to work through with your church council or mission action team that will help you see the clues as to whom your mission focus group could be. This is not intended to be a survey to produce a definitive answer—more a set of conversation starters and prompts for further thought.

History (both recent and distant)
- Who has come to faith and/or joined your church recently?
    - What are the characteristics most of them have in common?
    - Why did they come to your church—what was the need they were hoping would be met?
- What are you already doing to serve the community (that is, activities and initiatives you already have in place that serve unchurched people)?

- How many unchurched people are involved?
- What kind of unchurched people do you already come into contact with?
  - For example, you might have a lot of people seeking pastoral services like baptisms, weddings and funerals.
- What's your church's heritage? You may have a long history of reaching a particular group, or a long association with a particular organisation, or perhaps a community reputation for serving a particular group. While these may not reflect your current reality, it may be that God is inviting you to reconnect to your heritage.

Context

- Who are you close to geographically?
  - Your church building may be right next to a school, an aged-care facility or a health club.
- What's going on in your area?
  - Sometimes there will be high profile concerns that provide an opportunity to connect and serve.
- Who's moving into your area?
  - Often a change in the area's demographics is a mission opportunity.
  - Identify their needs and hopes and you might have opportunity to connect and serve.

Scripture

- What's your understanding of the Bible's teaching on those for whom God is especially concerned?
- Are there any themes in scripture that have particular poignancy for your church?
  - Some churches have particular passages that keep arising as especially meaningful or as the theme text for the church.
- If your tradition accepts prophetic ministry, are there any scriptural themes to the words spoken to your church over time?
  - Let me emphasise *scriptural*—prophets will often draw a leader's or congregation's attention to a biblical passage that could have specific implications for God's particular calling to a church.
  - Let me also emphasise *over time*—when it comes to all things prophetic, there is safety in numbers. I encourage churches

to look for themes where a number of trusted prophets have said similar things over a period of months or years.

Hearing God

I've walked with several churches (unsurprisingly, nearly all of them were charismatic in their leanings) through a process of discernment that prayerfully brings all of the other three 'circles' together. This may involve:

- Prayer-walking the neighbourhood over a period of time, listening for God's prompting. He might point out a school, a homeless person, a bunch of kids, a syringe on the ground—and use things like these as indicators as to his calling to your church.
- A prayer retreat where time is set aside to reflect on scripture, worship and listen for God's prompting.

As with prophetic ministry, there is wisdom in seeking to hear from a number people as to what is discerned as God's leading, especially people who would qualify as 'elders': people of character, wisdom and spiritual maturity, be they appointed or simply well-recognised.

These questions are not foolproof. Sometimes consensus can coalesce around other factors such as tradition, 'Sunday school' answers, politics or people's fears. If you sense that tradition, politics and/or fears are clouding things, it may be wiser to begin with a small side-project with some like-minded people who sense God's invitation to reach a particular group. If the project proves effective, it can be broadened over time.

Begin with questions

Once you've worked through some of the discernment process, you will probably come up with a shortlist of possible mission focus groups. Even if you only come up with one, I encourage you to pause before you jump in to do something to reach them.

The first question seems obvious: are you already reaching people from this group? If so, your effort is best directed toward the people already in your pathway. Let's imagine you shortlisted 'retired people' and your church already operates a men's shed with a dozen blokes from fifty-five to seventy-five tinkering around in there a few times a week. You might also have a knitting circle with a group of similar-aged women. Here you have two possible 'belonging' groups. Applying some thoughtful Pathways thinking would lead you to ask, 'How many of these people already profess faith in Jesus?' If the answer is 'all of them' you may have a fellowship group on your hands, and may or may not choose that demographic as your mission focus group. If the answer is 'only some of them', however, there's good reason to pursue this group as your mission focus, since you already have a bunch of people from that group in your pathway.

If you're not reaching your proposed mission focus group to any significant extent, there's a danger in assuming you know what these people want and need. I've lost count of the number of failed initiatives I've seen churches launch based on assumptions rather than solid missiology.

Your first step is to go and begin conversations with some people from your proposed mission focus group. You may need to do some work on where to find them and how to engage them. And you may need to go though 'ambassadors' to get there. For example:

- A school chaplain or principal may help you understand and begin some conversations with school kids.
- A local community house may put you in touch with unemployed people.
- A community housing agency or social worker may help you begin conversations with people vulnerable to homelessness.

Too often churches get a 'vision' for a particular program without understanding the people it's intended to serve. Be prepared to spend several months seeking to understand the people you're wondering about reaching. Be careful that your 'helping' is not accidentally perpetuating the problem you're trying to solve.

Solid missiology always involves a lot of direct conversations with people from the proposed mission focus group. If you're going to reach a particular people group, you will need to get used to being among them, learning about their ways and what makes them tick. If you can't make friends with people, you almost certainly can't reach them. And the more different they are from you, the harder it is.

In many ways, the willingness and effectiveness of you and your church or mission team to learn about and make friends with people from a particular group is a kind of acid test as to whether you're going to reach them. With this in mind, begin conversations a long time before you begin programs.

Pause to discern

Once you've done some learning and engagement with people from a proposed mission focus group, it may be time to take stock of what you've learned.

- This might include a time of prayer, seeking God's direction and being attentive to what he is showing you.
- You might also share observations and specific questions that help you gain clarity.

At this stage it's generally helpful to ask a couple of key questions about how you relate to your proposed mission focus group.

The first is about the basis of your interest in this group. If the main reason is because the group is already well-represented in your church (for example, your church has a lot of young families), it might make sense to decide to focus your mission on this group. The common ground provides ample opportunity for mission.

If the main reason is because the group is strongly represented in your community, I encourage you to be thoughtful and consider some experimental efforts to reach people from this group before committing a lot of effort and finance. What you learn through experiments will help you adapt and tailor your approach.

If your main attraction to a particular group is compassion or perceiving a significant need among them, you're in for some hard work. Well-meaning and poorly researched mission initiatives risk creating welfare traps characterised by reinforced helplessness, rewarding poor decisions and creating unwanted side effects.

Beware of unhelpful helping

Whole books have been written on misguided welfare, and I touch on this a little in chapter 5, so I'm not going to develop the idea beyond a few thought starters here. Ask yourself these questions before creating any kind of welfare-based ministry:

- Are you proposing a ministry that does for others what they should do for themselves (whether or not they are actually doing it)?
    - Is it about fixing people up?
- Will the ministry you propose create a one-up/one-down or professional/client kind of relationship?
    - Is it about being a therapist or telling people what to do?
- Will the ministry you propose place you in a position of playing 'authority figure' to adults?
    - Does it risk infantilising people?

If the answer is 'yes' to any of these, you may be in danger of simply perpetuating a problem. I strongly advise you to look at partnering with an agency or group that specialises in helping people with the same challenges as those you're hoping to reach.

Now ask yourself these questions:

- Will the ministry you propose call on people's strengths and not reinforce their weaknesses?
- Will the ministry you propose allow formation of equal and open friendships?
- Will the ministry you propose create environments that help a person feel they belong?

If the answer is 'yes' to all of these, you may well be on to something.

In this process you might pause to research what other churches, agencies or community groups are doing to serve the same group. Could you liaise with them? Learn from them? Cooperate? Join in?

You might take a little time to research strategies to serve people with similar challenges. Look to see if the strategies you observe actually make a difference and help people become more Christlike or whether they just relieve symptoms.

Choose and begin
Once you've worked through the thinking above, you're probably ready to settle on a mission focus group. There comes a time when the research and discerning is over and God's leading is clear enough for you to begin.

You don't have to be absolutely certain—just sufficiently confident of God's leading to take the risk of commitment.

Appendix 2: Rites of Profession

A profession rite serves as a public and personal marker of a person's commitment to follow Jesus Christ. Some traditions baptise people only on profession of faith; others baptise the infants of believers and offer the rite of confirmation on profession of faith. In the case of baptism, it also serves as an initiation into the community of believers.

Some have objected that we should not make distinctions as to who's an insider or an outsider. However, we find suggestion of a fairly clear distinction in Acts 2:41, where three thousand people accepted Peter's message at Pentecost, were baptised and were added to the group.

When we look at the practice of the Celtic monks, we find quite porous communities where inquirers were welcomed and enfolded into the rhythms of the community. Yet there was still a clear distinction between those inquiring and those who had vowed commitment. It's possible to be welcoming, hospitable and clear about where a person stands. Such a distinction serves to keep the main thing the main thing (that is, the goal of the community is to make disciples), and that distinction is drawn by a profession rite.

Some may protest that demanding a person undergo such a public declaration is placing too high an expectation on what may be a shaky faith, and time should be allowed to see if their faith commitment 'sticks'. Conversely, there is argument to be made that administration of a profession rite (or submission to a profession rite, depending on your perspective) actually serves to make a new commitment less 'shakeable'. And that leads me into the historically contested debate about sacraments.

The term 'sacrament' derives from the Latin *sacramentum*, which is the term used to describe an oath of allegiance taken by a soldier. It carries the idea of being dedicated to a particular cause or purpose—set apart or, literally, 'sacred'.

As Latin became the dominant ecclesial language of the Western church, *sacramentum* replaced the earlier Greek *mysterion*, which in the first couple of centuries seems to have been the collective term used for the rites of baptism and the Lord's Supper. It's important to get our heads around this idea, so strap in for some rough-cut theology.

Paul from time to time uses the term 'mystery' to describe God's eternal plan of salvation through the death and resurrection of Jesus (for example, Romans 16:25; Ephesians 1:9; Colossians 1:26–27). The custom and practice of the early church was to initiate a new believer into this mystery, 'Christ in you, the hope of glory', through the rite of baptism. Until a believer was baptised, they were not recognised as part of the church, and could neither participate in the Lord's Supper nor receive the kiss of fellowship (now there's a tradition that's no longer practised, a fact for which we Australian keep-your-distance blokes are particularly grateful).

The rite of baptism marked out the person as one who had entered into the mystery of the gospel and initiated them into the committed community of believers.

This begs the question: is baptism simply a ritual of recognition or does it have some kind of actual power? This is important, since that shaky faith may just be buttressed if there is actual power for renovation of the soul or transmission of grace in the administration of a sacrament.

As a kid growing up in the Baptist tradition, my earlier 'christening' by a Congregational clergyman when I was a babe-in-arms was ignored (a little arrogantly I must say, in hindsight), and I submitted to believer's baptism by full immersion at the age of fourteen. I expected nothing to happen other than some kind of vague spiritual high which would inevitably give way to spiritual oppression by the evil one. And I experienced more or less what I expected.

Reflecting more on my believer's baptism, I saw it at the time as an act purely of commitment and obedience (it was what a sincere teenager in the church did when they wanted to 'get serious' about their faith). Jesus commanded it, you should do it.

I've since wondered whether there may be more to it. My wondering comes from my examination of Romans 6, the practices of the early church and the Reformers' understanding of the rite.

In Romans 6 Paul teaches that those who have been baptised have been baptised into the death (and by strong implication, the resurrection) of

Christ (vv. 3-4). Is this simply the obedient symbolic acting out of our inner conviction, or is there something more at play here? Is this rite simply a public identification? Paul's language seems to imply something much more powerful.

The early church did not teach baptismal regeneration per se, but certainly saw baptism as the means by which membership into the body of Christ is conferred. One may be saved by faith, but one was viewed as sanctified—that is, set apart—by baptism.

Move on to the Reformers, who sought (although not always agreeing) to restore the church and it's doctrine to a more biblically orthodox stance— that is, closer to the foundational doctrine and practice as captured in the teachings of the apostles and canonised as the New Testament.

The battleground of sacraments at the Reformation centred on two main debates: first, what was the nature of the elements of the Lord's Supper (the transubstantiation versus consubstantiation versus consecrated symbols discussion) and second, the effect of sacraments—that is, what was the basis of them being a 'means of grace'? The traditional Roman Catholic view had been that the sacrament was a means of grace on the basis of the apostolic legitimacy of the priest (the status of the one administering the sacrament). The Reformers asserted that grace conferred was dependent on the sacrament being received in faith (the posture of the recipient). Cue lively debate.

What was not in dispute was that rightly receiving the sacrament, be it baptism or the Lord's Supper, was a means of receiving the grace of God— that is, that the sacraments were a 'means of grace'. It does the believer's faith good to receive sacraments, both the singular rite of initiation and the repeated rite of covenantal renewal.

Why all this dredging up of teachings and debates from centuries past? Simply this: for most of its history the church has held that baptism is a powerful means of conferring the grace of God upon a believer. Baptism is therefore beneficial to a person's faith. It seems from Paul's argument in Romans 6 that baptism conveys some kind of sanctifying power (that is, power to put to death the old self and to walk in the resurrected self). This seems to be supported in the teaching of the early church and the Reformers.

I can't technically define the exact nature of that power: perhaps that's why the early church referred to baptism as *mysterion*.

The foregoing notwithstanding, baptism is not presented in scripture, the early church or the Reformation literature as an optional extra, or a 'next step' separate from conversion designed to refill the grace tank. Conversion was *marked* by baptism. It was and remains the first step of tangible obedience in faith.

Appendix 3: Faith and Obedience

Getting clear on guilt, shame and judgment
When we do our own thing in contrast to the character of God, we should feel a pang of conscience. Conscience is a God-given reflex inviting us to repent. If we continue to obey our 'deceitful desires' while claiming to be followers of Christ, the internal conflict may be experienced as guilt or shame. These feelings too are helpful if they lead us to give up our self-destructive behaviours.

However, in themselves they can become destructive if they're perpetuated.

Guilt, that nasty, uncomfortable tightening of our gut, is actually a very useful emotion—for about ten seconds. That (in theory at least) is the time it takes to figure out whether we've done something wrong. After that, guilt is pretty much a destructive force.

If we've done something wrong, hopefully we'll feel guilty, that is, our inner being will react to the compromise of our integrity. We've not done what we know to be right, either by commission or omission. The helpful response in that instance is to confess, repent, apologise, make amends and thereby restore our integrity.

That's the normative ideal. Our lived experience, however, can be very different.

Without getting too much into the psychology of it all, some of us are primed for guilt—generally through past experiences, particularly in childhood. This sometimes comes about when a parent continually imposes blame on a child for their own (that is, the parent's) shortcomings. The child feels guilty but can't connect that guilt to any particular breach of their own integrity, and they have no pathway for reconciliation and restoration (the very things healthy guilt is designed to bring about). Being a child, they have neither the mental apparatus nor the positional power to rationalise the situation, see what's going on and assert themselves with the parent (or other guilt-projecting person). The child grows up both sensitised to feelings of guilt projected by others and ill-equipped to make healthy responses to their own sense of compromised integrity.

A person with this kind of priming is likely to experience some real difficulties with discipleship as a lifestyle of repentance (that is, putting off the sinful, putting on the godly). It may trigger their sensitivity and manifest in a range of less-than-helpful behaviours. That doesn't mean we should avoid the issue of repentance, but it does mean we should be alert to the possibility of this kind of priming and be thoughtful about our approach.

Shame is related to guilt but tends to run a little deeper. Shame goes from the sense of *doing* something wrong to the idea that there *is* something wrong. And here's where it gets confusing.

'Shaming' has become a bit of a buzzword in contemporary society, and most of the discourse is unhelpful enough to keep an army of psychologists in years of work. I recently read an article about a super plus-sized model, celebrating her healthy self-esteem evidenced by her willingness to put her size 26 physique on display for the cameras. The blogosphere went nuts, mostly with affirmation.

One columnist wrote a piece expressing concern about celebrating the physique of a person who on the face of it displayed a whole range of risk factors for future health problems. The columnist went on to observe that obesity was a major public health concern in most of the Western world. Again the blogosphere went nuts, hashtag fatshaming.

I was fascinated. The journalist's language had been moderate and objective, her tone calm, even understated. The reaction was personal, shrill and accusatory. Was the journalist shaming? Or were the bloggers sensitised to shame?

Many of us have a deep sense, perhaps even a fear, that there is something deeply wrong with us. When something or someone triggers that feeling, we can become upset with them, assigning responsibility to them for our own bad feelings.

The church cops its fair share of this kind of projection. Unfortunately, the church has a long and rather inglorious history of using shame as the basis for manipulating the hapless proletariat (as did the Pharisees in Jesus' time, much to his annoyance). And there are still some churches which, in the name of Jesus, project their collective pathology on those whose behaviour they believe to be sinful.

In a shame-sensitised society, and with a fairly chequered history, the church is apt to be regaled with criticism, even abuse, whenever it points out that some behaviour, policy or practice is not in accordance with their understanding of God's best for humanity.

All of this means that, as members of the church seeking to help people in their journey of discipleship, we're likely to hit some barriers around guilt and shame. This is rather paradoxical when we consider that Jesus holds out to us life free from guilt and shame.

Yet without experiencing a healthy pang of guilt (preferably just for the aforementioned ten seconds), repentance seems unlikely, and without repentance, following Jesus and taking seriously his rather revolutionary teaching will prove all but impossible. Our goal is not to make people feel guilty or ashamed, but neither should we avoid the possibility that people just might feel that way.

In our effort to avoid triggering reactions to guilt and thereby 'putting people off', we've all but eliminated an appropriate and godly call to repentance. This has led to the Western church largely being a collective of fairly 'undisciplined' believers. Yet I'm not sure that upping the guilt factor is the key to growing more and better disciples.

All of the foregoing is to say that 'just stop it' is not a particularly helpful jumping-off point for discipleship. While repentance is absolutely essential to discipleship, the primary motive can't be simply that of avoidance or alleviation of guilt and shame (nor, for that matter, escape from the ill-effects of judgment).

It's been used so much as to become passé, but God *loved* the world so much that he sent his Son to save it (John 3:16, in case you were wondering). God *is* love (1 John 4:8). We are objects of his love. His primary desire for us is that we might embody and experience all the fullness of Christ. Dare I say it, God's heart for us is to share his joy. Read Ephesians 1 and bathe in the sense of God's lavish generosity and delight to extend his grace to us.

Judgment flows out of his essential character of love. It is not loving to allow injustice to abide forever, to not bring to account those who cause the suffering of others. God is not essentially an angry person, but love gives rise to anger when love's object is harmed, even when the harm is caused by another of love's objects.

Appendix 4: Leadership Problems of Position, Authority and Power

I've lost count of the number of Christian authors I've read who react against any kind of large or hierarchically organised church structures. Big structures are bad, they maintain, because they're abusive. (Ironically, they type these opinions on computers that are only affordable to the general populace because of the economies of scale that ultra-mass production affords. Production on such a scale is in turn affordable only by really big companies like Intel and Samsung.)

I'm not here to defend the institutional church as pure and without stain or wrinkle (although that's Jesus' ultimate plan). History is littered with sad and even appalling stories of large organisations doing very harmful stuff in the name of Jesus. But here's the rider: it's also rich in stories of large organisations doing remarkable, magnificent redemptive stuff in the name of Jesus. Amazingly, sometimes the same organisation will feature in both kinds of stories.

Further, history generally does not record the harmful things that have gone on in smaller, independent, less-organised groups because these groups themselves largely go unrecorded in history, and the scandals are too isolated to make the headlines. But most of us have heard enough sad anecdotes to know that what happens on a big scale in big churches happens on a smaller scale in smaller churches.

The size of the institution is not the issue. Nor is the inherent nature of hierarchy. Let's just do a bit of organisational theory here, and the importance will become apparent.

Organisations by definition form and function around cooperation for mutual benefit. Let's take the organisation most familiar to all of us, the family. In my nuclear family there are four adults, each with varying degrees of responsibility and authority. This evening I enjoyed the benefit of eating a dinner cooked by my elder daughter. I benefited from her work. To gain that benefit, I had to give up some power—I didn't get my first choice for dinner. She's a vegetarian, and for this dinner, so were the rest of us.

I almost never buy groceries. That's a job willingly undertaken by my younger daughter (with my credit card in her hand!). What did she buy? Whatever was on the list that the family gradually compiled, and what in her best judgment was needed. I didn't determine her purchasing choices; she exercised authority delegated to her. And in so delegating the authority, my wife and I let go of some modicum of control.

For an organisation to work, the various players give some things in order to receive others. As the person who has the most actual power over the family's finances (my income presently contributes more to the family budget than the others'), I can either take a chokehold on the shopping or trust the judgment of others and enjoy the benefit of the pantry magically refilling each week. Cooperation requires letting go of power in order to gain a benefit.

Hierarchy arises when some people have responsibility for some aspect of the function or wellbeing of others. Another way of looking at it is that some of the power handed over for benefit accumulates with certain individuals. It's generally viewed pretty negatively—yet it is both efficient and inevitable.

Before I explain why, let me share a quick anecdote that I think helps bring the idea into focus. A colleague of mine relates a story of from her idealistic youth. Back in the 1970s, a lot of people had a crack at communal living—the Jewish kibbutz movement came to wider attention, neo-monastic movements like YWAM really took off and communities like the House of the Gentle Bunyip (true story) popped up in cities like Melbourne.

My colleague and a bunch of her friends were living in community, growing their own vegetables and trying to embody the way of Jesus in shared life. So far so good. In reaction to the perceived evils of hierarchy, they reached a consensus that every decision should be reached by consensus. And so came the conversation about relocating the shed. These people were all university-educated adults. Some were academics (that is, identifiably smart people). Yet the debate over the location of the shed raged for six months, and in the end a compromise consensus was reached to move the shed approximately two metres. Nobody 'lost'—and nobody 'won'. If the purpose of the community cooperating was mutual benefit, it's hard to see who was any the better for all the energy expended.

Consensus gives everyone equal authority and equal responsibility—and infinitely variable degrees of frustration. It gives the same authority to the least mature, least functional and least responsible participants as it does to the most. Personally, I'm pretty happy to benefit from handing a little of my power of decision to someone who will make a better decision than me.

While consensus and other flat-as-a-pancake structures have the apparent appeal of being abuse-proof, they're actually just as vulnerable—it's just that the abuse takes different forms. A consensus decision can be held to ransom by the least mature member of the group holding out, either from fear or bloody-mindedness. Further, consensus and other democratic processes can be manipulated through subtle and less-than-subtle manoeuvring outside of the main forum of conversation.

Every process for collective effort—from consensus at one end to dictatorship at the other—suffers from the same root problem. We humans are sinners: guilty of sin and damaged by sin. When issues of power come up, our sinfulness is brought into focus.

Sociologists studying leadership have discovered that hierarchy seems to emerge spontaneously. In group experiments, a bunch of strangers are thrown together and given a problem to solve. In next to no time people adopt functional positions of leaders and followers. And the groups that settle into some kind of structural functionality the quickest tend to solve the problem more quickly and efficiently, because they can more quickly put their best efforts toward the challenge at hand and expend less resource on the fairness of the process.

Hierarchy in various forms was evident in the New Testament church. In fact, the first problem the newly formed church tackled was one of position. Who would occupy the (much-esteemed) apostolic place of Judas Iscariot (Acts 1:15-26)? The apostles exercised authority over the fledgling church in teaching (Acts 2:42) and administration (Acts 6—see below) and in matters of doctrine and practice (Acts 15).

When the dispute arose over the distribution of food to widows (Acts 6), the apostles ignored the content of the problem and paid attention to function and structure. They insightfully realised that the real problem was that they could not give sufficient attention to the matter and still fulfil their core responsibilities. So they delegated authority to seven others and turned the responsibility over to them. Note there was a mix of group decision-making and delegation of authority to individuals who could make subsequent decisions. Note also that they chose godly and wise people for the task.

Hierarchy was also implicit in Paul's instruction to Titus to appoint elders in the church on Crete. Without leadership, people tend to do as they please and things inevitably turn to custard (for evidence, study the book of Judges, and observe that God restored his people through the ministry of godly leaders).

And now for the nub of it. Jesus had ample opportunity to dispel the notion of hierarchy since his disciples were perennially falling into dispute about the pecking order among them. Watch carefully how Jesus dealt with it in Mark 10:35–45. When James and John asked for the plum gigs in the anticipated kingdom, the rest of the apostles got their noses out of joint. So Jesus sat them down and went over it with them.

'You know how the Gentiles go about the exercise of authority? Don't do it that way. Instead, turn it upside down. In you want to be great, serve. If you want to be first, be like a slave.'

In other words, leadership is not about accumulating power and prestige to yourself. It's about acting for the benefit and welfare of others.

Note that Jesus didn't say, 'Now, kids, you're all equal and everyone has an equal say and an equal vote, so stop squabbling. Let's have a group hug and sing "Kumbaya".' Note also that he *did* hold up his own life as an example: 'The Son of Man did not come to be served, but to serve, and to give his life … '

Jesus did not dismantle the idea of leadership and authority afforded by structure. He simply inverted the aspiration of it. Around the same time he also said (but recorded in a different gospel), 'Whoever wants to be my disciple must deny themselves and take up their cross and follow me (Matthew 16:24).

When we throw out leadership and structure because we see these concepts as vehicles for abuse, we throw the baby out with the bathwater. In order for a group to cooperate and gain mutual benefit with any degree of efficiency, it's necessary for people to take up specific responsibilities. In order to fulfil those responsibilities, people must be afforded the power to decide and act.

And that power may include the power to direct the actions of others or to allocate resources.

The bigger the group, the more potential for collective good and the greater the power that may necessarily accrue to a small group of leaders. There is sound biblical precent for this in the New Testament. It's inherently neither right nor wrong.

For hierarchy and leadership to be beneficial and not abusive, the aspiration of those with power must be for the benefit of others, and their posture must be one of self-denial. The selection criteria for such roles should be bigger on godliness and maturity than on talent and charisma.

Appendix 5: If You're Planting

Let's begin with a definition. Church planting means establishing a new community of believers where one does not already exist and where the new community is intended to become autonomous and self-sufficient and to incorporate all seven steps of the Pathways model.

Beginning a new congregation within an existing church shares some of the same dynamics as church planting, but it does not need all seven steps of the pathway (that is, you can share some of step 6 and a lot of step 7 with other pathways).

Re-potting (planting a parallel congregation in a church with a long-standing but unviable congregation) is like congregation planting, except that the new congregation will quickly become the main event and the existing congregation will eventually either wind up or be absorbed into the new one (it's a useful model for helping declining congregations find a generative way forward).

This appendix is directed at church planting—it you're planting a congregation or involved in a re-pot, you'll need to do some translation.

Pathways has proven very helpful with church plants, both as a planning framework and as an assessment tool. If your plant is up and running with a range of groups and activities, you can probably use it as an assessment tool following the process set out in the body of the book.

If you're still in the early phases, the first thing you'll need to do is think about your model. This will determine how you apply Pathways philosophy.

Many of the church planting books published over the past twenty years presume that planting follows a given model. If a book uses phrases like 'launch' or the metaphor of conception-birth-adolescence, it's probably presuming a particular way of planting. If you read a bunch of books and they presume differing models, you're vulnerable to confusion.

Let's look at a few examples.

The model that thrived in the 1950s and 1960s and has now largely fallen from grace is what I like to call the 'field of dreams': if you build it, they will come. Back in those days, if you did (build) they did (come)—for a whole range of reasons better explained by sociology than missiology. Denominations are still doing this here and there. If the location is a new residential area and there are enough Christians moving into the area who are interested in joining, this model is actually pretty effective in getting a new church off the ground and established. However, if there is not the ready-made congregation among the influx of new residents, it can be a very expensive learning experience.

Nowadays the most commonly understood model is what I have labelled the 'hive-off': gather about sixty people from an existing church (the number may vary from thirty to over two hundred depending on whom you talk to), form them into a discreet congregation and open up shop in another location. This is a favourite of large churches, and very large churches will use this or a similar approach to plant interstate or even overseas.

Similar to the 'hive-off' is the 'recruit-a-congregation-and-launch' model, whereby a planter gathers a team and then a congregation from the area surrounding the proposed planting site. Once sufficient numbers have been gathered, the church is 'launched' with a public worship service. This model often uses momentum-builders such as 'preview services'. It may also use mass-communication methods like radio advertising and mass call-outs.

The similarity between all three of these models is that they tend to focus on the middle steps of the pathway: those who are believers interested in a new church, or seekers on the cusp of a faith commitment.

The next variation is a favourite of those in the cell-and-celebration movement, whereby the planter plants a cell group that grows and multiplies (hopefully by making new disciples, but not always or exclusively). Once there are sufficient numbers among the cluster of cells, a celebration service is launched, perhaps only monthly to begin with, then with increasing frequency.

Recent movements like SOMA and 3DM are not too different to the cell-and-celebration model above, although their basic units of missional communities may be larger than the traditional twelve-person cell. Further, while most will end up establishing a gathered celebration or public worship service, some may not.

Among those that may not are the house church movement and its variants. These movements simply establish multiplying communities of believers small enough to meet a house (generally fewer than twenty-five people). These movements will often set up in a third space like a pub or café and make it their lounge room, hanging out there multiple times a week.

Done well, these approaches tend to pay more attention to the beginning steps of the pathway: people who are within reach but may have no real interest in faith as yet.

Last but not least is the pioneer planter, who heads out to a new location, armed usually with a data projector, a portable PA system and a banner, accompanied by their spouse and kids (if they have them). This model has seen the Pentecostals plant in literally hundreds of country towns across Australia. It's not all that different to a Wesleyan pioneer establishing a new circuit in the American Midwest two centuries ago. It's got 'runs on the board' as a model, but the attrition rate is huge.

Think mission focus group
If you're working with a model that puts the public worship service front and centre, you have some broad questions to ask about your mission focus group. The flavour, language, location, timing, venue, structure, duration and supportive programs that you choose will, either deliberately or accidentally, exclude a huge range of other possibilities. What you choose will suit some people and not others. If you just replicate your previous experience or create the kind of service you'd like for yourself, you may find you simply attract a bunch of dissatisfied Christians from other churches, which creates problems later on.

Think carefully. In Australia, Sunday morning is all about kids' sport. If you decide to schedule your service for 10.00 am on Sunday morning, you're setting up in competition to footy, netball and nippers. If you hope to attract families with school-aged kids, this could be a challenge.

A venue with no car parking (like a CBD cinema) will be fine for young adults accustomed to using public transport, but a real challenge for parents with young kids and all the paraphernalia that goes with them.

Conversely, if you're working initially with smaller groups with no immediate expectation to begin a worship service, you have the flexibility of allowing each group to discern a distinct mission focus group and tailor their activity to suit. Each group can uniquely ask and answer the questions pertaining to the first three stages of Pathways ('potential contact', 'in touch' and 'belonging'). If you're hoping to form the cluster of smaller groups into a congregation, it's probably wise to consider all the groups using common 'embracing the gospel' and 'following Jesus' processes. It makes equipping and resourcing the group leaders much simpler.

If you're right at the beginning of your planting odyssey and you have just yourself or a small group, it's worthwhile having a fairly narrow mission focus group in the early stages. This is why the 'third space as lounge room' approach works well. The café or pub becomes the defining characteristic of your mission focus group. Equally, you could take the same approach with a sporting club or other community group.

If you're still wondering about your exact mission focus group, you may need to begin with a loosely defined mission focus group (for example, defined by a suburb or town) and work through a process of refining. This is generally achieved by trial and error: try a few contexts, groups, ideas and see where God grants the openings. All the while pray, listen, seek to discern God's leading. It's usually best if you can get the definition down to a fairly narrow slice so you can concentrate the efforts of your team. Dispersed effort is usually not all that effective.

Refer to Appendix 1 on identifying a mission focus group if you want more detail.

Begin at both ends
Even if you're from a really big church and you're about to do a hive-off, I encourage you to begin thinking about the people you're called to reach, not just the congregation you hope to gather. Focusing on a public worship service may mean you have something visible, have a gathering point for believers and have the opportunity to take up an offering (always a plus when you're planting). But at the same time it may suck up all the resources in your group and leave little time and energy for engaging the unchurched.

I've lost count of the number of young churches I've served or know about that have either grown entirely by transfers from other churches or not grown much beyond their launch size. If you 'launch' with a group that is already a viable congregation, you're especially vulnerable.

Instead, you might be better served slowing things down and planting something besides a worship service in the first instance. Here's an example.

A planting couple were commissioned by their denomination to plant in a growth corridor in the north-west of Sydney in the early 2000s. While the couple gathered a small team in the nearby church, the denomination presciently purchased one of the few larger parcels of land remaining in anticipation of building a church and a school. The new suburb had turned a bunch of small farms into a seemingly endless sea of McMansions almost overnight.

Into these 'dream homes' moved mostly two-income-no-kids couples who worked long hours, usually in city-based, professional careers, paying down eye-wateringly high mortgages with a view to beginning a family in a couple of years. Chances of reaching these people? Not much better than nil.

Things changed when the young couples in the McMansions began to have kids. All of a sudden professionally competent, socially adept, high-achieving women found themselves feeling isolated and occasionally frazzled, imprisoned in their dream homes with unreasonable toddlers.

Typical of growth corridors, the town planners had not given much thought to public facilities where opportunities to connect would be created. Seeing the opportunity, the planting team organised funding for some demountable buildings, playground equipment and safety fencing to be installed on the site of the future church.

Instead of commencing a worship service, they began playgroups and other opportunities for the new mums to connect and commiserate while their kids played safely. In time the team began inviting the mums to Alpha, and then Bible studies. About a year after the demountables arrived, a worship service was commenced. Six months later the congregation numbered about 120.

Hopefully you can see the pathways steps.

If you begin mission (reaching the unchurched) you'll probably, in time, get a church. It's much harder to get mission by beginning with a church. This is why I try to encourage people to think of church planting more in terms of a local mission endeavour than an exercise in reproducing a worship service.

A worship service focus is difficult to break out of when you plant with a denomination, because denominational executives often see church planting as not much more than establishing another franchise. The franchise mindset tends to carry the same assumptions as the 'field of dreams'. Planters who head down that track are in danger of merely gathering service attenders and consumers—particularly if those people are leaving a nearby church disappointed, disillusioned or dissing everything.

Think team
Now let's think about planting and the other end of the pathway—that is, serving and leading.

I spent a fair bit of time in the body of the book looking at the idea of a mission focus group, and made a comment that Jesus chose for his team (perhaps a planting team) a bunch of guys who didn't quite fit his mission focus group. While his focus was on Galilean Jewish outcast kinds of people, his team were all Jewish, mostly Galilean but mostly from the middle class, as Jesus was himself.

You might be drawn to a mission focus group because of need, but you should definitely recruit your planting team on the basis of potential—or else be prepared for a very long period of discipling a small group until their lives display the order and discipline necessary to carry responsibility. If you're pursuing a high-need mission focus group, long experience with challenging people leads me to advise you to take a decent-sized team of fairly well-sorted people—or be prepared for a very long haul.

I've watched pioneer planters arrive in a town, start a service, attract a motley crowd and empower them to take up responsibility in the church. More often than not it works for a while, until the character issues surface. It's dangerous to put a person into a position of responsibility when they don't yet have the character required to sustain them.

My counsel, therefore, is to be patient and thoughtful in building your planting team. Be prepared to set a reasonably high standard of commitment (Jesus called people to leave what they were doing to follow him, and he seemed to do okay).

In creating your team, build in the disciplines of discipleship, service and leadership development right from the get-go. Once you start a worship service it's too easy to put these off until later, and later is when the immature, undisciplined behaviour erupts and threatens your sanity.

In summary: when planting, start at the ends—engagement with the harvest-field and leadership—and you'll almost inevitably get to the middle. Start at the middle and you may not get to the ends. Churches that stay small tend to put all their effort into the middle and have no resources left for the ends—it's a trap that may leave you working hard to hold together a small number of immature people who expect a lot and give very little.

Appendix 6: The Fundraising Trap

They say every church is unique—each has its own story, its own culture, its own collective personality. Like families, churches over time develop their own ways and quirks. Some are endearing. Some are, well, quirky.

A few years ago I began a pilot program group of seven small churches (that is, an average Sunday attendance of less than fifty people). While they're all very different, as each has completed the Pathways workshop, some common elements have emerged.

One of these is what I've begun to call 'the fundraising trap'. It begins when finances are a little short and the church council agrees to take on some fundraising activity just to 'top-up' the bank account.

Small churches generally have at their heart a group of determined and hard-working stalwarts: willing hands that sizzle sausages, bake cakes, sort bric-a-brac and do whatever it takes to raise the funds to keep the minister paid-up and the church doors open.

Next time there's a shortfall, those same hands work to achieve the same result. When finances tighten, fundraising activities increase. Over time, fundraising can become almost a preoccupation.

As it has been throughout history, the future of the church is determined more than anything else by its capacity to make disciples—whether we think in terms of whole nations and denominations, or at the level of a local church youth group.

The 'trap' becomes evident when church leadership teams realise that although their fundraising activity may bring them into contact with unchurched people, it doesn't do much to help new people become committed followers of Jesus. And without new disciples, the church at every level has a limited lifespan.

Although members of churches caught in the fundraising trap usually recognise that significant effort must be committed to reaching and discipling those who are currently outside the church, there's seldom any spare energy. At the suggestion of introducing yet another demand on church members, I usually hear, 'We're working as hard as we can just to keep things afloat as it is.' And no doubt that's true.

Simply moving all the effort from fundraising to making disciples seems too risky to contemplate. If a church ceases its fundraising activities, it may not have the funds to pay clergy or keep the lights on. The dilemma seems intractable.

Churches can escape the fundraising trap, although it requires some disciplined thinking and perhaps some discomfort. Some parishes have begun by evaluating their fundraising, and found that, by the time they add up their input costs, they could cease some activities, put the money saved in the offertory and come out of it just about even.

Others have sought to integrate their fundraising activities into their mission pathway. This usually means personally inviting people with whom they come into contact through fundraising activities (for example, fetes and op shops) to the next stage in the pathway (perhaps a social event or an interest group).

Far and away the most effective strategy is to change the position description of the paid clergy. Research by Thom Rainer has been validated to some extent by our experience in the pilot program.[63] When the clergy spend a significant proportion (in this pilot program we specify one-third) of their time intentionally reaching the unchurched, there's a much greater likelihood that new people will join the church and stay.

Of course, this strategy means a change of expectations and possibly some raised levels of anxiety. Ministers may feel a little unsure of themselves outside the safety of the church, and the congregation may resent their reduced availability. And there's no ironclad guarantee it will work.

Yet for those who dare, becoming a missionary-priest offers the possibility of leading the church into a new season of outreach, of revitalisation as new disciples are made, and ultimately of hope that the best days of the church may still be ahead.

---

[63] Rainer, Thom S. *Surprising Insights from the Unchurched and Proven Ways to Reach Them* (Zondervan, Grand Rapids, 2001).

www.ingramcontent.com/pod-product-compliance
Lightning Source LLC
Chambersburg PA
CBHW051937290426
44110CB00015B/2020